Anglican Con·cil·i·a·rism

The Church Meeting to Decide Together

Phil Ashey

Anglican House

Published by Anglican House Publishers

ISBN 978-0-9979211-9-9

About the Cover Art

The Council of Nicaea (A.D.325), an assembly of bishops representing all of Christendom, was the first effort to attain consensus in the Church through rigorous Conciliarism. The resulting Nicene Creed, as lightly amended in 381, is to this day the consensus statement of the Christian faith. Every week in church services around the world hundreds of millions of Protestants, Catholics, and Eastern Orthodox confess their personal faith in Jesus Christ by reciting the Nicene Creed.

The iconic style of the cover artwork depicts Emperor Constantine I, who summoned the Council of Nicaea, presiding as Bishops receive the bread and wine of the Holy Eucharist. Note the Word of God lying open on the altar, signifying Conciliarism's submission to the ultimate authority of Holy Scripture.

The date of the work and the artist are unknown.

Contents

Page

Eleven Principles and Practices of Conciliarism v
Dedication 1
Preface 3

PART ONE

One Anglican Conciliarism 11

Two Principles and Practices of Decision Making in the Mother Church 21

Three Conciliarism at Work Elsewhere in the Anglican Communion 45

PART TWO

ANGLICAN CONCILIARISM: CATHOLIC *AND* REFORMED

Four The Medieval Church, Great Schism and "Strict Conciliarism" 87

Five Reformation Anglicanism and The Supreme Authority of Holy Scripture 95

PART THREE

THE LOSS AND RECOVERY OF CONCILIARISM

Six The Loss of Conciliarism in Principle and Practice 105

Contents

		Page
Seven	Deficit of Authority in the Anglican Communion and the North American Revitalization	125

PART FOUR
A WAY FORWARD

Eight	Recovery of Conciliarism within the Anglican *Communion*	145
Nine	The *Sine Qua Non* of Conciliarism: *Fundamental Declarations*	171
Ten	Communion & The Common Good	187
Acknowledgements		205
About the Author		207
Appendix		209
Glossary of Latin Terms		245
Bibliography		249
General Index		269

The Eleven Principles and Practices of Conciliarism

1. SYNODOL GOVERNMENT IS NECESSARY, REGULAR AND PERMAMENT.
2. THE WHOLE CHURCH IS REPRESENTED IN SYNOD
3. THE MIND OF THE CHURCH IS DISCERNED IN A RIGOROUS SYNODAL PROCESS
4. BISHOPS HAVE A PARTICULAR ROLE AS GUARDIANS OF THE FAITH, ORDER AND LITURGY
5. DIOCESAN SYNODS ARE LIMITED IN THEIR SCOPE
6. SYNODAL GOVERNMENNT MUST EXIST AT THE DEANERY, DIOCESAN AND NATIONAL CHURCH LEVELS, AND MAY EXIST AT THE LEVEL OF THE LOCAL CHURCH
7. SYNODS MANIFEST ECCLESIAL DENSITY
8. THE WHOLE CHURCH GATHERS IN SYNOD AROUND ITS BISHOP(S), BUT NEVER OVER AND AGAINST THEM
9. SYNOD IS CONCERNED WITH THE CHURCH'S MISSION TO THE WORLD, NOT JUST WITH THE INTERNAL LIFE OF THE CHURCH
10. A SYNOD ALSO EXPRESSES THE SPIRITUAL LIFE AND EVENT OF THE CHURCH THROUGH DAILY WORSHIP AND PRAYER, AND THE HOLY EUCHARIST
11. THE WORK OF SYNODS AS CONFORMING TO THE ULTIMATE AUTHORITY OF THE HOLY SCRIPTURE

Dedication

I give thanks to God for the gift of my children Carol, Jake, Kirsten and Meghann, who patiently endured my absence while I was long hours away researching and writing. But above all I give thanks to God for Julie, my wife and friend, who has not only endured those absences, but also lovingly prayed and labored with me every step of the way. "Many women do noble things, but you surpass them all." (Prov. 31)

Preface

I will never forget the words of then Archbishop Henry Luke Orombi of Uganda, who said "I thank God for this crisis in the Anglican Communion, because it has caused us to find each other!" He was speaking at a conference in Pittsburgh on the Hope and Future for Anglicanism in North America, and around the world. He was speaking about the journey that many North American Anglicans had made to places like Uganda, Kenya, Nigeria, Rwanda and South America to rediscover what it means to be in communion and on mission with other Biblically faithful Anglicans.

The pastoral oversight and refuge we sought in these Anglican Churches was our way of maintaining our Anglican bona fides as we left the Episcopal Church and the Anglican Church of Canada over irreconcilable doctrinal differences. But in the process we were humbled, convicted, inspired and instructed in what it means to be in Communion with other Biblically faithful Anglicans across the globe.

In fact, Archbishop Orombi was speaking of the heart of what it means to be in Communion: *that we find each other.*

Very simply, this book is about how we as Anglicans can find each other again around a common confession of faith and doctrine, worship and mission with a coherent order that is Biblical, apostolic, catholic and classically Anglican. This book is about Anglican decision making in a conciliar way that other Christians will recognize, *so that we may also find each other again* – around shared faith and decision makingThe premise of this book is simple: the *conciliar* way of decision making in the Church (also called "conciliarism") has never been practiced at the global level of Anglican Communion organization and governance. This goes all the way back to the first Lambeth Conference of Bishops in 1867 – a conference rather than a "council," by deliberate choice of the Archbishop of Canterbury. Since then, the structures for organizing and governing the Anglican Communion have developed in ineffectual fashion, holding the Communion together through relational "bonds of affection," at least while there was still a shared faith and doctrine among the Churches of the Communion.

That doctrinal consensus collapsed during the 20th Century. Behind the bonds of affection the existing Instruments of Communion have expressed a deficit of authority to deal with accelerating doctrinal innovations and practices in the largely Western and Global North Churches of the Communion. These innovations have broken the bonds of affection as well as communion around Anglican identity, polity and mission. In short, the very survival of the "Communion" of Anglican Churches is now in question.

To carry the premise of this book one step further, what would it look like if, at the global level of Anglican Communion governance, we were to make our decisions together around a shared faith and confession, and with the same conciliar way of decision making that we find at the level of national/regional Anglican Churches, their sub-jurisdictions, dioceses, deaneries, and even local congregations? In a sense, this book is about an "ecclesiology from below," an extrapolation to the global level of Communion certain well defined Anglican principles and practices of conciliarism that we find at all other levels of Anglican churches. "From below" means that we look at the laws of Anglican Churches themselves to see what those common principles and practices of Anglican *conciliarism* may be.

So this book proposes to examine the future of conciliar theory and practice as a viable organizing principle for the Communion of Anglican Churches – from a canonical approach, that this, from an examination of the laws of Anglican churches:

- In Chapters ONE and TWO we examine the evidence for the principles and practice of conciliar decision-making in the laws and canons of the Church of England, from before the Reformation to the present.
- In Chapter THREE we examine the evidence of such principles and practices within the Anglican Communion from four representative Churches (Australia, South East Asia, Nigeria, and Ireland) with two of their dioceses each. Since this is a canonical study "from below" of the actual laws (constitutions and canons) of these Churches, the Chapter is heavily footnoted with citations to those laws.
- Chapters FOUR and FIVE we focus on the development historically of eleven (11) principles and practices of conciliarism, from the Great Schism of the 14th and 15 century Medieval Catholic Church through the Reformation and Richard Hooker.
- In Chapter SIX we examine the "devolution" and loss of conciliar principles and practices at the

global level of Anglican Communion governance in light of unilateral actions by some Churches in the last 50 years, with respect to doctrine, discipline and order that have stretched the current "Instruments of Communion" beyond the breaking point.

- Chapters SEVEN documents this devolution and loss in rather excruciating detail, around the timeline provided by the Province of South-East Asia in its letter of Accession to the now defunct Anglican Communion Covenant. We see the fruit of the loss of Anglican Conciliarism in North America, where there are significant differences in the principles and practice of conciliarism between the contrasting Provinces.
- Chapter EIGHT extrapolates the evidence for conciliarism from the laws of the Churches examined in Chapters One through Three (and in the Appendix), as well as the *Principles of Canon Law Common to Churches of the Anglican Communion*, in order to propose a model for conciliarism at the global level of Communion governance. This proposed model seeks to overcome the "deficit of authority" in the current Instruments through the adoption of Fundamental Declarations, enhanced responsibility of Primates for doctrine, discipline and order, and a Council of the Anglican Communion.
- Chapter NINE explains why the proposed and failed Anglican Communion Covenant is no substitute for Fundamental Declarations of faith and doctrine.

- Chapter TEN explains why a shared and common good is essential to the very nature of Communion, and how that common good is rooted in the Scriptures themselves – specifically in Philippians 2:5-11.

Included as an Appendix is a comparison and contrast between the laws of the Churches in North America – The Episcopal Church USA and the Anglican Church in North America, and two of their dioceses each – around the same eleven principles and practices of Anglican conciliarism. It may be a bit of a trek for those who are not used to canon law, but it is well worth the climb.

The conciliar principles in this proposed model seek to promote "communion" and mission that is both loyal to its Christological center and intelligible to Anglicans and other Christians all over the world.

Part I

Con·cil·i·a·rism

The Church Meeting to Decide Together

ONE

Anglican Conciliarism

Conciliarism is the Church meeting to decide together. Anglican theologian Paul Avis has declared:

> "Within the range of political options available within the Church's tradition, Anglicanism is an expression of conciliar Catholicism."[1]

Many Anglicans would agree that conciliar practice (if not theory) is the organizing principle of Anglican polity at all levels of the Church, indeed it is a unique and essential characteristic of Anglicanism. But since the 1970s, if not before, Anglicans have been embroiled in controversies over the limits of sexual expression, marriage, and leadership within the church that have tested the limits of conciliarism as defined by Avis and others. In fact, these controversies reflect much deeper differences in doctrine, discipline and order among the Churches of the Anglican Communion. The unilateral decisions some Churches have

---

[1] Paul Avis, *"Anglican Conciliarity: History, Theology and Practice,* 11. Documents of The Lambeth Commission on Communion <http://www.anglicancommunion.org/commission/process/lc_commission/docs/200402conciliarity.pdf> Accessed 11 November 2015.

made as to doctrine, disciple and order – and the response of others – have brought into question the very survival of conciliar theory and practice as an essential organizing principle of Anglicanism.

On September 16, 2015, the Archbishop of Canterbury announced a gathering of Primates in January 2016 "to look afresh at our ways of working together as a Communion and especially as Primates, paying proper attention to developments in the past, especially recent events."[2] At least two prominent observers of the Anglican Communion speculated that the Archbishop of Canterbury would encourage the Primates to step back from a "Communion" model and embrace a "Federal" model (such as the Lutheran World Federation) – both as a concession to deep disagreements among the Churches on fundamentals of the faith, and to enable joint mission among Anglican Churches who choose not to be in Communion with each other.[3] On the other hand, would this gathering be a reaffirmation of a way of addressing the tensions between "Communion" and the autonomy of Anglican Churches – the tension between the universality and the particularity of the Church, "the one and the

---

[2] "Archbishop of Canterbury calls for Primates gathering," *Justin Welby, The Archbishop of Canterbury* (16 September 2015) <http://www.archbishopofcanterbury.org/articles.php/5613/archbishop-of-canterbury-calls-for-primates-gathering> Accessed 17 October 2015.

[3] Ruth Gledhill, "How to understand Justin Welby's vision for Christian unity," *Christian Today* (17 September 2015) <*http://www.christiantoday.com/article/how.to.understand.justin.welbys.vision.for.christian.unity/65040.htm* > Accessed 17 October 2015, and Andrew Brown, "Archbishop of Canterbury plans to loosen ties of divided Anglican Communion," in *The Guardian* (Wednesday 16 September 2015) <http://www.theguardian.com/world/2015/sep/16/archbishop-of-canterbury-urges-breakup-of-divided-anglican-communion> Accessed 17 October 2015.

many" – through a return to historic conciliar principles of gathering the Church together in councils or synods? [4]

Just what are these historic "conciliar" principles? Is "catholic conciliarism" the particular brand of conciliar theory and practice that Anglicans have appropriated as an essential organizing principle for their Churches? If so, at what levels of the church – local, deanery, diocesan, national and global – do we find such principles and practices alive and well in the Mother Church of England and other Churches of the Anglican Communion? Are these principles and practices threatened with extinction by the crises within the Anglican Communion – not because they have failed, but because they have never been fully implemented (See Chapter 6). Or are these crises a call to replace mere shadows of conciliarism with deeper recovery of conciliar principles and structures at the Global level of Anglican Communion governance, with powers that are

---

[4] See John Zizioulas, *The One and the Many: Studies on God, Man, the Church and the World today* New York: St. Vladimir's Seminary Press, 1993), at 339-341: Zizioulas recommends an historical solution – synodality – an institution that ensures the right balance between the "one" and the "many." Synods serve as "instruments of communion" of churches to safeguard unity and harmony. To do this, synods must not interfere with the "internal affairs" of the local church. But what are the limits of those "internal affairs"? Some will certainly argue that they include the presenting issues of human sexuality, marriage and Holy Orders that currently divide the Anglican Communion. But elsewhere Zizioulas makes it clear that there are matters of doctrine discipline and order that are binding on all Churches by virtue of the same enunciated in the first Seven Ecumenical Councils. See John D. Zizioulas, *Lectures in Christian Dogmatics*, edited by Douglas Knight (London: T&T Clark, 2008), 141-142. Thus what may appear to be a merely "internal affair" may have underlying issues of doctrine, discipline and order that affect the whole church, and not just the particular.

dispersed but not suffering a deficit of authority – including a pan-Anglican Council and other structures that could change the very face of Anglicanism?

The answer to these questions is the subject matter of this book. But before answering there are several ways to narrow and thus focus the discussion.

DEFINING THE SHAPE OF "ANGLICAN" CONCILIARISM

First, with regard to the definition of conciliarism, the Catholic canonist Jean Gerson (1363-1429) described the conciliar ideal in his 1415 sermon *Ambulate* that stiffened the resolve of the great Council of Constance (1414-1418) to exert its authority over rival Popes and end the "Great Schism":

> "The Church, or a general council representing it, is so regulated by the direction of the Holy Spirit under authority from Christ that everyone, of whatever rank, even papal, is obliged to hearken to and obey it… [It] is an assembly called under lawful authority, at any place, drawn from every hierarchical rank of the whole Catholic Church, none of the faithful who requires to be heard being excluded, for the wholesome discussion and ordering of those things which affect the proper regulation of the same Church in faith and morals." [5]

But this practice of gathering in councils is distinct from the doctrine of *conciliarity.* "Conciliarity" is the practice of Ecumenical Councils of the *whole Church* to address matters of doctrine, discipline and order. Strictly speaking, these are no longer possible since 1054 AD when there was a great schism between the Churches of the east and west. Despite the practical impossibility of bringing *all Christians*

---

[5] Paul Avis, *Beyond the Reformation? Authority, Primacy and Unity in the Conciliar Tradition* (London: T&T Clark, 2006), p. 85

together in a genuinely "Ecumenical Council," Edith Humphrey recently observed by contrast that "*Conciliarism* is the practice of the Church expressing its life together in different kinds of councils until we can return to the truly Ecumenical Council."[6] It is the practice of the Church meeting at various levels not always to "trouble shoot," but as an essential expression of our life together. These kinds of councils have an old and "august provenance" beginning in the Fourth Century AD and the great councils of Metropolitans beginning later in that same century.[7] In fact, conciliarism was practiced far and wide and for centuries in Catholic Christianity before Gerson and others formulated a conciliar ideal and its principles.[8]

Secondly, we must acknowledge how the tension between catholicity and enculturation of the Gospel shapes both the ideal and the practice of conciliarism. Catholicity may be defined as that which Christians believe and practice "according to the whole" (literally *kat holon*) Church.[9] A major function of councils is to express this

---

[6] Edith Humphrey, *"The Nature of the Church: Apostolic, Conciliar and Concrete,"* lecture delivered at the International Anglican Catholic Conference, Ft. Worth TX (USA), July 15 2015, <http://www.kendallharmon.net/t19/index.php/t19/article/61253/> Accessed 16 August 2015.

[7] Ibid. [n6].

[8] Paul Valliere, *Conciliarism: A History of Decision Making in the Church* (Cambridge: Cambridge University Press, 2012), p. 90. *See also* Ramsey MacMullen, *Voting about God in Early Church Councils* (New Haven and London: Yale University Press, 2006), 7 in which MacMullen estimates that in the period 325-553 AD, after the Council of Nicaea mandated semi-annual provincial synods, some 15,000 ecclesiastical councils must have taken place within the Roman Empire—making conciliar practice a norm for most bishops.

[9] Humphrey, [n6], Ibid. See also *The Commonitorium of St. Vincent of Lerins,* Ch. II.6: "Moreover, in the Catholic Church itself, all possible care

consensus fidelium of and for the whole Church, including Anglicans. Yet the very first "proto-council" in Acts 15 was called because of that missional question of first impression: how to communicate the gospel of Jesus Christ to a new culture, a new context, a new people – the Gentiles. Specifically, should Gentile followers of Christ be required to obey the whole faith as it had been received at that time, including Jewish laws on circumcision and diet? Or was justification by faith in Christ alone enough? The dynamic interplay of scriptures, visions, the living life of the faithful church in the wisdom and authority of the Apostles and other godly leaders of the Church in Acts 11-15 provide a biblical precedent for the practice, if not the ideal, of conciliarism today.[10]

Almost 2,000 years later, the same tension between catholicity and enculturation of the Gospel is at the heart of the difference between the Churches of the Anglican Communion on matters of human sexuality, holy orders and authority in the Church. In their treatise, *To Mend the Net*, Archbishops Drexel Gomez and Maurice Sinclair named this tension in their proposals for a new conciliar response to divisions among Anglicans over such issues:

> "How, in the midst of the pressures of time, do the churches both remain faithful to the teaching and practice of the apostles and yet witness relevantly and in context to

---

must be taken, that we hold that faith which has been believed everywhere, always, by all. For that is truly and in the strictest sense 'Catholic' which, as the name itself and the reason of the thing declare, comprehends all universally." <https://www.crossroadsinitiative.com/library_article/1049/Commonitorium_Vincent_of_Lerins.html> Accessed 16 August 2015.

[10] Humphrey, [n6] ibid. See also Chapter 5, the discussion of Hooker's hermeneutical framework, from Acts 15, for discerning truth in councils when controversies touch upon matters of faith and doctrine.

the truth of the Gospel amongst these changes and chances of history?"[11]

Insofar as the Church of England herself may be characterized as a distinctive "enculturated expression" of Medieval Western Catholicism – adapted to the theological convictions and necessities of the English Reformers while maintaining in large part Catholic canon law and structures – the Anglican practice of conciliarism may have a genius in holding together "elements that are opposed in other traditions."[12] Does this include faithfulness and relevance in mission? Whatever the case may be, any discussion of Anglican conciliarism must recognize its mission focus and its ability to hold apparent opposites in faithful tension.

Finally, if Anglicanism is an expression of Catholic conciliarism, we must ask "what version of Catholic conciliarism – episcopal reforming, quasi-oligarchic or strict constitutional conciliarism? (See Chapter 4). It appears that the Reformers embraced the strict Catholic "constitutional" conciliarism (sometimes called "conciliar constitutionalism") of the Council of Constance and its

[11] Drexel Gomez and Maurice Sinclair, eds., *To Mend the Net: Anglican Faith and Order for Renewed Mission* (Carrollton TX: Ekklesia, 2001), 28.

[12] Paul Avis, *The Identity of Anglicanism: Essentials of Anglican Ecclesiology* (London: Bloomsbury T&T Clark, 2008) at 168-169. But see N Doe, *Christian Law: Contemporary Principles* (Cambridge: Cambridge University Press, 2013), at 120-124, 153, who observes that among Anglicans, Lutherans, Methodists and Reformed/Presbyterians alike, the opposing elements of autonomy and coercive legislative authority are present in the way each Church structures its international and national church structures, with coercive legislative authority present only at the national level, and autonomy subject only to moral suasion and coordination of common mission at the international.

champions such as Jean Gerson. This strict Catholic conciliarism was marked by what Oakley and Tierney describe as a *communio ecclesiology*, being the fundamental conviction that unity and authority is found in a corporate association or "communion" of believers rather than in a single person. Since authority resides in and flows from the whole body of the Church, authority is exercised even in the absence of a singular or effective "head" or "Pope" of the church.[13] This is manifest in the synodal practice that characterized the ancient church for long centuries after the Council of Nicaea (325).[14] Therefore it follows that a council is superior to any bishop, including the Pope, and that such councils are a remedy for errant bishops (including a heretic Pope), with the power even to remove the Pope.[15] Moreover, the corporate nature of the Church

---

[13] Authority in the church flows from the corporate association of its members *(communio)* found in such passages as Acts 11-15, I Corinthians 12 and Ephesians 4. See Francis Oakley, *The Conciliarist Tradition: Constitutionalism in the Catholic Church 1300-1870* (Oxford: OUP, 2003) at 106-107, summarizing and citing Brian Tierney, *Foundations of the Conciliar Theory* (Cambridge: CUP, 1955, reprinted 1968) at 240: "But side by side with this [familiar doctrine of papal sovereignty] there existed another theory [developed notably by the great thirteenth century decretalist Hostiensis] applied first to single churches and then at the beginning of the fourteenth century, in a fragmentary fashion, to the Roman Church and the Church as a whole, a theory which stressed the corporate association of the members of the Church as the true principle of ecclesiastical unity and which envisaged the exercise of corporate authority by the members of the Church even in the absence of an effective head."

[14] Oakley, [n13] at 106.

[15] See Tierney [n13} at 245, where he states that strict Catholic conciliarism is ultimately a restatement of certain early Decretist statements that implied a limitation on papal authority, "impregnated" by Decretal corporation concepts: "The Decretist assertions that only the whole Church was unerring in faith, that a pope could not act against the general well-being of the Church, that, in the last resort, he could be deposed by the Church, provided essential ingredients in all the later theories of conciliar authority."

and its authority means that councils are enduring, and not merely emergency, expression of the authority of the whole Chuch.

However, Anglican Reformers did not embrace the Medieval Catholic provenance of conciliarism without substantial modifications. Above all, and because councils "can and do err," they placed the meeting and decisions of the councils of the Church under the supreme authority of the Holy Scriptures. (See Chapter 5) In short, while conciliarism seems to be an organizing principle of governance within Anglicanism – beginning with the mother Church of England and its Reformational ecclesiology – it is very clearly "a modified conciliarism" (Avis). It may best be described as *episcopally led and synodically governed* as Podmore observes in *Aspects of Anglican Identity*:

> "It is still led and governed by its bishops, but the bishops act not in isolation but in partnership and constant dialogue with the clergy and the laity through the synods of the church, and with their consent."[16]

Anglican conciliarism is characterized by councils or synods that meet as a fundamental expression of the life of the church, and not merely for emergencies. Anglican conciliarism is shaped by the missional tension between Catholicity and enculturation: between faithfulness and relevance. And athough it is an expression of Medieval Catholic strict constitutional conciliarism, nonetheless it is circumscribed by the requirement that the councils or synods of the Church must conform their deliberations,

[16] Colin Podmore, *Aspects of Anglican Identity* (London: Church House Publishing, 2005) at 123.

actions and decisions to the Holy Scriptures as the ultimate standard and rule of faith and practice.

TWO

Principles of Anglican Decision Making in the Mother Church

In *Aspects of Anglican Identity*, Colin Podmore deduces the following ten principles of synodal government in the Church of England[17] which are the roots of Anglican conciliarism, and to which we will add an eleventh—the ultimate authority of Holy Scripture. Since the laws of the Church of England are the primary evidence of whether these principles operate or not, let us examine each of these principles in turn in light of those laws.

1. SYNODICAL GOVERNANCE

[17] Ibid. [n16] at 119-123. We begin with these principles or "roots" of conciliarism within the Mother Church of England. But they have developed into a larger *ius commune* or "Common Law" of the Anglican Communion as they have been applied and developed in different contexts throughout the world. In Chapter 3 we compare Podmore's Principles to *The Principles of Canon Law Common to the Churches of the Anglican Communion (PCLCCAC)* (London: Anglican Communion Office, 2008), which include principles of conciliarism practiced by the Churches of the Anglican Communion.

Synodical government is a permanent, regular and necessary feature of the Church. Podmore traces its history in the Provinces of Canterbury and York back to 601 AD. While the increase of papal power from the 11th Century diminished the role of provincial councils or synods, by the thirteenth century England saw an increase in the number of synodal gatherings. "The councils—sometimes national, sometimes provincial – were of course primarily gatherings of bishops," sometimes attended by abbots, priors, deans and archdeacons.[18] In diocesan and lower assemblies, and when gatherings were called to address the taxation of the clergy, representatives of the lower clergy participated.[19] By the mid-fourteenth century these ad hoc meetings had developed into two conciliar bodies within each Province – the Provincial Council and the Provincial Convocation. By the beginning of the fifteenth century and right up to the Reformation, these two conciliar bodies fused into one body within each province, the Convocations of Canterbury and York. One result of this fusion was the removal of the distinction between council and convocation with regards to the role of the House of Clergy. In Provincial Convocation, the Clergy exercised a right to withhold consent to proposals from the House of Bishops. - and not simply to provide counsel.[20]

The Reformation made no change to the structure and procedures of the Provincial Convocation (other than eliminating abbots and priors from membership). But under the Submission of the Clergy Act (1534), the right to call a convocation passed to the Crown, and no canons could be promulgated that conflicted either with the royal prerogative or Parliament. Convocation was further

[18] Podmore, (n16) at 105.
[19] Ibid.
[20] Ibid. at 105-106.

diminished in 1664 when the Archbishop of Canterbury surrendered the right of the clergy to tax themselves in and through the Convocation. As Podmore notes, "Now that the Crown no longer needed to summon the Convocations in order to obtain taxation, it felt no need to summon them at all."[21] For twenty five years the Convocations did not meet. The Crown summoned the Convocations again in 1689, 1701 and 1717, but disputes and controversies marked these gatherings such that, except for an isolated meeting in 1741, the Convocations were not allowed to transact any business until the mid-nineteenth century.[22]

By that time, the pace of social change exceeded the capacity of Parliament to enact corresponding ecclesiastical legislation. Moreover the presence of Protestant dissenters and Roman Catholic laymen in Parliament led to increasing pressure from the Church of England to allow Convocations to transact business again. While Convocations were allowed to meet and transact business, they still had no legislative or executive powers until 1919, when Parliament passed the Church of England Assembly (Powers) Act, which established a "national assembly" of the Church of England.[23]

The Church of England Assembly consisted of the Convocations of Canterbury and York (bishops and clergy only) and a House of Laity. The Act gave the Assembly power to enact "measures" ***subject to*** review by a joint ecclesiastical committee of both Houses of Parliament and approval as a whole by resolution of both houses. It would then receive the royal assent and become the statutory law

[21] Ibid. at 107-108.

[22] Ibid. 108.

[23] Ibid. at 108-109.

of England, as if by Act of Parliament. As Podmore notes, "this system of legislation by measure remains unchanged today."[24]

However, the Church of England Assembly (Powers) Act (1919) proved too cumbersome. There was no provision for the two Convocations and the House of Laity to discuss canonical revisions *together.* This resulted in the Synodical Government Measure (1969) that established the General Synod effective 1970. The General Synod consists of the Convocations of Canterbury and York with a House of Laity *meeting together* – the upper houses of the Convocations forming the House of Bishops and the lower houses forming the House of Clergy. While the Convocations may and do meet apart from General Synod, it is only the Synod that has inherited the powers from the Church Assembly Act (1919) to pass measures which, if approved by both houses of Parliament and receive the Royal assent, become the law of England.[25]

The purpose of the Synodal Government Measure (1969) is "to rename and reconstitute the Church Assembly as the General Synod *and to make further provision for the synodical government of the Church of England* "(emphasis added).[26] General Synod is a permanent, regular and necessary expression of the life and governance of the

[24] Ibid. at 109.

[25] Ibid. at 109-110. See also the distinction in Synodal authority between measure and canon: "in the case of a measure it is the royal assent that gives it the force of law, whereas in the case of a canon the royal license and assent only empower the Synod to 'promulgate and execute a canon'—it is the action of the Synod (not the Crown) that gives a canon its legal validity."

[26] Synodical Government Measure 1969 (*SGM)* Introductory Text 25th July 1969 < http://www.legislation.gov.uk/ukcm/1969/2/contents > Accessed 29 August 2015

Church, which can trace its roots all the way back to the 7th Century. It meets at least twice a year, and at such other times as it may provide – not just in emergencies.[27] The same is true for diocesan synods[28] who also specify the minimum number of meetings for all deanery synods each year.[29] Parochial Church Councils (PCC) meet at least four times per year, and additional meetings may be convened by the Chair or not less than one-third of the members of the PCC.[30]

By its constitution,[31] General Synod exercises a legislative and a deliberative function only.[32] The work of the General Synod continues between their meetings, and when the Synod is dissolved at the end of an electoral period, its work is prorogued, the new synod is immediately elected and carries on its business.[33] Although the Synodical Government Measure is silent on the matter,

---

[27] *SGM*, [n26] Sched. 2, Article 3(1).

[28] Ibid, Sched. 3 at s.34 (1) (c-d): "in the case of a diocese in which area synods have been constituted in accordance with section 17 of the Dioceses Measure 1978, not less than one and in the case of any other diocese not less than two shall be held in each year," and "a meeting of the diocesan synod shall be held if not less than a specified number of members of the synod so request."

[29] Ibid, Sched. 3 at s.28 (1) (c).

[30] Ibid, Sched. 3, Appendix II, ss.2-3.

[31] Ibid, Sched 2. Art. 6.

[32] M Hill, *Ecclesiastical Law, Third Edition* (Oxford: OUP, 2007) As Hill observes at 43, "First, it is to consider matters of concerning the Church of England and make provision for them by measure, canon, order or act of synod and, secondly, it is to consider and express its opinion on any other matters of religious or public interest. It has no judicial function."

Synod lacks any executive function, and the Archbishops Council now undertakes those functions between meetings formerly discharged by the Standing Committee.[34]

Diocesan synods have a bishop's council and standing committee that may carry out the advisory and consultative functions of the synod between meetings.[35] Diocesan Synod may also delegate executive functions to the deanery synods between meetings.[36] Deanery synods have a standing committee that carries on their work between meetings.[37] PCCs also have a standing committee with power to transact the business of the council between its meetings and subject to its directions,[38] and may appoint other committees to carry on the work of the church.[39] In other words, the length and continuity of synods at every level of the Church, both during meetings and between, can be said to reflect the councils of the Medieval Catholic conciliarists of the 14th and 15th centuries.

2. REPRESENTATIVE GATHERING OF THE WHOLE CHURCH

Synods are a representative gathering of the whole church: Bishops, clergy and laity, with clergy and laity involved in equal numbers. In the Church of England, the General Synod is a gathering of the whole Church through the House of Bishops and the House of Clergy in the Convocations of Canterbury and York, and a House of

---

[33] *SGM,* [n26], at Art. 3(3): "Business pending at the dissolution of the General Synod shall not abate, but may be resumed by the new Synod at the stage reached before the dissolution."

[34] Hill, [n32] at 43.

[35] *SGM,* [n26] s.4 (4) and Sched. 3, s.34 (l).

[36] Ibid, s.4 (5).

[37] Ibid, Sched 3. at s.28(1)(e)

[38] Ibid, Sched. 3, Appendix II, s. 14(a)(b)

[39] Ibid, Sched. 3, Appendix II, s.15

Laity.[40] The bishops of both Convocations form a single, upper House of Bishops, while the clergy of both Convocations form a single, lower House of Clergy, to which are added the House of Laity representing lay members from across the entire Church.[41] According to Podmore, since 2005 there are 52 bishops in the upper House: 44 diocesans, the Bishop of Dover and 7 elected representatives of the other suffragan and assisting bishops.[42] The House of Clergy includes persons representing clergy of the dioceses, university clergy, deans and provosts of cathedrals, archdeacons, chaplains of the armed forces, and religious communities.[43] The House of Laity includes four classes of communicant lay people: those elected by the diocesan electors of each diocese, lay persons chosen by lay members of religious communities, ex-officio members and co-opted members.[44] The lower Houses of Clergy and Laity are roughly equal in number, with approximately 205 clergy and 207 laity (since 2005).[45]

A diocesan synod consists of a house of bishops, a house of clergy and a house of laity. The house of bishops includes the diocesan bishop, suffragan bishops and any such assisting bishops nominated by the diocesan and

---

[40] Ibid, Sched. 2, Arts. 1 and 2.

[41] Ibid.

[42] Podmore, [n16] at 112. See also N Doe, *The Legal Framework of the Church of England* (Oxford: Clarendon Press, 1996) at 57: "The House of Bishops consists of the members of the Upper Houses of both Convocations (which include the two archbishops and all diocesan bishops as well as bishops elected by and from the suffragan bishops of the two provinces).

[43] *The Canons of the Church of England, Seventh Edition* (London: Church House Publishing, 2012), Can. H2.

[44] *SGM*, [n26] Sched.3, Pt. V, *CRR* "Church Representation Rules," rr. 35-42.

[45] Podmore, [n16] at 112.

approved by the provincial archbishop.[46] The house of clergy includes *ex officio* members, those elected by the houses of clergy in the deanery synods, and not more than five co-opted members.[47] The house of laity includes *ex officio* members, those elected by the houses of laity in the deanery synods, and not more than five co-opted members who are actual communicants.[48] The numbers of the houses of clergy and laity are approximately equal.[49]

A deanery synod consists of a house of clergy and a house of laity. The house of clergy includes beneficed or licensed deanery clergy, extra-parochial clergy serving institutions in the deanery, clerical members of General Synod or diocesan synod resident in the deanery, and any other clergy resident or working in the deanery. The house of laity includes representatives elected to the synod by the annual meetings of deanery parishes, lay members of General Synod, diocesan synod or an area synod whose names are on the electoral roll of a deanery parish, lay representatives of a community under the care of a chaplain licensed by the bishop, deaconesses and lay-workers licensed by the bishop to work in any part of the deanery, and co-opted members who are actual communicants,[50] with the provision that "the house of laity is not less in number than the house of clergy."[51]

---

[46] *SGM*, [n26] Sched 3., *CRR* r.30(2)
[47] Ibid, r. 30(4).
[48] Ibid, r. 30(5).
[49] Ibid, Sched. 3 at rr. 30(1) and 31(8). See also r. 33(1) which provides that the diocesan synod may vary the rules of representation on the diocesan synods "*to secure better representation* of clergy or laity or both on the diocesan synods." (Emphasis added).
[50] Ibid, Sched. 3 at rr. 24(6) and 24(7).
[51] Ibid, Sched. 3, rr. 24(1) and 25(6). See also r.26 (1) which provides that the diocesan synod may vary the rules of representation on the deanery

In short, under the Measure and its Church Representation Rules, each level of conciliar governance (synod) within the Church of England is representative of the breadth and width of the whole Church, "none of the faithful who requires to be heard being excluded" (Gerson).

3. *CONSENSUS FIDELIUM* (THE MIND OF THE WHOLE CHURCH)

Important and controversial matters of faith, doctrine and order must be guided by the mind of the whole church (the "*consensus fidelium*"), with the support of all three houses (bishops, clergy and laity) voting separately.

The Constitution of General Synod provides that final approval of *any* Measure or Canon requires a vote "on a division by Houses" and the assent of the majority of the members of each House present and voting.[52] But there is no such discretion when it comes to matters touching "doctrinal formula," services, ceremonies, administration of the Sacraments, or sacred rites of the Church. Such provisions shall be submitted for final approval "in terms proposed by the House of Bishops and not otherwise."[53] While General Synod has unlimited power at law to

synods *"to secure better representation* of clergy or laity or both on the deanery synods." (Emphasis added).

[52] Ibid, at Art. 5(1). However, this requirement may be dispensed with by permission of the chair and with the leave of the General Synod in accordance with Standing Orders.

[53] Ibid, at Art.7 (1). See also S Slack, "Synodical Government and the Legislative Process," *14 Ecc LJ 43-81* (2012), at 57, where he narrows the definition of Article 7 business to any "provisions"— and not merely resolutions—"relating or pertaining to...doctrinal formula, services and so forth of the Church of England."

change the doctrine of the Church, it can do so only by observing rigorous procedures which reflect the mind of the whole Church, as Doe observes:

> "(B)y requiring the participation of the whole church as represented in General Synod, they give juridical expression to the theological principle that doctrines ought to be derived from a *consensus fidelium*...If they so require, the two Convocations (or either of them) or the House of Laity may insist on the provision being referred to them [in the form proposed by the House of Bishops] by Convocations sitting separately and by the House of Laity... A provision which fails to secure the approval on a reference by each of the four Houses of Convocation or by the House of Laity [is] not to be proposed again in the same or similar form until a new General Synod comes into being."[54]

However, if only one House of one Convocation objects, a second reference may be made to the Convocations. If there is a second objection from one of the Houses of Convocation, the provision may be referred to the General Synod's Houses of Bishops and Clergy, and their approval by a two-thirds vote in each House is sufficient and operates in lieu of approval by the four Houses of Convocation.[55]

There are also rigorous procedures which reflect the need for approval by the whole Church (*consensus fidelium*) with regards to permanent changes in the Sacraments of Baptism, Holy Communion or the Ordinal, "or a scheme

---

[54] Doe, [n42] at 258-259.

[55] Doe, [n42] at 259 citing *SGM* Sched. 2, Art.7 (5). See also Slack, "Synodical Government and the Legislative Process," [n53] at 56-57, who describes the power conferred on the Houses of Convocation and Laity as one to delay or veto Article 7 business, and "qualified" in that their veto can be overridden by a 2/3 majority in each of the Houses of Bishops and Clergy.

for a constitutional union or a permanent and substantial change between the Church of England and another substantial Christian body" (whose members reside in Great Britain). Any such changes by Measure or Canon must first be approved by a majority of the dioceses of the Church at meetings of their Synods.[56] Any permanent changes in the Services of Baptism, Holy Communion or the Ordinal require the assent of a two-thirds vote in each House of the General Synod.[57] By resolution of General Synod, a scheme of constitutional union or permanent and substantial change of relationship between the Church and another Christian body in the U.K. may also require a special majority of each House or the whole Synod or both.[58]

4. BISHOPS HAVE A PARTICULAR ROLE IN FAITH, ORDER AND LITURGY

Within the General Synod the bishops have a particular role as the guardians of the faith and order of the Church and its liturgy. As noted above, Article 7 of the Synod's constitution preserves the ancient and catholic role of bishops as guardians of the faith and order of the Church

[56] *SGM*, [n26], Sched. 2, Art.8(1) see also Art.8(1A) which provides that the Archbishops may also require approval by a majority of dioceses for a scheme of constitutional union or substantial change in relationship with a Christian body whose members do not reside in Great Britain.

[57] Ibid, at Art.8 (1C). See also Slack, [n53] at 58: Article 8 business requires approval by majority of dioceses *before* it may proceed to General Synod, and final approval by at least a 2/3 majority in each House "and may be made subject to the requirement of the assent of such special majorities (whether of each House or the whole Synod or both) as the Synod may provide for by resolution.

[58] *SGM,* [n26], at Art.8 (1B).

and its liturgy.[59] Synod may only consider a provision which touches the doctrinal formula, the services and ceremonies of the Church, the administration of the sacraments or sacred rites thereof, or the identity of the Church "on terms provided by the house of Bishops and not otherwise."[60] In other words, any proposed changes in doctrine or liturgy must first be referred to the House of Bishops and can only be submitted for final approval in terms proposed by the bishops. If Convocations or the House of Laity require the provision to be referred to the Convocations before Synod, they cannot change the terms or the text proposed by the bishops. Synod may only give final approval on the terms and the text proposed by the bishops. Moreover, the ability of any 25 members (which is just under half the membership of the House of Bishops) to require a majority vote by Houses means that a majority of the House of Bishops can prevent any proposal from being enacted.[61] For all these reasons, Podmore observes,

> "Here the bishops' role as guardians of the faith and liturgy is preserved. Thus the Church of England remains an episcopally led as well as synodically governed church."[62]

---

[59] See Slack, [n53], at 56: the requirement that Article 7 business must be (1) referred to the House of Bishops *before* being finally approved by the Synod and (2) must be submitted for Final Approval *only* in terms proposed by that House recognizes "the special position of the House [of Bishops] in the polity of the Church; its members having been ordained as 'teachers' and 'guardians of the faith'." (Emphasis added) Slack goes on to give an example in 2009 of the Bishops' unfettered power of Amendment conferred by Article 7, with respect to their amending a draft Canon relating to the celebration of the Holy Communion in local ecumenical projects.

[60] Ibid, at Art.7 (1).

[61] Ibid, at Art. 5(2).

[62] Podmore, [n16] at 115. But see Slack, [n53] at 44, who takes issue with the term "episcopally led, synodically governed" as misleading because (1)

This last point is crucial. Even though Article 7 safeguards the prerogatives of Bishops to state the terms and the text of any changes to doctrine and liturgy, the House of Clergy and the House of Laity have the right to delay or veto those changes and send them back to the Bishops for further work. Episcopal leadership which may be in error on matters of doctrine and liturgy can be "checked and balanced" in synod by the Houses of Clergy and Laity, as well as the Convocations. This is a living example of the inheritance from Medieval Catholic constitutional conciliarism.

5. DIOCESAN SYNODS ARE LIMITED IN THEIR SCOPE

Subsidiarity applies: Diocesan Synods are limited in their scope and may not make decisions unilaterally which touch upon the faith and order of the Church. Under the *SGM* 1969, a diocesan synod has no authority to issue any statement purporting to declare the doctrine of the Church on any question.[63] The same limitation applies to deanery

---

it suggests that episcopal leadership is exercised outside the context of synodical government, (2) it fails to take account of the subtlety and complexity of the relationships between bishops, clergy and laity in Synod, and (3) it suggests that Synod enjoys executive power "rather than the legislative and deliberative powers of a parliament." Slack would prefer the term "bishop in synod' because it more accurately reflects the limitations on Synod not to usurp the role of bishops as guardians of the faith, or to pass legislation to which they are opposed, while ensuring that bishops hear the views of the representatives of the clergy and laity. So long as this is the context in which "episcopally led, synodically governed" is understood, it seems to be a helpful shorthand for understanding the conciliar nature of synodal government.

[63] *SGM*, [n26] "Constitution and functions of Diocesan Synods", s. 4(2).

synods[64] and Parochial Church Councils.[65] This reflects the principle of subsidiarity within conciliar governance – namely, that problems should be addressed at the most immediate level consistent with their solution. And since the doctrine of the Church must be a reflection of the whole Church (the *consensus fidelium*,) it is reserved to the whole Church meeting in General Synod.[66] In fact, it is the whole Church meeting in Synod which can, as a matter of both supremacy and subsidiarity, "extend, amend or further define" the functions of diocesan synods.[67]

Instead, the diocesan synod is primarily a deliberative, advisory and consultative body whose functions are enumerated in section 4(2) of the Synodical Government Measure.[68]

At the same time, the diocesan synod "shall make rules for deanery synods" (at a lower level of governance) which shall provide for such matters as the appointment of a clergyperson and a layperson as joint chairs of the deanery synod, the minimum number of meetings, how votes may

---

[64] Ibid, "Constitution and Function of Deanery Synods," s.5 (3).

[65] Ibid, "Functions of Parochial Church Councils," s.6 (2) (2) (b).

[66] See definition of the doctrine of subsidiarity in Wikipedia, <https://en.wikipedia.org/wiki/Subsidiarity> Accessed 29 August 2015. For discussion of application of this doctrine to legislation in the Church of England, see N Doe's discussion of "The Supremacy of General Synod" in *The Legal Framework of the Church of England* [n42] at 56-70, and for "The power to Formulate and Authorize Liturgy" at 287-291.

[67] *SGM*, [n26] "Constitution and functions of Diocesan Synods" at s.4 (6).

[68] Ibid., at s. 4(2): "...to consider matters concerning the Church of England and to make provision for such matters in relation to their diocese, and to consider and express their opinion on any other matters of religious or public interest...[and] to advise the bishop on any matters on which he may consult the synod." By amendment in 2003, the functions of a diocesan synod also include consideration of the annual budget for the dioceses and to approve or disapprove them, and to consider the annual accounts of the diocesan board of finance. S. 4(2) (d) and (e) (as amended).

be taken "and such other matters…as the diocesan synod sees fit."[69] In this case, subsidiarity empowers the diocesan synod to address some deanery level issues at a level it feels itself most competent to address.

6. SYNODAL GOVERNANCE FOR ALL LEVELS OF CHURCH

Synodal government must exist at the levels of deanery, diocese and national Church, and may exist at the local church level. Diocesan Synods "shall be constituted" for all dioceses of the Church of England.[70] While conciliar governance at the diocesan level continues to be "episcopally led and synodically governed," "it shall be the duty of the bishop to consult with the diocesan synod on matters of general concern and importance to the diocese."[71] The functions of a diocesan synod include those typically associated with a "council" at this level: considering matters concerning the Church and making provision for such matters in relation to the diocese, advising the bishop on matters for which he is seeking their counsel, and considering and expressing an opinion on any matters referred to them by General Synod.[72] The relationship between diocesan bishop and synod reflects the principles of strict constitutional conciliarism formulated by the Medieval Catholic conciliarists (see Chapter 4).

Likewise, Deanery Synods shall be constituted for all deaneries in the Church of England.[73] Under the principle

---

[69] Ibid, Sched. 3, s.28.

[70] *SGM*, [n26] "Constitution and functions of Diocesan Synods", s.4 (1).

[71] Ibid, at s. 4(3).

[72] Ibid, at s.2.

[73] Ibid., "Constitution and functions of Deanery Synods," s.5(1)

of subsidiarity, the deanery synods address problems which are appropriate to the level at which the deanery functions. Those functions include considering matters concerning the Church of England and making provision for those matters in relation to their deanery, gathering the parishes of the deanery together to formulate common policies on common problems, to implement provisions made by the diocesan synod, to provide "sound parochial opinion" when required or appropriate to do so, and to raise matters of concern to the Diocesan Synod.[74] Like the diocesan synod, the deanery synod may not issue any statement purporting to declare the doctrine of the Church on any matter.[75]

Although the mandatory language in *SGM* 1969 requiring synods for all dioceses and deaneries within the Church is lacking for Parochial Church Councils, the Parochial Church Councils (Powers) Measure 1956 provides that "it ***shall be the duty*** of the minister and the parochial church council to consult together on matters of general concern and importance to the parish."[76] It is significant that the Measure describes Parochial Church Councils as "the Council."[77] In keeping with the principle of subsidiarity, the functions of the PCC are appropriate to the problems and solutions they face at the parish level.[78]

---

[74] Ibid., at s.5(3)

[75] Ibid.

[76] Parochial Church Councils (Powers) Measure 1956 <http://www.legislation.gov.uk/ukcm/Eliz2/4-5/3/contents> Accessed 23 October 2015, at s.2 (Emphasis added). See also *SGM* [n26], "Functions of Parochial Church Councils," s.6 (2) (1).

[77] Parochial Church Councils, [n76] at s.1 "Definitions" and throughout the Measure.

[78] Ibid, at ss. 2 and 7: power to frame an annual budget, levy and collect as needed for the maintenance of the church; power with the minister to determine the objects to which all income shall be allocated and to making

Annual meetings of the PCC elect in every third year parochial representatives of the laity to the deanery synod, and any person entitled to attend the meeting "may ask any question about parochial church matters, or bring about a discussion of any matter of parochial or *general interest*"(emphasis added).[79] As Hill observes:

> "...the contemporary model of the relationship between a minister and the PCC is one of mutual co-operation and support, combining joint decision-making and a cross-fertilization of ideas and initiatives. The keynotes are interaction and consensus in what is often styled a collaborative ministry."[80]

Such councils (PCC) are in fact a regular feature of conciliar governance, their meetings must reflect the participatory nature of councils, and they are a necessary and regular part of the governance of the Church at the parish level.

7. EACH MEMBER OF SYNOD REPRESENTS "THE WHOLE"

Synods manifest "ecclesial density": The presence of Synods at the national and provincial levels of a Church indicate a corporate identity and "wholeness" of which

---

representations together to the bishop on any matters affecting the welfare of the church, considering matters concerning the Church of England "or many other matters of religious or public interest, *but not the declaration of the doctrine of the Church on any question*" (emphasis added), making known and implementing provisions made by the diocesan and or deanery synod, giving advice to the diocesan and or deanery synod, and raising such matters as the PCC considers appropriate with the diocesan or deanery synod. See also *SGM*. [n26] s.6 (2) (2).

[79] Ibid, Sched. 3, ss.9 (5) (a) and 9(7).

[80] Hill [n32] at 75.

each participating member is a representative (rather than as an advocate for a competing group within the whole).

Although *SGM* 1969 is silent on this principle, Podmore observes:

> "The fact that synods, and not mere conferences, exist at the provincial and national levels is an indication of 'ecclesial density' at those levels. The Church of England has a corporate identity at the national level,"

and he goes on to observe that this is represented by the bishops sitting together at Synod "mainly" as the corporate episcopal leadership of the Church at the national level, and around which the rest of the Synod gathers (see Principle 8, below). He then concludes,

> "The General Synod is not a federal conference at which largely autonomous dioceses are represented by delegations casting 'block votes.' Each member speaks and votes as an individual member of the whole Synod (or of his or her house within the Synod) and exercises those responsibilities on behalf of the whole church at the national level."[81]

8. A SYNOD IS A GATHERING AROUND BISHOPS

---

[81] Podmore, [n16] at 121. His authority for this proposition seems to lie in the definition of the word "synod" which means "a body of people who are together on the way." It is in the sense that the General Synod is a body of people who are elected for five year terms, who meet together two or three times a year during that term and in that process develop a "corporate life" or identity in which each member, ideally, seeks the good of the corporate whole. This continuous expression of synodality—of "a body of people who are together on the way"—is what Podmore describes as "ecclesial density." See also C. Podmore, "A Tale of Two Churches: The Ecclesiologies of The Episcopal Church and the Church of England Compared," *International Journal for the Study of the Christian Church*, Vol. 8, No. 2, May 2008, 124-154 at 131. First published in *Ecclesiastical Law Journal* (2008), 10 Ecc. LJ 34-70.

A Synod is a gathering of the whole church around (and indeed under) its bishops, never over against them. The Procedures of Diocesan Synods in the ***SGM*** 1969 make it difficult, if not impossible, for the clergy and laity to pass any measure or policy over and against the diocesan bishop. In the case of a particular question before the synod (except a matter referred to the Diocesan Synod by the General Synod under Article 8 of its constitution), there can be no assent to the question by the house of bishops unless there is a majority ***including the diocesan*** (emphasis added). In addition, the diocesan bishop may require a vote by orders, may cast a second or casting vote if there is an equal division in the house of bishops, and shall have the right to have his opinion on the question recorded in the minutes.[82] However, Rule 53(2) of the ***SGM*** 1969 prohibits a bishop from giving any direction within the bishop's diocese contrary to any resolution of the General Synod.[83]

9. A SYNOD'S CONCERNS TRANSCEND CHURCH LIFE

A Synod is concerned not only with the internal life of the Church but also with the needs and issues of the world

---

[82] *SGM*, [n26], Sched 3., s.34(1)(e-g, i-j); see, e.g., *The Standing Orders and Constitutions of the Exeter Diocesan Synod*, <http://www.exeter.anglican.org/wp-content/uploads/2014/10/Diocesan-synod-standing-orders.pdf> Accessed 31 August 2015, SO 60, 61, 64A and 64B and *The Standing Orders of the Synod of the Diocese of Liverpool*, < http://www.bing.com/search?q=Standing+Orders+of+the+Synod+of+the+Diocese+of+Liverpool&form=PRDLCS&pc=MDDCJS&mkt=en-us&refig=c33286b68c3344df985e767bc358c075&pq=standing+orders+of+the+synod+of+the+diocese+of+liverpool&sc=0-26&sp=-1&qs=n&sk=&cvid=c33286b68c3344df985e767bc358c075> Accessed 31 August 2015, SO 57(b), 58(b), 62, 63 and 66.

[83] *SGM*, [n26], Sched. 3, s.53 (2).

and with the Church's *mission to the world.* Both the General Synod and Diocesan Synods are to "consider and express their opinion not only on matters relating to the diocese, but "on any other matters of religious or public interest."[84] A more robust focus on mission is vested in the Archbishop's Council, whose objects are "to co-ordinate, promote, aid and further *the work and mission of the Church of England.*"(Emphasis added).[85] The Archbishops' Council is accountable to General Synod but not subordinate to it, and must cause a report of its work and proceedings to be laid before Synod.[86]

It seems another expression of subsidiarity that the clearest expressions of mission are found in the functions of deanery synods and parochial councils – where mission to the world is most immediate. Synods in the deaneries "promote…the whole mission of the Church, pastoral, evangelistic, social and ecumenical,"[87] while the PCC is

---

[84] Ibid, [n26] "Schedule 2: Constitution of the General Synod," Art. 6(b) and "Constitution and functions of Diocesan Synods," s.4 (2) (a).

[85] Hill, [n32] at 38-39, citing National Institutions Measure 1998 <http://www.legislation.gov.uk/ukcm/1998/1/introduction > Accessed 1 September 2015, s. 1(1). However, as Podmore notes in "A Tale of Two Churches," [n81] at 149: "The Archbishop's Council, as the Church of England's executive council is called—and the name is significant—is expected not so much to have its own vision for the Church of England *as to implement that of the House of Bishops. On major issues of policy, the Archbishop's Council cannot in practice act without the agreement of the House of Bishops."* (Emphasis added).

[86] National Institutions Measure 1998, [n85] s. 4(1) (2). See also s. 9 (a) (b): General Synod must be given an opportunity at each group of sessions to question representatives of the Archbishops' Council in connection with any reports, budgets, draft legislations to be passed by Synod, and any other matters referred to Synod by the Council.

[87] *SGM,* [n26], "Constitution and functions of Deanery Synods," s.5 (3) (b).

charged to work with the incumbent in promoting that "whole mission of the Church" in the parish.[88]

10. A SYNOD IS A SPIRITUAL GATHERING

A Synod is a gathering for more than governance: it is a gathering which expresses the spiritual life and event of the Church through daily worship and prayer, and Holy Eucharist. Although ***SGM*** 1969 is silent on this matter, Podmore observes from the life of Synod itself that "a synod is a liturgical—indeed, a Eucharistic—and spiritual body."

> "Each day's session of the General Synod begins with prayer and ends with a blessing given by one of the presidents; the inauguration of a new General Synod begins with a celebration of the Eucharist at Westminster Abbey, there is a big celebration of the Eucharist in York Minister on the Sunday morning of the July group of sessions in York, and about once a year there is also a celebration of the Eucharist in the Synod chamber; in addition there are celebrations of the Eucharist each day outside the session for those who wish to attend. When final decisions are taken about weighty and controversial matters, it is customary for the chairman to call for a period of silent prayer before the Synod votes, and for the result to be heard in silence."[89]

11. A SYNOD MUST CONFORM TO THE AUTHORITY OF HOLY SCRIPTURE

Any and every decision of a Synod must conform to the ultimate authority of Holy Scripture. Although ***SGM*** 1969

[88] Ibid, "Functions of Parochial Church Councils," s.6 (2) (a).
[89] Podmore, [n16] at 122.

is silent on this matter, the Thirty-Nine Articles of Religion are not. Article VI "Of the sufficiency of the holy Scriptures for salvation,"[90] Article XX "Of the authority of the Church"[91] and Article XXI "Of the authority of general councils"[92] together establish the Scriptures as the ultimate source of doctrine, authority and rule of faith and practice within the Church – including its councils or synods. With respect to ordained ministers (who make up two of the three houses of General Synod), Avis observes that in the law of the Church of England we have "a convenient and succinct account of Anglican confessional identity" in the Preface to the Declaration of Assent in Canon C15.[93] This includes the inheritance from Article

---

[90] J.I. Packer, *The Thirty-nine Articles: Their Place and Use Today* (Oxford: Latimer House, 1984) at 7, citing Ar. VI: "Holy scripture contains all things necessary to salvation: so that whatsoever is not read therein, nor may be proved thereby, is not to be required of any man, that it should be believed as an article of the Faith, or be thought requisite or necessary to salvation."

[91] Packer, [n90] at 12-13, citing Ar. XX: "The Church hath power to decree rites or ceremonies, and authorities in controversies of faith: and yet it is not lawful for the Church to ordain anything that is contrary to God's Word written, neither may it so expound one place of Scripture , that it may be repugnant to another."

[92] Ibid, [n90] at 13, citing Ar. XXI: "General councils...when they be gathered together, (forasmuch as they be an assembly of men, whereof all be not governed with the Spirit and the Word of God,) they may err, and sometimes have erred, even in things pertaining unto God. Wherefore things ordained by them as necessary to salvation have neither strength nor authority, unless it may be declared that they be taken out of holy Scripture."

[93] Avis, P. *The Identity of Anglicanism,* [n12] at 10; *The Canons of The Church of England 2012* [n42]: The Preface of the Declaration of Assent in Canon C 15 reads as follows: "The Church of England is part of the One, Holy, Catholic and Apostolic Church worshipping in the one true God, Father, Son and Holy Spirit. It professes the faith uniquely revealed in the Holy Scriptures and set forth in the catholic creeds, which faith the Church is called upon to proclaim afresh in each generation. Led by the Holy Spirit, it has borne witness to Christian truth in its historic formularies, the Thirty-

XXI specifically, that councils can and do err, "wherefore things ordained by them as necessary to salvation have neither strength nor authority, unless it may be declared that they be taken out of holy scripture."[94]

Of course, it may be argued that there is liberty with regards to matters that are not "necessary to salvation," or where Scripture is silent, as well as matters that do not touch on the more rigorous procedural and voting requirements under Articles 7 and 8 of the constitution of General Synod touching doctrinal formulas, the services, the ceremonies or the administration of the Sacraments or sacred rites of the Church. Even so, the Scriptures remains the standard against which such exceptions may be argued.

nine Articles of Religion, *The Book of Common Prayer* and the Ordering of Bishops, Priests and Deacons. In the declaration you are about to make will you affirm your loyalty to this inheritance of faith as your inspiration and guidance under God in bringing the grace and truth of Christ to this generation and making him known to those in your care?" (Emphasis added).

[94] Packer, [n90] at 13.

THREE

Principles of Conciliarism at Work Elsewhere in the Anglican Communion

The laws of the other Churches of the Anglican Communion are the evidence from which we may conclude whether conciliarism remains an essential organizing principle of Anglican polity and governance. If we examine four representative Churches of the Communion across the globe – Australia, South-East Asia, Nigeria and Ireland – we find that the same eleven principles of conciliarism we saw in the last chapter, as well as shared principles of conciliar governance in the "common law" of the Anglican Communion,[95] are indeed present and active in the constitutions and canons of these four Churches and their dioceses.[96] Let us examine each of

[95] See the *PCLCCAC,* [n17], Definitions, at 95-96: "A 'principle of canon law' is a foundational proposition or maxim of general applicability which has a strong dimension of weight, is induced from the similarities of the legal systems of churches, derives from the canonical tradition or other practices of the church, expresses a basic theological truth or ethical value, and is about, is implicit in, or underlies canon law."

[96] Two representative dioceses were chosen from each Church. The Dioceses of Adelaide and North Queensland for Australia, the Dioceses of Singapore and Kuching for South East Asia, the Dioceses of Ogbia and

these eleven conciliar principles in practice in other Churches of the Anglican Communion.

1. SYNODOL GOVERNMENT AS NECESSARY, REGULAR AND PERMAMENT

All four Churches have a national[97] or Provincial assembly, namely, a synod, council or other body,[98] that is

---

Etsako for Nigeria, and the Dioceses of Connor and Down and Dromore for Ireland.

[97] Is "national" the best term to describe the "Provinces" of the Anglican Communion? In *Canon Law in the Anglican Communion: A Worldwide Perspective* (Oxford: Oxford University Press, 1998) at 9-10, Norman Doe observes that churches within the Communion fall into five broad categories: (1) National, corresponding to the territorial boundaries of the secular state in which they exist; (2) Provincial, corresponding to secular jurisdictional divisions within a state; (3) Regional, operating territorially over a number of secular states; (4) Extra-Provincial, organized as a diocese which is not part of a province but comes under the direct jurisdiction of the Archbishop of Canterbury or another Church, and (5) United, founded as a result of a constitutional union between Anglican Churches and other Christian Churches. In this Chapter, Australia and Nigeria are national, while South East Asia and Ireland are regional. In Chapter 7, The Episcopal Church USA is national (organized as well around several provinces), while the Anglican Church in North America is regional (covering the United States, Canada and now Mexico).

[98] The variety of usage among the Churches of the Anglican Communion with respect to the name of the "central church assembly" (synod, council, convocation or convention) raises the question whether those differences are meaningful. On the one hand, the *PCLCCAC* defines the central church assembly simply as the highest representative and legislative authority within a church "which may have the title General Synod, General Convention, Provincial Council or other style." On the other hand, Podmore says the difference is not without a distinction. Synods, councils and convocations are all convened by a lawful ecclesiastical authority, namely the Bishop, whereas a "convention" connotes a voluntary gathering and association within an ecclesial body initiated by clergy and laity. C. Podmore, "A Tale of Two Churches: The Ecclesiologies of The Episcopal Church and the Church of England Compared," [n81] at 128-129. In practice, whether called by bishops or by authority of the constitution and

the permanent, necessary and regular feature of the life and governance of the Church, and not merely episodic.[99] The Provincial or General Synod is the supreme legislative body of the Church,[100] although Australia reserves such power for "the several synods" subject to the provisions of

---

canons of the Church, the distinction seems to be one without much difference.

[99] *PCLCCAC,* [n17], Principle 15.6; *The Constitution Canons and Rules of the Anglican Church of Australia 2014, Tenth Edition* (Sydney: The Anglican Church of Australia Trust Corporation, 2014) <http://www.anglican.org.au/governance/Documents/Green%20Book%202014_120215.pdf> Accessed 17 July 2015, Constit, II.5, IV.15 ("General Synod"); *Constitution and Canons of The Province of The Anglican Church in South East Asia* (Received by email dated 12 August 2015 from Stephanie Ng, Bishop's Office, Diocese of Singapore), Constit., VII(a) ("Provincial Synod"); *Constitution and Canons of The Church of Nigeria (Anglican Communion)* (Received by email dated 22 July 2015 from Gbenga Fatoye on behalf of Abraham Yisa, Registrar of the Church of Nigeria), Constit. II.5 ("General Synod"); Brenda Sheil, ed., *The Constitution of The Church of Ireland as set out in the First Schedule to the Statute of the General Synod, Chapter XV of 2003 and An Appendix comprising the standing orders of General Synod, the provisions relating to the constitution, duties and powers of the Standing Committee and the Board of Education of the General Synod, etc.* (Dublin: The General Synod of the Church of Ireland, 2003) (Received by email 21 July 2015 from Dr. Catherine Smith, Synod Officer, Church of Ireland House, Dublin), Ch.I.1.1 ("General Synod").

[100] See *PCLCCAC,* [n17], Principle 19.1: "The power to legislate is vested in the representative assemblies of a church." See Australia [n99], Constit. II.5 ("plenary authority and power to make canons, ordinances and rules") and V.26; South East Asia [n99], Constit. VII (a) ("Provincial Synod...shall be the legislative body of this Province"); Nigeria [n99], Constit. III.22 ("For the avoidance of doubt, the General Synod... shall be the legislative body of the Church of Nigeria and every enactment, resolution or directive of the said Synod shall have effect and be binding upon the Church..."); Ireland [n99], Constit. Ch. I.III.28 ("The General Synod shall have power...to make all such regulations as shall be necessary for the order, good government and efficiency of the Church of Ireland").

the constitution of the Church.[101] It has broad powers to ensure the order, administration and good governance of the Church[102]. Nigeria includes the consideration of any matters concerning the Church and promoting the spiritual welfare of its members" among the broad powers of General Synod.[103] But its powers may also be specifically enumerated. In Australia this includes canons in respect of ritual, ceremonial and discipline, making statements of faith, declaring the view of the Church on any matter affecting the Church or affecting spiritual moral or social welfare and necessary steps for union with other Christian communions.[104] In South East Asia this includes power to vary or rescind provisions of the constitution, canons, and standing orders of Synod, to interpret provisions of Constitution and establish rules of procedure for ecclesiastical discipline.[105] Ireland includes the power of General Synod to unite, separate, subdivide, and transfer dioceses and provinces, and to create new dioceses.[106]

The Church of Nigeria adds to all of the above the powers of its General Synod to protect the corporate identity of the Church, regulate relationships with other Churches in the Anglican Communion, set standards for

---

[101] Australia [n99], Constit. II.5

[102] Ibid, Constit. II.5 ("for the order and good government of the Church"); South East Asia [n99], Constit. VII(c) ("for the general management and good government of the Province"); Ireland [n99]. Constit. Ch.I.III.28.

[103] Nigeria [n99], Constit. III.21(a) ("consider matters concerning the Church of Nigeria, make provision for the administration of its affairs, and promote the spiritual welfare and well-being of its members")

[104] Australia [n99], Constit. V.26

[105] South East Asia [n99], Constit. VII(d)(e) and (l)

[106] Ireland [n99], Constit. I.III.31 (1). See *PCLCCAC,* [n17], Principle 20.3: "Formation, alteration or suppression of a diocese is in the keeping of the central church assembly and may be effected in such cases and manner as are allowed by law."

the ecclesiastical discipline of laity, minimum standards for theological education, regulations for inter-diocesan transfer of clergy, administration of all Church funds, trusts, and group insurance.[107]

The permanence of the Provincial or General Synod is reflected in the duration of the Synod "session" for which representatives are elected and appointed. Among the four Churches the session is anywhere from three to six years in duration.[108] The regularity of these Synods is reflected in the set times they are scheduled to meet.[109] Under certain circumstances and emergencies, special sessions of the Synod may also be convened.[110]

---

[107] Nigeria [n99], Constit. III.22.

[108] Australia [n99], Constit. IV.23 (a)(b) (at least once every six years, normally four years); South East Asia [n99], Constit. VII (f) ("A Session of the Provincial Synod shall be for a period of not more than four years."); Nigeria [n100], Constit. Ch. II.11 and Can. XII.15 ("ordinary session of General Synod shall take place every three years"); Ireland [n99], Constit. Ch.I.I.5(1) (Three years: "Beginning 2005 and triennially thereafter").

[109] Australia [n99], Constit. IV.23 (a)(b) (once every four to six years); South East Asia [n99], Constit. VII(g) (Every other year); Nigeria [n99], Constit. Ch. II.11 (Every three years); Ireland [n99], Constit. Ch.I.II.14 (Every year).

[110] Special circumstances for convening a Special Session of the Synod include the discretion of the Archbishop/Primate and/or written request by bishops, clergy and/or laity. See Australia [n99], Constit. IV.23(a)(b) (convened by Primate on resolution of not less than ½ of House of Bishops or 1/3 of House of Clergy or 1/3 of Laity or resolution of Standing Committee); South East Asia [99], Constit. VII (h) (Urgency and with written request of not less than ½ members of either of the three Houses); Nigeria [n99], Constit. Ch.II.11 (whenever requested to meet by petition of 1/3 of any House, but within the discretion of the Primate alone to call); Ireland [n99], Constit. Ch.I.II.15 (special meetings may be convened at discretion of Archbishop(s), or bishop next in order of seniority and shall be convened by written request of not less than 1/3 of any order).

As a matter of subsidiarity, the constitutions of the four Churches establish diocesan synods with powers to be determined by the diocesan constitutions but subject to the constitution of the Church.[111] Sessions of diocesan synods are of lesser duration and meetings more frequent than those of the Provincial or General Synod of the Church.[112]

---

[111] Australia [n99], Constit. VIII.47-51; South East Asia [n99], Constit. XIV (a)(b); Nigeria [n99], Constit. Ch. IX.38-39; Ireland [n99], Constit. Ch.II.I.1.

[112] See, e.g., Australia: *The Constitution, Canons and Regulations of the Diocese of Adelaide*, <http://www.adelaide.anglican.com.au/leadership/governance/constitution/> Accessed 6 October 2015, Constit. III.15(1): Synod meets at least once in each calendar year, and in special circumstances by request specifi9c numbers of clergy and lay delegates from 3 congregations supported by Diocesan Council, and *The Constitution of the Anglican Church of Australia in the Diocese of North Queensland*, <http://www.anglicannq.org/governance/diocesan-constitution-and-canons> Accessed 6 October 2015, Constit. Non-Fundamental Provision 6: Synod convened and held at least once every two years, otherwise whenever Bishop may determine it is desirable to do so, or by special session where requested by 2/3 Diocesan council or 10 clergy and 20 lay delegates; South East Asia: *Constitution of the Diocese of Singapore* (Received by email dated 12 August 2015 from Stephanie Ng, Bishop's Office, Diocese of Singapore), Constit. IV(1)(2)(3): Session is not less than 2 and not more than 3 years. Bishop gives notice of time and place of each meeting, with no more than 18 months elapsing between one meeting and another. Extraordinary meetings convened by bishop upon a request by not less than 1/5 of Clergy and 1/5 of Lay delegates. Sessions may be adjourned or prorogued, and *The Constitution of the Synod of the Church in the Diocese of Kuching* (Received by email dated 18 August 2015 from Stephanie Ng, Bishop's Office, Diocese of Singapore), Constit. VIII(1): every second year at time and place determined by Bishop and Standing Committee; Nigeria: *The Principles, Constitution and Regulations of the Anglican Diocese of Etsako* (Received by email dated 22 July 2015 from Gbenga Fatoye on behalf of Abraham Yisa, Registrar of the Church of Nigeria), Constit. Ch. III.3.1-2: The life of the Synod shall be three years, and it shall convene at least once annually at such times and places as the Bishop may appoint, and *The Constitution and regulations of the Diocese of Ogbia* (Received by email dated 22 July 2015 from Gbenga Fatoye on behalf

The powers of diocesan synods, both broad and enumerated (mostly fiduciary), do vary from Church to Church. But whether broad, enumerated or a combination of both, the function of Diocesan Synods is to deal with matters of concern to the diocese.[113] In Australia and Kuching (South East Asia) the powers of diocesan synods focus on the life, growth, order, good government and "efficiency" of the Church in the diocese.[114] In Ireland the

---

of Abraham Yisa, Registrar of the Church of Nigeria), Constit. Ch.III.8a: Silent on duration of Session; Synod convened at least once a year by Bishop in Advent; Ireland [n100], Constit. Ch.II.I.4, 21: Life of the Synod is three years beginning in 2005, meeting ordinarily once a year at such time and place as the Bishop prescribes. In Ireland all dioceses are governed by the General Constitution and canons of the Church, Ireland [n100], Constit. Ch. I.III.28-31.

[113] See *PCLCCAC,* [n17], Principle 20.5: "The diocesan assembly, namely synod, council or other such body, may have authority to legislate for the diocese."

[114] See, e.g., *The Constitution, Canons and Regulations of Adelaide* [n112] which gives broad powers to the diocesan synod "to provide for the life, growth, order and good government of the Church in the Diocese," Constit. Ch. III.2.8, and enumerated powers that include beyond fiduciary duties the power of legislation, consultation with bishop, appointment delegation and dissolution of committees, employment and dismissal of employees and officers, "and all such other acts, matters or things as shall be or may appear to be incidental or conducive to the life and growth and order and good government of the Church in the diocese," Constit. Ch.III.2.9(1); see also *The Constitution of the Anglican Church of Australia in the Diocese of North Queensland* [n112], Constit. Non-Fundamental Provision 11: same broad and enumerated powers as Adelaide, but adding power to nominate and elect the Bishop, establish rules for the election and composition of Synod, establish judicial tribunals to hear all questions of doctrine and discipline "touching any person clerical or lay," appointment of Standing Committee, exercise of all patronage, and providing assistance to infirm or disabled clergy, clergy widows and orphans; *The Constitution of the Synod of the Church in the Diocese of Kuching* [n112], Constit. VII(1) ("consider,

Constitution provides for the daily management of the diocese, including administration, "efficiency and good government," with enumerated powers of General Synod to "unite, subdivide, transfer and create new dioceses" and to prevent the admission in legislation of any principle "inexpedient to the common interest of the Church."[115] But in the Diocese of Singapore (South East Asia) the priority of the Diocesan Synod is to fulfill "the Statement on the Spiritual Background of the Diocesan Synod,"

> "To make the Church in the diocese to be ever more and more truly a body, a small living organism within the body of Christ, working in Him for the salvation of men and for the Kingdom of God…"

with broad administrative and governmental powers flowing out of and in support of that spiritual, missional priority.[116] This is also true of the power of the General Synod of the Church of Nigeria, to which its diocesan synods expressly conform their powers.[117] The Diocese of Singapore expresses the conciliar principle that neither Bishop nor Synod shall act without consulting each other:

---

determine and take requisite action with regard to all matters concerning the life, work and administration of the Church in the Diocese");

[115] Ireland [n99], Constit. Ch. I.III.28-31

[116] *Constitution of the Diocese of Singapore* [n112], Constit. III.1 "In carrying out these responsibilities, the Synod shall consider, determine and take requisite action with regard to all matters concerning the life, work and administration of the Church in the Diocese…"

[117] Nigeria [n99], Constit. Ch.III.21 (a): General Synod shall consider matters concerning the Church of Nigeria and make provision for the administration of its affairs *and for the promotion of the spiritual welfare and well-being of its members…"* (Emphasis added); see also *The Principles, Constitution and Regulations of the Anglican Diocese of Etsako* [n112], Constit. Ch. III.1.i: "The Diocese shall have power to enact laws and make regulations for the Diocese in conformity with its Constitution of Church of Nigeria (Anglican Communion)."

> "The very existence of the Synod secures that in all matters the bishop will not go forward with any project without consent and cooperation of clergy and laity, and they will not attempt to take action without bishop's approval."[118]

Between sessions the Provincial or General Synod continues to work through a Standing or Executive Committee of the Synod.[119] In Nigeria, the Standing Committee is so large that it functions as a "council" itself and has its own "Secretariat" with a General Secretary who reports from the Standing Committee to the General Synod.[120] The Standing Committee carries on the work of Synod through members elected from Synod and those appointed by the Archbishop or Primate even if not

---

[118] South East Asia: *Diocese of Singapore,* [n112], Constit. Preface: Spiritual Background, at 4. This accords with *PCLCCAC,* [n17], Principle 20.6: "A diocesan bishop may give or withhold consent to proposed diocesan legislation to such extent as is provided by law, but may not legislate unilaterally."

[119] This power of delegation accords with *PCLCCAC,* [n17], Principle 17.4: "Bodies which or persons who exercise ecclesiastical functions may delegate to others only such functions as they are not required to perform themselves provided the delegation is carried out with care, with the consent of those to whom the function is delegated, *and in the manner and to the extent prescribed by law."* (Emphasis added). See Australia [n99], Constit. V.34; South East Asia [n99], Constit. VIII (a); Nigeria [n99], Constit. VI.31 (1) and XII. 49: Also defined as "The Executive Committee" of General Synod, Constit. XVII.5(19); Ireland [n99], *Appendix: The Constitution, Duties and Powers of the Standing Committee as provided by the resolution of General Synod 9 May 1967, as amended 2013,* Constit. I.2-6

[120] See *Communique of the Standing Committee of the Church of Nigeria, October 1, 2015* <http://anglicanmainstream.org/nigerian-anglican-communique/> Accessed 7 October 2015: "One hundred and forty seven bishops, One Hundred and Fifty-Two clergymen, and Sixty-Eight members of the House of Laity were present," See also Nigeria [n99], Constit. XI.48, 51.

members of Synod.[121] In order to carry on the work of Synod between sessions, the Standing Committee is given broad administrative powers and discretion.[122] The necessary and regular function of the Synod as an expression of conciliar governance is demonstrated by the times prescribed by the Church (with the exception of Ireland) for the Standing Committee to meet between sessions.[123] Except as otherwise provided in the constitution

---

[121] Australia [n99], *Rules for the Appointment of a Standing Committee of General Synod,* Rule II.2; South East Asia [n99], Constit. VIII.2; Nigeria [n99], Constit. XII.49(2) (includes all bishops and one clerical and one lay representative of each Diocese, seated and elected by General Synod upon the nominated of their respective dioceses); Ireland [n99], *Appendix: The Constitution, Duties and Powers of the Standing Committee as provided by the resolution of General Synod 9 May 1967, as amended 2013,* Constit. I.2-6: *ex officio,* elected and co-opted members of General Synod.

[122] Such broad powers typically include: advising the Primate or Archbishop on matters of concern to the Church and matters referred by the Primate; assisting in implementing the resolutions passed by Synod, communicating such resolutions, canons and regulations to the dioceses; managing all trusts, properties, finances and funds of the Church, setting and preparing the agenda and reports for Synod (including audited financial reports of the Church's accounts); proposing the business Synod needs to address and apportioning to the dioceses the working expenses of Synod; appointing committees to help expedite its work, and exercising all such powers and duties vested in the Synod which it may delegate to the Standing Committee from time to time. See Australia [n99], *Rules for the Appointment of a Standing Committee of General Synod,* Rule II.5; South East Asia [n99], Constit. VIII (e); Nigeria [n99], Constit. XII.50; Ireland [n99], *Appendix: The Constitution, Duties and Powers of the Standing Committee as provided by the resolution of General Synod 9 May 1967, as amended 2013,* Powers and Duties, II.9-11.

[123] Australia [n99], *Rules for the Appointment of a Standing Committee of General Synod,* Rule II.4(1): "within six months of the close and not more than nine nor less than six months prior to an ordinary session of Synod, upon written request of the Standing Committee, and at other times as the Primate deems advisable; South East Asia [n99], Constit. VIII(f): "at least once a year"; Nigeria [n99], Can.XIII.1: at such time and place as the Primate or Dean may appoint

and canons, Nigeria also empowers the Standing Committee to "determine all disputes" arising within the Church.[124] Ireland empowers its Standing Committee with many powers, ranging from monitoring legislation that may affect the Church to governing local ecumenical partnerships that do not affect the rubrics, rites and formularies of the Church.[125]

In general, diocesan synods carry on their work between sessions through the same kind of Standing Committee or Council.[126] In some dioceses the Diocesan Council acts as a council of advice for the Bishop in carrying out the business of synod.[127] In others, the diocesan council serves the bishop and synod in deed only through enumerated powers.[128] In Ireland, the enumerated powers of Diocesan

---

[124] Nigeria [n99], Constit. XVI.78: The judgment of the Standing Committee shall be final and binding unless varied or reversed by General Synod.

[125] Ireland [n99], Constit. IX.I.11A, *Appendix: The Constitution, Duties and Powers of the Standing Committee as provided by the resolution of General Synod 9 May 1967, as amended 2013,* Powers and Duties, II.12.

[126] Australia [n99], Constit. XII.74 (1): "'Diocesan Council' is the body exercising powers and functions of the synod on its behalf when it is not in session." See also *Diocese of Adelaide* [n112], Constit. IV.22: Diocesan Council is the executive committee of the Synod; South East Asia: it is the Standing Committee of Diocesan Synod that conducts its business when synod is "not sitting," *Diocese of Singapore* [n112], VI.1.1 (a), and "acts for synod between ordinary sessions," *Diocese of Kuching* [n112], Constit. XI(4); Nigeria: The "Diocesan Board" is the Standing Committee and "shall act in the intervals between sessions of the Synod," *Diocese of Ogbia* [n112], Constit. Ch.V.15 and *Diocese of Etsako* [n112], Ch. IV; Ireland [n99}, Constit. II.II.34-36: Diocesan Synod shall assign and limit by its rules.

[127] Australia: *Diocese of Adelaide* [n112], Constit. IV.22 and *Diocese of North Queensland* [n112], Constit. Non-fundamental provision11 (f); South East Asia: *Diocese of Kuching* [n112], Constit. XI.4.

[128] South East Asia: *Diocese of Singapore* [n112], Constit. VI.5: Enumerated powers include administration and management of all trusts, properties and funds of the diocese, management of all its financial affairs, and "other

Councils are fixed by the Constitution of the Church, and circumscribed by the enumerated powers of Diocesan Synods.[129] In almost all cases, diocesan councils meet several times per year, or as needed, during the intervals between ordinary sessions of the diocesan synod.[130]

2. THE WHOLE CHURCH BEING REPRESENTED IN SYNOD

---

duties as may be committed by resolution of Synod"; Nigeria: *Diocese of Ogbia* [n112], Constit. V.21 Enumerated powers of Diocesan Board include in the following priority: developing evangelistic and pastoral work of this Church, promoting Christian education of the community, deliberating upon any matter referred up by Archdeaconry Board, dealing with all matters of diocesan finances, fixing the rate of remuneration for all church workers, and appointing other committees as needed for "expeditious execution of its functions," and *Diocese of Etsako* [n112], Constit. IV (same priorities and powers);

[129] "Subject to the control of the Synod, the Diocesan Council shall exercise the powers conferred on the Synod in the following matters: Sections 5, 31, 32, 42 of Chapter 2, Sections 6, 7, 24, 27 and 35 of Chapter 3, and Sections 14 and 16 of the Appendix...and the Synod shall have power to alter, repeal or supersede all or any of such acts of the Council," *Diocese of Connor Diocesan Regulations 2010 with Proceedings and Standing Orders of The Diocesan Synod (Passed by the Diocesan Synod 9 September 2010, Amended 3 October 2013)* (Received by email 30 July 2015 from Tracey Taggert, Assistant to the Secretary of the Dioceses of Connor, Down and Dromore, Church of Ireland), reg. 4.8.2 and *Diocese of Down and Dromore Diocesan Regulations 2010 with Proceedings and Standing Orders of The Diocesan Synod (Passed by the Diocesan Synod 17 June 2010, Amended 20 June 2013*), (Received by email 30 July 2015 from Tracey Taggert, Assistant to the Secretary of the Dioceses of Connor, Down and Dromore, Church of Ireland), reg. 4.11.

[130] Australia: *Diocese of North Queensland* [n112], Can. 5.9: at least once every three months, with two meetings per year in person (otherwise by telephone or video conference); South East Asia: *Diocese of Kuching* [n112], Constit. XI (10): at least twice and year and otherwise as needed; Nigeria: *Diocese of Ogbia* [n112], Constit. V.17-18: at least once every four months and by emergency summons as needed; Ireland: Diocesan Council shall fix the time and place of its meetings. See *Diocese of Connor* [n129], reg. 4.8.1 and *Diocese of Down and Dromore* [n129], reg. 4.10.

Representation of the whole Church (Bishops, clergy, and laity) is manifested in council. The conciliar principle of representation of the whole church[131] is evident in the constitution and canons of these Anglican Churches and their synods. All three orders – bishops, clergy and laity – are represented in both Provincial and diocesan synods.[132] However, unlike the Church of England, every Church here provides greater representation of the laity within the synods, either through a higher ratio of laity to clergy,[133] or

---

[131] Principle 2, *supra,* in Chapter 2; See also *PCLCCAC,* [n17], Principles 15.9: Bishops, clergy and laity share authority in synodical government, Principle 18.1: Representative government is fundamental to church polity and "in matters which touch all, all should have a voice," and Principles 18.2-3: the central assembly of a church includes bishops, clergy and laity, who may be represented by Houses or other cameral arrangements. See also Definitions at 95: At the diocesan level the assembly consists of the bishop, the clergy and the laity of the diocese, and at parochial or other level of clergy and laity.

[132] Australia [n99], Constit. IV.15, see also *Diocese of Adelaide* [n112], Constit. III.10 and *Diocese of North Queensland* [n112], Constit. Fundamental Provision 4; South East Asia [n99], Constit. VII (b), see also *Diocese of Singapore* [n112], Constit. II and *Diocese of Kuching* [n112], Constit. V (2); Nigeria [n99], Constit. II.6, IX.39 and Can. XII.1, see also *Diocese of Ogbia* [n112], Constit. I.xx, III and *Diocese of Etsako* [n112], Constit. III; Ireland [n99], Constit. Preamble and Fundamental Declaration IV, Ch. I.I.1, and II.I.2 (same representation of all three orders in diocesan synods).

[133] Australia: *Diocese of North Queensland* [n112], Synod Can. 3.3: Two lay and one clergy representative to diocesan synod from each parish; South East Asia [n99], Constit. VII (b)(ii): Four lay and three clergy representatives to Provincial Synod from each diocese; Nigeria [n99], Constit. II.8(2) and 9(2): Three lay and two clergy representatives to General Synod from each diocese, see also *Diocese of Etsako* [n112], Constit. VI.6(i-iv): same; but see *Diocese of Ogbia* [n112], XI-XII: Four laity and three clergy elected to General Synod; Ireland [n99], Constit., I.I.2: Two lay and one clergy representative to General Synod from each diocese, and II.I.2: for each diocesan synod, two to five laity for every clergy with a cure, and no more

in diocesan synods lay representation according to the size of the congregation.[134] The one exception to this among these Churches is the General Synod of Australia, where clergy and lay representatives are equal in number according to the quota of clergy in each diocese.[135]

3. THE MIND OF THE CHURCH AS DISCERNED IN A RIGOROUS SYNODAL PROCESS

Discerning the Mind of the Church (*Consensus Fidelium*on) on faith, order, worship and other matters important and controversial takes place through a rigorous synodal process. At the heart of conciliar governance is the principle that any definition of doctrine requires the participation of the whole Church – indeed, that any "juridical expression" of doctrine through a synod must

---

than two laity for every clergy without a cure but licensed in the diocese. See also *Diocese of Connor* [n129], reg. 1.1, 2, 2 (in diocesan synod, two laity for every clergy "officiating in each cure") and *Diocese of Down and Dromore* [n129], reg. 1.2 and 2.2 (same as Connor). This accords with *PCLCCAC,* [n17], Principle 22.3: "Lay participation in church government is subject to the conditions prescribed in the law of a church as to eligibility, membership, selection and admission."

[134] Australia: *Diocese of Adelaide* [n112], Constit. III.15 (3); South East Asia: *Diocese of Singapore* [n112], Constit. XV.2 and Schedule A, Reg. 4: Election of House of Laity according to number of persons on Parish electoral role, and *Diocese of Kuching* [n112], Constit. XXI (1): One or more lay representatives from each parish as decided by Standing Committee; Nigeria: *Diocese of Ogbia* [n112], Constit. III.5(g) and *Diocese of Etsako* [n112], Constit. XI.

[135] Australia [n99], Constit. The Table Annexed to the Constitution: Clerical and Lay Representatives in General Synod, 1: "The number of clerical and lay representatives respectively of each diocese shall be in proportion to the number of clergy in the diocese and shall be determined by dividing that number by a quota, namely twenty, and if on the division there is a remainder of ten or more the diocese shall be entitled to one more clerical and one more lay representative." See also *Diocese of North Queensland* [n112], Synod Can. 3.3: equal representation to diocese lay representative.

give expression to the mind of the Church, the *consensus fidelium.*[136] Accordingly, the Churches of Australia, South East Asia, Nigeria and Ireland have elaborate provisions in their constitution, canons and regulations to reach that *consensus fidelium* on doctrine and other important and controversial matters.

It should be noted first that Australia, Nigeria and Ireland provide a posture in synods for achieving the *consensus fidelium* – namely, that all three orders of ministry sit together in synod to deliberate and decide on such matters.[137] Secondly, when voting by orders, there is also an order in which those votes are taken and received that enables the whole Church to discern its mind – typically the laity voting first, then the clergy, and finally

---

[136] Doe [n42] at 258-259. See also *PCLCCAC,* [n17], Principle 50.1: A church's own doctrinal formulas shall be compatible with the faith "received, practiced and held by the church universal." This receiving, holding and practicing expresses integrity with the scriptures, and both the geographical and the temporal dimensions of catholicity. See Valliere, [n8] at 111: "Ecclesial consensus may be gauged spatially or temporally... Consensus in time is the agreement of one generation of Christians with its predecessors... likewise the church in the mode of *universitas* [spatially] depends upon a common confessional and canonical core, a substantive ecclesial consensus." But note the ongoing tension between faithfulness and mission in *PCLCCAC,* [n17], Principle 50.2: The church may draw up its formularies so that the faith may be presented both loyally and intelligibly.

[137] Australia [n99], Constit. IV.15: "The three houses shall sit together in full Synod and shall deliberate and transact business therein and shall vote together unless a vote by houses is required"; see also Nigeria [n99], Constit. II.15-17 and Ireland [n99], Constit. I.I.4. See also *PCLCCAC,* [n17], Principles 50.3: The competence to develop, reformulate or alter doctrine vests in Provincial Synod, and 53.5: "The width of permissible theological opinion in a church is determined (a) legislatively, by its central assembly; (b) executively, by its bishops, individually or collectively, and (c) judicially, by its courts and tribunals."

the bishops, with no matter resolved until it has received a vote of the majority of those present in each of the three houses.[138] In these three Churches, the discernment of the laity and clergy must be received by the bishops before they can pronounce the *consensus fidelium*.

When matters are deemed important and controversial, a rigorous procedure is required to achieve the *consensus fidelium.* Each of the four Churches does this by first defining what particular matters qualify as important and controversial, followed by the juridical process itself. The first step is to determine whether the matter before the Synod is ordinary or special. Ordinary legislation is that which does not touch upon the faith and order of the Church, and may or may not affect any change to its constitution or canons. In Australia "ordinary" legislation "shall be deemed to be resolved in the affirmative" simply by a vote of the majority of those present in each of the three houses of General Synod.[139] Even if it does not alter or amend the constitution and canons, the other Churches have elaborate requirements for such legislation.[140] But in

[138] Australia [n99], Constit. IV.15. See also Part III, Rule 1: *"Rules for the Conduct of all Business coming before The General Synod,"* SO 47(b); see also Nigeria [n99], Constit. II.16 and Can. XII.16; Ireland [n99], Constit. I.II.22: "The bishops shall not vote until after the declaration of the votes of the clerical and lay representatives."

[139] Australia [n99], Constit. IV.15

[140] South East Asia [n99], Constit. XVIII: rules, regulations and by-laws "not inconsistent" with the constitution and Fundamental Declarations of the Church must first be submitted in writing to the Standing Committee with a statement of the reasons why the bill is desirable, forwarded to all members of Provincial Synod not less than six months prior to its meeting, approved by a two-thirds majority of each house voting by orders, and assented to by the Archbishop. See also Ireland [n99], Constit. I.II.21, 25: In Ireland, even an ordinary bill must survive a process that includes a motion to introduce, three separate readings of the bill, review "clause by clause" with opportunities to amend by the whole Synod, debate at every stage and

South East Asia and Nigeria, amendments to constitution and canons require even more elaborate procedures.[141] In short, with the exception of Australia, even ordinary legislation is subject to rigorous procedures to ensure it reflects the mind of the Church.

By contrast, legislation that touches on the faith and order of the Church requires even *more* rigorous *consensus fidelium*, including the faith of the church universal.[142] In Australia faith and order includes doctrine, discipline, ritual, ceremonial and "any bill which imposes a financial

---

a final vote in the affirmative that requires no less than a majority of each house voting together or by orders.

[141] South East Asia [n99], Ibid. XIX: Alterations or amendments to the constitution and canons may only be moved by the House of Bishops, Provincial Synod, Provincial Standing Committee or a diocesan synod. The motion must include the same form of written notice, but to the Archbishop—who shall then forward it immediately to the dioceses for their consideration. If the Provincial Synod approves the amendment by a simple majority of each house voting separately, it must then allow at least six months for consideration by the dioceses, Then, if there are no adverse votes or comments by any diocesan synod "or others," Provincial Synod must vote again and approve by no less than a two-thirds majority of each house voting separately, and receive the assent of the Archbishop. See also Nigeria [n99], XV.71-74: The legislation must first go to the Standing Committee. If it is resolved there in the affirmative, it must be sent to all the dioceses for approval of two-thirds of all the Diocesan Synods in the Church—unless the matter involves only the amendment of the Canons. Then it goes to General Synod for final approval, which requires a majority vote of two-thirds of each house in Synod. If it fails to obtain approval by the two-thirds majority of all diocesan synods, it may be referred back to the Standing Committee who may, in their discretion, submit the matter to General Synod for approval by the required two-thirds majority.

[142] *PCLCCAC,* [n17], Principle 50.4: "the development of doctrinal formulae by a church assembly may be subject to such substantive limitations and special procedures as may be prescribed by the law of a church to ensure the protection of the faith of the church universal."

liability upon a diocese."[143] South East Asia defines faith and order to include the historic formularies and its Fundamental Declarations.[144] Nigeria defines faith and order most comprehensively, including amendments to constitution and canons.[145] Ireland defines a special bill as any modification or alteration in "the articles, doctrines, rites, rubrics or formularies of the Church."[146]

In South East Asia bishops are competent themselves to discern the *consensus fidelium*.[147] But in the other churches

---

[143] Australia [n99], Constit. V.28 and V.28A (3).

[144] South East Asia [n99], Constit. II.

[145] Nigeria [n99], Constit. IV.23-25: "Faith and order" includes provisions touching the doctrinal formulae of the services or ceremonies of the Church, the administration of the Sacraments, permanent changes to the services of Baptism, Holy Communion and the Ordinal, the circumstances under which a bishop may be permitted to authorize a trial use of such changes, or a "permanent and substantial change of relationship between the Church and another Christian body in Nigeria." In this context, "order" includes any amendments to the constitution which touch upon the faith of the Church See also *PCLCCAC,* [n17], Principle 55.6-7, which vests approval of liturgical adaptations and innovations, and new forms of service for experimental use, in the central assembly of a church provided such changes are in keeping with the Scriptures and the Book of Common Prayer 1662.

[146] Ireland [n99], Constit. I.II.26 (1).

[147] South East Asia [n99], Constit. III: Bishops are themselves competent "to interpret all matters" concerning doctrine, life and worship according to the Holy Scriptures, the Thirty-Nine Articles and the Fundamental Declarations of the Church. But where they are unable to reach consensus after consultation, prayer and "seeking the mind of the Lord in accordance with the Holy Scriptures," then the Archbishop on behalf of the House of Bishops shall refer the matter to the Archbishop of Canterbury for guidance with guidance from other Primates "as he (the ABC) thinks fit". But see also Fundamental Declaration 7 which provides for some review by Provincial Synods and the dioceses. See also *PCLCCAC,* [n17], Principle 53.10: "The interpretation of the standards and formularies of, and all questions of faith and doctrine arising in, a church shall be determined within that church save to the extent that its law permits reference for the purpose of

the levels of legislative review and participation of clergy and laity are rigorous. In Australia, it is impossible to reach the mind of the church without the nearly unanimous consent of the dioceses. Legislation from the General Synod touching faith and order is provisional only until it is approved by all the dioceses and enacted by their synods.[148] In Nigeria there are at least five levels of review for legislation. Legislation touching faith and order as defined in Article IV[149] must first be referred to the

---

consultation or determination of such matters to a body external to that church."

[148] Australia [n99], Constit. V.28 (3) and V.30: The dioceses seem to exercise a virtual veto over legislation by the General Synod. Whether the special bill touches the ritual, ceremonial or discipline of the Church, imposes a financial liability on the diocese, or amends the constitution of the Church without touching any matter of ritual, ceremonial or discipline, it must be agreed to by at least two-thirds of the members of each of the three houses of General Synod present. It then becomes a provisional canon subject to approval by each diocese within a specified period. If *every* diocesan synod assents to the provisional canon it shall be deemed to have duly passed, it comes into effect no later than one month from that date and any diocesan ordinance inconsistent with that canon is voided. But if *any* dioceses *do not* assent, their report and recommendations shall be sent to General Synod. Synod may by simple majority decide to repeat the process from the beginning, or to go ahead and duly pass the provisional canon by at least two-thirds of the members of each of the three houses. Even so, if the canon affects the ritual, ceremonial or discipline of the Church in the diocese, it has no effect until the diocese by ordinance adopts it! Likewise, if General Synod says that any other canon it passes affects "the order and good governance of the Church within the diocese," it has no affect until the diocese adopts it. And if General Synod fails to make that declaration, *the diocese may do so*—in which case the canon has no effect until the diocese adopts it. Finally, even if it adopts the canon by ordinance, *a diocese may by ordinance exclude it "at a subsequent date."* (Emphasis added).

[149] Nigeria [n99], and further including Canons I-XX, the "Canons of the Constitution" which may not be altered, amended or repealed, Ibid., XV.74.

Theological and Doctrinal Department or Committee of the Church of Nigeria, whose recommendations will be forwarded to the Episcopal Synod.[150] The Episcopal Synod then submits the bill on behalf of the bishops of Nigeria to the Standing Committee, the dioceses and finally the members of General Synod "for final approval in terms proposed by the House of Bishops *and not otherwise*" mirroring exactly the language of the *SGM* 1969.[151]

Although the levels of review are less rigorous than Nigeria, a special bill in the Church of Ireland must survive the same process for an ordinary bill with several rigorous additions, including notice to all diocesan synods, multiple readings of the legislation at General Synod.[152] Whereas

---

[150] See *PCLCCAC,* [n17], Principle 50.6: A church may have a Doctrinal Commission or similar body to advise on and propose doctrinal development to the extent and in the manner prescribed by law.

[151] Compare Nigeria [n99], Constit. IV.23-25 with *SGM* [n26], Art. 5(1). The five step process is outlined in IV.23-25 and XV.72-73: If the legislation touches any matter of faith and doctrine, notice must go from the Episcopal Synod to the Standing Committee for resolution. If the Standing Committee agrees that the legislation may go to the next ensuing session of General Synod, it must first be submitted for approval by the synods of at least two-thirds of the dioceses of the Church. If the bill fails to receive approval by two-thirds of the diocesan synods of the Church, the Standing Committee has discretion to decide whether the legislation should go on to the General Synod. Whether it receives the approval of two-thirds of all diocesan synods, the legislation shall not be finally approved until it is passed by at least two-thirds of the members of each House voting at General Synod. But see XV.71: If the legislation does not touch on faith and doctrine, but amends, alters, repeals or adds to the Constitution, it may come from the General Synod, or its Standing Committee or a diocesan synod without first going through the Theological and Doctrinal Department of the Church. See also *PCLCCAC,* [n17], Principle 50.5: "No new doctrinal formulae may be approved by a central church assembly without the consent of the House of Bishops or equivalent episcopal collegial body."

[152] Ireland [n99], Constit. "Appendix: Standing Orders Adopted by The House of Representatives May 1965, amended 2011," SO 30: First, the resolution for motion to introduce must be approved by no less than two-

Nigeria places review by the bishops at the beginning of the process, Ireland seems to place them at the end.[153] If by majority vote the bishops approve the bill, it becomes a statute binding on the Church of Ireland. If the bishops do not approve by a majority, at the next ordinary session of General Synod the clergy and laity may "re-affirm" the special bill by a two-thirds majority vote conjointly or by orders. However, the bishops may still have the last word by voting against the special bill by no less than two-thirds of their members present and voting "and giving their reasons in writing."[154] This somewhat tortuous process confirms the critical role bishops play in the Church of Ireland discerning the *consensus fidelium*.

4. BISHOPS HAVE A PARTICULAR ROLE AS GUARDIANS OF THE FAITH, ORDER AND LITURGY

---

thirds of each order of the House of Representatives (clergy and lay representatives) present and voting. Secondly, after the resolution has been approved, the bill shall not be processed further until copies of the motion are sent to each diocesan synod within one month of its approval. Thirdly, the second reading, the amendments, the third reading and final passage must also be approved at each step by no less than two-thirds of the clergy and laity present and voting.

[153] Ibid, I.II.21-22: Bishops vote separately from the House of Representatives (clergy and laity), they shall not vote until *after* the declaration of the votes of the clerical and lay representatives, and they may withdraw from General Synod for a day for the purpose of voting. See also "Appendix: Voting by Bishops in Synod," SO 20-22. But see also Constit. I.II.20 and "Appendix: Voting by Bishops in Synod," SO 20: At any time in Synod, the bishops may make a request to consider any matter—ordinary or special—apart from the clergy and laity, and this shall have the effect of postponing any further discussion of the bill until they have done so.

[154] Ibid, I.II.21 and SO 21.

Within the synod or council Bishops have a particular role as the guardians of the faith and order of the church and its liturgy. This is resoundingly true within the General Synods of South East Asia and Nigeria. In their constitutions and canons, both recognize bishops have a special authority, duty and responsibility to preserve the truth of the doctrine of the Church, the purity of its life and the worthiness of its worship.[155] In both Churches the role of the Bishop as guardian of faith and order is rooted in the New Testament "distribution of gifts" according to the Holy Spirit.[156] In the preface to its constitution, from the Statement by the Archbishop of Canterbury in the original preface (1973),[157] the Diocese of Singapore

---

[155] Nigeria [n99], Constit. I.4 (a); South East Asia [n99], Constit. III (b) (c) and Can.6.1: The House of Bishops shall interpret "all matters concerning the preservation of the Church's doctrines, its life and worship in accordance with the Holy Scriptures, the 39 Articles and the Fundamental Declarations… [and] these matters [are] placed solely within authority of bishops, their decisions are binding on the whole Province," and XVII: Any dispute in the interpretation of any provisions of the Constitution shall be referred to the House of Bishops whose decision shall be final and binding. See also *PCLCCAC*, [n17], Principles 37.4: In Diocesan episcopal ministry, "the bishop must teach, uphold and safeguard the faith and doctrine of the church," 48.3: In the presentation of doctrine, bishops have the special responsibility to "teach the faith, to state publicly the doctrine of the church, and expound their application to the people and issues of the age," and 56.7-8 and 60.1: In liturgical administration, the bishop has the authority to order liturgy, liturgical practice and worship within the diocese.

[156] Nigeria [n99], Can. I.6 "Fundamental Declarations." South East Asia [n96]], Constit. III (b): "in accordance with the Holy Scriptures." See also *PCLCCAC,* [n17], Principle 16.1: Leadership and authority are "gifts of God" mediated through the church.

[157] South East Asia: *Diocese of Singapore*, [n112], Constit. "Statement on the Spiritual Background of the Diocesan Synod," at 1-4. Modifications and alterations (in italics) were made to reflect the new "charismatic" experiences of the Diocese of Singapore since its formation—but this statement on the role of bishops is otherwise unabridged.

explains the catholic and apostolic reasons for the unique role of bishops:

> "The Priests and the laity bring the fruits of the experience gained in parish, profession or home into the consultations and discussions of the Synod. Their outlook may often be limited by their experience. It needs to be balanced by an outlook gained from the history of other ages or the examples of other parts of the Church of today. Although much of the business of the synod will be homely matter, unconnected with great principles or doctrines, any important question about the Church's action may involve an issue of doctrine or of moral principles, *on which the Diocesan Bishop must express, and if necessary insist on the teaching of the universal Church.*" [158] *(Emphasis added).*

Accordingly, while both Churches provide that matters of faith and order – including doctrine and worship – shall be referred to the bishops meeting as a House or Synod together, both also provide that where the bishops cannot come to a consensus, they may appeal to other Metropolitans of the Anglican Communion, including Canterbury, for guidance.[159] This is a commitment to the role of Bishop that is classically conciliar and goes well beyond those principles at work in the ***SGM*** 1969.

The Church of Ireland seems to preserve the special role of bishops as guardians of faith and order at the end of the legislative process, when they may defeat by a two-thirds majority vote of bishops present and voting in General Synod any special bill touching faith and order approved

---

[158] Ibid, at 3.

[159] Nigeria [n99], Constit. Canon XI.3 "Of Episcopal Synod" and South East Asia [n99], Constit. III (d). See also *PCLCCAC,* [n17], Principle 53.10.

by a two-thirds majority of the clergy and laity.[160] But bishops are also "guardians" in the ecclesiastical discipline of the Church, where judicial proceedings include matters of doctrine and ritual at issue, [161]as well as in dioceses where changes in liturgy are of "substantial importance."[162] The role of bishops in Australia is more ambiguous. While they may meet together as a House apart from Synod as needed for the discharge of their "functions" under the constitution,[163] the constitution, canons and regulations are virtually silent on their "duties" with regards to matters of faith and order.[164] In short, three of the four Churches preserve the role of bishops as guardians of faith and order, with two of the three (South East Asia and Nigeria) in the most robust and classically conciliar terms.

5. DIOCESAN SYNODS THAT ARE LIMITED IN THEIR SCOPE

Other Anglican Churches also practice the principle of subsidiarity: specifically, that diocesan synods are limited in their scope and may not take unilateral action touching upon the faith and order of the Church. The mind of the whole Church is likelier to be found in the meeting of the whole Church in General Synod rather than in any one diocese.[165] This limitation is explicit in the law of the

---

[160] See n.154, *supra.*

[161] Ireland [n99], Constit. VIII.39: where the matter of doctrine or ritual is necessary for adjudication, the Disciplinary Appeals Tribunal shall suspend all proceedings until it has received a statement from the House of Bishops.

[162] Ibid, IX, Cans. 2 and 5(4): When a change in liturgy is of "substantial importance" it is beyond the authority of the clergy to enact and must therefore be referred to the Ordinary for pastoral guidance.

[163] Australia [n99], Constit. III.11-13.

[164] But see "Strategic Issues, Commissions, Task Forces and Networks Canon 1998," where the Primate may receive questions of doctrine and decide whether to refer them to the Doctrine Commission, Ibid, at 348.

[165] Principle 5, *supra.*

Churches of Australia, South East Asia and Nigeria,[166] and implicit in the Church of Ireland. But for the same reasons of subsidiarity, the Bishop and the Diocesan Synod are competent to discern the mind of the Church, especially when it relates to any changes or additions to the Diocesan Constitution.[167] Local matters of lesser importance and

---

[166]See Australia [n99], Constit. XII.71 (1-2): No Diocesan or Provincial Synod shall make any alteration in faith ritual or ceremonial, and discipline of this Church except in conformity with an alteration made by General Synod; South East Asia: *Diocese of Singapore* [n112], Constit. Part II "Fundamental Declarations" 4 and 7: Any alteration in the Fundamental Declarations of the Diocese, including the formularies. doctrine, discipline, worship and forms of service of the Church, require the written approval of the Provincial Synod, following a four step process within the Diocesan Synod, and *Diocese of Kuching* [n112], Constit. Part II: "Fundamental Declarations" 3: "No act, determination, canon or rule made by the Diocesan Synod shall be of any force if it is inconsistent with anything contained in the said Declaration [of Provincial Synod]," and VII(2)(a)(b): Diocesan Synod has no power to determine matters of faith and Order, any legislation on Faith and Order has no validity or effect other than as an advisory opinion to the Bishop, and if the Bishop seeks to promulgate a ruling concerning Faith and Order the laity by a two-thirds majority vote may refer the matter directly to the Archbishop; Nigeria [n99], Constit. IX.41: General Synod allows Dioceses to deal with matters "which concern only the members of the Church within each Diocese: Provided that no enactment of any Diocesan Synod shall have any force in the Diocese if it conflicts with any enactment of the General Synod." If it does, it has no force or effect within the Diocese," see also *Diocese of Ogbia* [n112], Constit. II: Fundamental Principles 1: "The diocese disclaims for itself the right as an individual dioceses of altering any of the aforesaid standards of faith and doctrine," and *Diocese of Etsako* [n112], Constit. III.3.12: "Provided always that nothing be ordered or enacted by the Synod contrary to the provisions of this Constitution and that of the Church of Nigeria."

[167] See, e.g., Australia [n99],"Constitution of a Diocese Alteration Canon 1995," Can.3.2: alteration of the diocesan constitution requires a majority vote in diocesan synod of 2/3 of house of laity, 2/3 house of clergy at same sitting of synod, confirmation by resolution of Synod passed in like manner

controversy are entirely within the competence of the Bishop and Diocesan Synod.[168]

With respect to other matters touching the conciliar principle of subsidiarity[169] the General or National Synod of each of the Churches defines the authority, limits and rules for its diocesan synods.[170] The constitution of the Church of Ireland goes on to define the authority, limits and rules for smaller units of the Church, including Archdeaconries, Parish Annual meetings and Vestries,[171] while Nigeria leaves such matters to the dioceses themselves.[172]

---

within 3 years, and assent in writing by bishop, and *Diocese of North Queensland* [n112], Constit. Non-Fundamental Declaration 13: Diocesan Synod competent to alter Non-Fundamental Declarations in constitution not touching doctrine; see also Nigeria: *Diocese of Etsako* [n112], XIX: Requires notice to all members of synod stating reasons for the amendment and text, 2/3 majority approval and assent by Bishop; But see South East Asia: *Diocese of Kuching* [n112], Constit. XXV: Where amendments by Diocesan synod must still obtain the approval of the Provincial Synod.

[168] See, e.g., Ireland: With Bishop's consent, Diocesan synods may suspend, alter, repeal or supersede any acts of diocesan council, and take appeal from disputed elections within parishes, *Diocese of Connor* [n129] rr. 4.8.2 and 8.1-5 and *Diocese of Down and Dromore* [n129], rr. 4.12 and 8.1-5.

[169] Principle 5: "Subsidiarity applies: Diocesan Synods are limited in their scope..." *supra,* p. 34.

[170] Australia [n99], Constit. VIII.47-51 "Diocesan Synods"; South East Asia, [n99], Constit. XIV "Diocesan Synods"; Nigeria [n99], Constit. IX.39-41: "Dioceses: Diocesan Synods"; and Ireland [n99], Constit. II: "Dioceses and Diocesan organization."

[171] Ireland [n99], Constit. II.III "Archdeacons and Rural Deans," and III "Parishes and Parochial Organizations."

[172] See Nigeria: *Diocese of Ogbia* [n112], Constit. X "Archdeaconries" and XI "Parishes" and *Diocese of Etsako* [n112], Constit. VI "Archdeaconries and Parishes."

6. SYNODAL GOVERNMENNT EXISTING AT THE DEANERY, DIOCESAN AND NATIONAL CHURCH LEVELS, AND PERHAPS AT THE LEVEL OF THE LOCAL CHURCH

In each of the four Churches synodal government exists at the level of national and diocesan governance. But what about synodal government at other levels, such as the deanery or parish?

First, it should be noted that the Churches in Australia and Nigeria have made provision for synodal government through groupings of dioceses that function as an ecclesiastical sub jurisdiction or Province of the Church. These Provincial Synods function above diocesan synods with such powers as are granted by the constitution of the Church, and are representative of the whole Church in the Province through the participation of bishops, clergy and laity.[173] The Church of Ireland has a variation on this theme: an "Episcopal Electoral College" whenever there is

---

[173] Australia [n99], Constit. VII.36-42: see especially s.40 where the powers of a Provincial Synod or Council are determined "as the diocesan synod of each of the dioceses to be included" see fit, and subject to approval by the General Synod., see also *Provincial Synod Constitution Amendment Ordinance 2011 Assenting Ordinance 2011 (New South Wales)* <http://www.sds.asn.au/assets/Documents/ords/2011/41ProvSynConstitutionAmendOrd11.AssentOrd2011.pdf> Accessed 12 October 2015: Provincial Synod consists of House of Bishops, House of Clergy and House of Laity according to a schedule of representation from each diocese in the Province; Nigeria [n99], Constit. VIII.33: Provincial Archbishop presides, representation from all three houses from each diocese, with higher two lay representatives for each clergy representative elected from each diocesan synod within the Province. By contrast to Australia, the powers of the Provincial Council are enumerated by the constitution of the Church, not the dioceses, and include the right of appeal to Provincial Archbishop of any dispute which cannot be resolved by the Diocesan Bishop, Ibid, at VIII.36-37.

need for an episcopal vacancy in a diocese (except Armagh), through a college of electors which include three bishops nominated by the House of Bishops, and twelve clergy and twelve laity from the diocese where the see is vacant.[174]

Secondly, Nigeria alone provides synodal governance within an "Archdeaconry." Diocesan constitutions provide for the organization of the diocese through Archdeaconries consisting of not less than three parishes, approved by the Bishop with the consent of the diocesan board, and with representation of all clergy and a higher number of laity from within each parish in the archdeaconry. The Board of the Archdeaconry functions synodally as a council of clergy and laity, the Archdeacon presiding, and meeting at least twice a year to address "the internal affairs" of the Archdeaconry.[175] But it is not as defined as the Deanery Synods in the Church of England.

Finally, all four of the Churches provides for synodal government at the parish level, through diocesan constitutions that include provisions on the election to a Parochial Church Council or Vestry at an annual meeting of the parish,[176] the composition of the PCC or Vestry as

---

[174] Ireland [99], Constit. IV.I.8.

[175] Nigeria: *Diocese of Ogbia* [n112], Constit. X.34 and *Diocese of Etsako* [n113], Constit. VI.2.

[176] Australia: *Diocese of North Queensland* [n112], Constit. "The Parishes Regulation Canon 2009'" r. 27.1; South East Asia: *Diocese of Singapore* [n112], Constit. "Schedule N: Regulations on Parishes, Congregations and Matters Connected Therewith," r.5 (Electors must be subscribing members of the parish and qualifications for PCC may be established by the constitution of the Parish itself); Nigeria: *Diocese of Ogbia* [n112], Constit. XI. 36, 38: (Electors and those who serve on PCC must be "subscribing members" as determined by clergy), ibid, *Diocese of Etsako* [n112], Constit. VI.3; Ireland [n99], Constit. III.13 (only registered vestry members may be electors). This accords with *PCLCCAC,* [n17], Principle 21.5: Lay members of

clergy and laity, with a higher representation of laity,[177] the regularity of their meetings[178] and their powers or function.[179] In short, there is ample evidence for synodal government at the parish level as a joint responsibility of the clergy and the laity.

7. SYNODS AS MANIFESTING ECCLESIAL DENSITY

Other Anglican Churches also promote "ecclesial density" at synodal gatherings – a common good or

---

the parish assembly are selected or appointed by way of election or other lawful process from "such classes of qualified persons as are prescribed by law."

[177] Ibid, Australia: *Diocese of North Queensland;* Nigeria: *Diocese of Ogbia,* XI.36-37, 39 and *Diocese of Etsako,* VI.3.3; Ireland, Constit. III.13(c) and III.18; this accords with *PCLCCAC,* [n17], Principle 22.4: A parish has a representative assembly consisting of clergy and laity. See also South East Asia: *Diocese of Singapore,* [n112], Schedule N, r.9 where Bishop may visit at any time and preside as Chair of PCC.

[178] Ibid., Australia: *Diocese of North Queensland* [n112], r.27.1: not less than six times per year, and at least every three months; Nigeria: *Diocese of Ogbia,* XI.36 (j): Monthly; Ireland, Constit. III.19 (At times fixed by the select vestry or Diocesan synod).

[179] Ibid., Australia: *Diocese of North Queensland* [n112],r.27.1: "The ministry and management of the parish is the joint responsibility of the incumbent, wardens and PCC" (emphasis added); South East Asia: *Diocese of Singapore,* Schedule N, r.7(b): The clergy shall approve, "in consultation with the parochial Church Council," all activities of the parish, (Emphasis added); Nigeria: *Diocese of Ogbia,* XI.44-46: No mention of consultation between clergy and laity on PCC. Powers enumerated to include control, management and annual accounting for all church accounts and property, and payment of the Diocesan assessment; Ireland, Constit. III.24, 25: Enumerated powers for Vestry, to be shared by clergy, wardens and other vestrypersons. This accords with *PCLCCAC,* [n17], Principle 21.6: The parish assembly has such functions as are prescribed by law to promote the whole mission of the church, pastoral, evangelistic, social and ecumenical.

corporate identity which each member of synod represents above and beyond any personal or group interests. In light of the demonstrably rigorous processes required of members of Synod in all four Churches to discern the mind of the Church, the *consensus fidelium,* on matters important to the Church (especially faith and order),[180] there is evidence of a "corporate identity" or "wholeness" of which each participating member of Synod is a representative. By virtue of discerning the mind of the Church, there is the discernment of a higher "common good" which is at the heart of the mind of the Church, and therefore its corporate identity or wholeness.

Two of the Churches also articulate a corporate identity and wholeness at the Provincial or national level. In the constitution of the Church in South East Asia, a distinction is made between matters of concern "common to the whole Province" which affect both the communion of the dioceses within the Province and "of the Province with other Provinces of the Anglican Communion," and matters of local concern in the dioceses. But the constitution reserves to Provincial Synod the determination of whether a matter is of concern to the whole, or of local interest to the diocese, and restricts the liberty of the dioceses to that which is "compatible with the unity and good order of the Church of the Province."[181] The Diocese of Singapore carries this further by distinguishing between the separate responsibilities and the *corporate responsibilities* of the members of Diocesan Synod, whose *one common duty* is "to witness to Christ in word and deed," and to do so "in conscious harmony and deliberate agreement" with each

[180] See discussion, *supra,* at Principle 3.

[181] South East Asia [n99], Constit. XVI.

other.[182] Likewise, in Nigeria, the corporate identity of the Church lies not simply in a general statement of the good government and well-being of the Church, but in the authority of the General Synod to guard "the national character, constitution, integrity and autonomy of the Church of Nigeria."[183] In both cases there is an articulation of a corporate identity, common good or wholeness beyond persons and dioceses, whether it is witnessing to Jesus Christ or guarding the national character and integrity of the Church. But there is also an express subordination of individuals and dioceses to that common good.[184]

In Ireland and Australia, the corporate identity and wholeness is more difficult to articulate. In Ireland, General Synod has power to control, alter, repeal or supersede any regulation made by a diocesan synod, "so far as may be necessary to prevent the admission of any principle inexpedient to the common interest of the Church."[185] However, the constitution never defines what that "common interest" might be. In Australia, General Synod has power to make canons, rules and regulations "relating to the order and good government of this Church," without defining those corporate goods elsewhere in its governing documents.[186] In short, the Churches in Asia and Africa seem to have a sense of the common good

[182] South East Asia: *Diocese of Singapore* [n112], Constit. "Preface: Statement on the Spiritual background of the Diocesan Synod," at 2.
[183] Nigeria [n99], Constit. III.22.
[184] Ibid, IX.38(h): In approving Diocesan Constitutions, General Synod shall provide liberty to meet local conditions and desires and shall secure "a degree of uniformity...as may be desirable for the well-being of the Church."
[185] Ireland [n99], Constit. I.III.29.
[186] Australia [n99], Constit. V.26.

of "the whole Church" which they can and do articulate as a corporate identity and responsibility – in contrast to the more western Churches of Ireland and Australia.

8. THE WHOLE CHURCH GATHERING IN SYNOD AROUND ITS BISHOP(S), NEVER OVER AGAINST THEM

Other Anglican Churches gather in Synod around their bishops – but never over and against them. Episcopal leadership is fundamental to the polity of a church.[187] We see this principle of episcopal leadership operating broadly in three ways in all four Churches. First, the "principal bishop" (Archbishop, Provincial Archbishop or Metropolitan) or bishop diocesan summons the Synod at a time and place fixed by the constitution, or at his own discretion, and sets the agenda for the Synod.[188] Secondly,

[187] *PCLCCAC,* [n17], Principle 15.10.

[188] Australia [n99], Constit. IV.23(b): Special session convened by Primate on request of bishops, clergy, laity or Standing Committee, *Provincial Synod Constitution Amendment Ordinance 2011 Assenting Ordinance 2011 (New South Wales)* [n173], Constit. s.15, and *Diocese of North Queensland* [n112], Constit. Non Fundamental Provision 6; South East Asia [n99], Constit. II (b): Archbishop summons and presides over both Provincial Synod and House of Bishops; Nigeria [n99], Constit. V.26(2): "The Primate shall summon and preside over meetings of the General Synod, Episcopal Synod, and the Standing Committee and is the principal minister of the Church of Nigeria (Anglican Communion), *Diocese of Ogbia* [n112], Constit. I.xvi, III.8(a) and *Diocese of Etsako* [n112], Constit. Definition 25, III.3.3: The Bishop shall summon Diocesan Synod at least once per year and at other times at his discretion; Ireland [n99], Constit. I.II.14-15, 17: Archbishop or bishop next in seniority *may* convene ordinary and extraordinary sessions of General Synod as prescribed by constitution, and *shall* do so upon written request of 1/3 of members of House of Bishops or House of Representatives (emphasis added). See also II.21: Bishop *shall* prescribe ordinary annual meeting of diocesan synod at a time and place of his choosing, and *may* convene special meetings of the diocesan synod upon written request of not less than ½ of members of diocesan council or 1/3 of members of synod (emphasis added), and VI.I.8: Archbishop convenes Episcopal Electoral

the "principal bishop" (the diocesan bishop, the bishop commissary or bishop next in line of seniority) presides over meetings of the synod, and may exercise considerable power over the proceedings during synod.[189] Thirdly, no act of a diocesan synod has any effect until it has received the assent of the Bishop.[190]

College. See also *PCLCCAC,* [n17], Principles 39.6-7: The principal bishop (Archbishop, Presiding Bishop, Moderator or other office having archiepiscopal or metro political authority) exercises authority and leadership over the province, convenes and presides at its legislative and episcopal assemblies, enjoys precedence over other bishops and oversees the bishops, and Principle 37.5: The bishop has a role of leadership in the governance of the diocese, and is president of the diocesan synod, council or equivalent assembly.

[189] Australia [n99], Constit. IV.20, *Diocese of Adelaide* [n112], Constit. III.17, 18: Bishop shall preside and have a casting vote as well; Nigeria [n99], II.12(1): Primate is the President of General Synod and presides at all sessions, *Diocese of Ogbia* [n112], Constit. VIII(g) and *Diocese of Etsako* [n112], Constit. III.3.8-9: Bishop also sets the agenda for Diocesan Synod; Ireland [n99], Constit. I.II.17: Archbishop (Armagh, or Dublin if Armagh is absent) presides at General Synod. See also *Appendix to the Constitution: Standing Orders approved by the House of Representatives,* SO 15-17: President shall decide who will speak, confine speaker to subject matter, and when he rises all others sit so that he may be heard without interruption, and SO 26, 40, 41: President may direct the reading of Bills on the same subject matter, the order of their consideration and voting, and decide whether motions to close debate or to move to other business are an abuse of Standing Orders; see also *Diocese of Connor* [n129], Standing Orders 6-12: and *Diocese of Down and Dromore* [n129] "Standing Orders of The Synod" SO 6-11: "All questions of order shall be decided by the President," including time limits of speakers."

[190] Australia: *Diocese of North Queensland* [n112], Constit. Non-Fundamental Provision 6; South East Asia: *Diocese of Kuching* [n112], Constit. X (6): Nothing shall be determined by the Diocesan Synod unless it has been accepted by the Bishop with the concurrence of the majority of the members present and voting together or by orders, and *Diocese of Singapore* [n112], Constit. "Constitutional Declarations by the Archbishop of

However, it would be incorrect to conclude that a bishop's veto is final. All four Churches provide leave to appeal the bishop's veto or dissent from an action of the diocesan synod by a process which includes a vote by the clergy and laity reaffirming the vetoed legislation at the next ordinary or special meeting of synod, and if the bishop still dissents, an appeal to the General Synod or House of Bishops whose decision shall be final and binding on bishop and diocese.[191]

---

the Anglican Church in South East Asia 1998," Declaration 5: The Bishops decisions may not be overruled by the other Houses of Diocesan Synod, but right of appeal lies to the Provincial House of Bishops; Nigeria [n99], Can. VII.1: The Bishop may veto any resolution of his Diocesan Synod which he considers to be "a detriment to the interest of the Church,"; Ireland [n99], Constit. II.I.28-30: Acts of Synod have no effect until approved by a majority of clergy and lay representative present and voting together, or by orders, and assented to by the Bishop. If the bishop dissents from the clergy and laity, all action on the matter is suspended until the next annual meeting of the synod. See also *PCLCCAC,* [n17], Principle 50.5: No doctrinal changes without the consent of the Bishop.

[191] Australia: *Diocese of North Queensland* [n112], Constit. Non-Fundamental Provision 10: When the bishop dissents from a canon or resolution approved by a majority of the diocesan synod, it is suspended until the next general or special synod, when the matter may be resubmitted for a 2/3 majority vote by the clergy and laity. If the bishop dissents again, appeal lies directly to the Provincial Synod whose decision shall be final. Until the Provincial Synod is constituted, appeal lies directly to the Primate; Nigeria: *Diocese of Etsako* [n112], Constit. III.3.11 (b): Appeal lies directly to Archbishop and bishops of the Ecclesiastical Province of Bendel from bishops dissent without a second vote by clergy and laity. Archbishop and bishop's decision shall be final and binding on diocesan bishop and synod. See also *Diocese of Ogbia* [n112], Constit. III.8(l): Direct appeal is to Standing Committee of the Church, and through Primate to the Archbishop of the Province whose decision shall be final and binding; Ireland [n99], Constit. II.I.30: Bishop's dissent from action at diocesan synod suspends all action until next annual meeting of synod, and if reaffirmed then by 2/3 majority of Clergy and Laity, and Bishop still dissent, matter goes to General Synod for final decision—provided Bishop may refer matter

In short, there is ample evidence from all four Churches that synods gather around bishops and that their leadership is crucial, though not without some checks and balances at the diocesan level. For all of these reasons, and for all of the principles of conciliar governance at work in its constitution and canons, the Province of the Anglican Church in South East Asia concludes that "the Province with the constituent dioceses is episcopally led and synodically governed."[192]

9. SYNOD AS CONCERNED WITH THE CHURCH'S MISSION TO THE WORLD, AND NOT JUST WITH THE INTERNAL LIFE OF THE CHURCH

Other Anglican Churches are also concerned with the Church's mission to the world, and not just the internal life of the Church. There is evidence of this in the constitutions

---

at any time to General Synod. The Diocese of Singapore puts the case most clearly with regards to disagreements between the Bishop and the clergy and laity in Synod: *"He may be wrong, or they [clergy and laity] may be wrong, for no man is infallible*. If, in such a case, a large number of them is strongly persuaded that the Diocesan Bishop has made a mistake, they have an appeal to the House of Bishops of the Province of the Anglican Church in South East Asia. Such an appeal may be made if the proposal which was rejected by the Diocesan Bishop was supported by two-thirds of those present and voting in the House of Clergy and two-thirds of those present and voting in the House of Laity at two separate sessions of the Diocesan Synod." South East Asia: *Diocese of Singapore* [n112], Constit. "Preface: Spiritual Background of the Synod," at 4. But see *Diocese of Kuching* [n112], Constit. XXVI where the requirement for appeal is only 1/3 of the clergy and laity at a subsequent session of Synod. See also *PCLCCAC,* [n17], Principle 16.4: "Leadership and authority should be exercised in an accountable manner, within the episcopal and synodical structures of a church, with respect for others in authority, and with regard for the common good and the dignity, rights, needs and gifts of all."

[192]South East Asia [n99], Can. 6.1.

of the Churches of South East Asia and Nigeria and its dioceses. South East Asia declares the Church exists to proclaim the Gospel of Jesus Christ "in obedience to his Great Commission," to make disciples, to extend God's Kingdom, and even to plant new dioceses beyond its boundaries,[193] Nigeria prioritizes evangelism, discipleship, Christian education and care for the poor and needy above the internal needs of the Church and creates jurisdictions of "likeminded faithfuls" beyond its boundaries.[194] There is virtually no evidence of this in the Churches of Australia[195] and Ireland, although the Diocese of North Queensland does at least mention mission[196] and the Standing

[193] South East Asia [n99], Constit. Preamble at 5, *Diocese of Singapore* [n112], Constit. III.1: "The Synod shall fulfill the responsibilities placed upon it by the Statement on the Spiritual Background of the Diocesan Synod... working in Him for the salvation of men and for the Kingdom of God," and XIII "Clergy Leadership in the Diocese outside Singapore": the Bishop shall appoint clergy to prepare for the eventual creation of a Diocese "in that country where that is appropriate."

[194] Nigeria [n99], Constit. I.2(2): "The aims, objectives and principles of the Church of Nigeria (Anglican Communion) are: (a) to evangelize, and promote the knowledge of God and the adherence to the teaching and examples of Jesus Christ, (b) to promote Christian education, morals and values, (c) to assist in the care and welfare of the people , particularly the poor, the aged and the needy, (d) to provide for the spiritual welfare of her members..." and IX.38: General Synod shall have power to create convocations of like-minded faithfuls outside Nigeria under the oversight of the Primate; see also *Diocese of Etsako* [n112], Constit. "Fundamental Aims and Principles" at 4 incorporating the aims, objectives and principles of the Church of Nigeria I.2(2).

[195] Australia [n99], Constit. V.26: General Synod may "declare its view on any matter affecting this Church."

[196] Australia: *Diocese of North Queensland* [n112], Constit. Canon 3: Diocesan Council, 10.2 (amended 2013): Priorities in the disposal of income may include "any strategy in the mission of the Church" expressed by resolution of Synod.

Committee of Ireland monitors civil legislation that may affect the Church.[197]

10. SYNOD AS EXPRESSING THE SPIRITUAL LIFE AND EVENT OF THE CHURCH THROUGH DAILY WORSHIP AND PRAYER, AND THE HOLY EUCHARIST

Among our four Churches, South East Asia has the greatest commitment to this principle when bishops gather together to decide any matter of faith and order referred to them, in the election of an Archbishop and in the celebration of Holy Communion daily at Synod.[198] Nigeria requires every session of General Synod to begin with Holy Communion, as well as for the elections of the Archbishop and Bishops.[199] Ireland begins each day of General Synod with a reading from Holy Scripture and

---

[197] Ireland [n99], Constit. Appendix: The Standing Committee of the General Synod (Resolution of the General Synod 9 May 1967, Amended 2013), II.12.

[198] South East Asia [n99], Constit. III (d): The House of Bishops should always seek to achieve consensus on any matter of faith and order referred to it "only after consultation, prayer and seeking the mind of the Lord in accordance with the Holy Scriptures," and I (a), Regulation A: Election of the Archbishop: "The election of the Archbishop is a matter of spiritual importance and must be conducted as an act of worship in true spirit of unity, love, humility and submission to God." See also *Diocese of Kuching* [n113], Constit. X (2): "The Holy Communion shall be celebrated daily when the diocesan synod is in session."

[199] Nigeria [n99], Constit. Can.XII.14 and Cans.II.7 (1) and IV.15 (2): On the day of the election of the Primate and other bishops, Holy Communion shall be celebrated, and daily thereafter until there is an election. See also *Diocese of Ogbia* [n112], Constit. III.8(d)(e): Each session of Synod preceded by Holy Communion, each subsequent day begin with prayer or Holy Communion as Bishop may direct, and Bishop shall preach a Synod sermon, and *Diocese of Etsako* [n112], Constit. III.3.6: Same as *Ogbia* except no requirement of bishop to preach.

prayer behind closed doors, and diocesan synods with Holy Communion and prayer.[200] In Australia, General Synod opens each day with prayer.[201]

11. THE WORK OF SYNODS AS CONFORMING TO THE ULTIMATE AUTHORITY OF THE HOLY SCRIPTURES

Synods must conform to the ultimate authority of the Holy Scriptures. This follows from Articles VI, XX and XXI of the Thirty-Nine Articles, which together provide that no decision of any Council is valid unless it is consistent with and supported by Holy Scripture. Article XX specifically provides that the Church may not ordain anything "contrary to the Word of God, neither may it so expound one place of Scripture, that it may be repugnant to another."[202] Therefore, we would have evidence of this

---

[200] Ireland [n99], Constit. Appendix: Standing Orders Approved by the House of Representatives, SO 1, 2; *Diocese of Connor* [n129], "Order of Proceedings and Ordinary Meetings of The Diocesan Synod," Item. 2: the proceedings shall begin with the reading of Holy Scripture and prayer, and "Standing Orders of the Synod," SO 1: every meeting of Synod preceded by a Celebration of Holy Communion," Ibid., *Diocese of Down and Dromore* [n129], "Proceedings of the Synod" items 1 and 2. See also VI.I.9 "Episcopal Electoral College": On day appointed for election, college meets in church or cathedral for celebration of Holy Communion, and charge to College on the office and work of a bishop in the Church "and the qualities of heart and mind required in those who are called to that sacred office."

[201] Australia [n99], Constit. Rule I: Standing Orders, r.3: "The Synod shall be opened each day with prayers by the President."

[202] *Supra,* pp. 42-43, and *PCLCCAC,* [n17], Principles 49.4 and 49.5, which affirm the 39 Articles as being "grounded in the Holy Scriptures, and in such teachings of the ancient Fathers and Councils of the Church as are agreeable to the Holy Scriptures" and as representing the sources of *"lawful doctrine"* for a church. (Emphasis added). However, it must be noted that the *PCLCCAC* affirms the Holy Scriptures of the Old and New Testaments as not only containing "all things necessary for salvation" but as therefore "the rule and ultimate standard of faith," quite apart from the 39 Articles, at Principle 49.2

principle of the supremacy of Holy Scripture as the ultimate rule and standard for faith and practice, including conciliar decision-making in synods, wherever a Church has adopted the Thirty-Nine Articles of Religion and/or "The Chicago Lambeth Quadrilateral"(1888)[203] for a fundamental statement of doctrine.

We do have such evidence in the Fundamental Declarations, Ruling Principles and Canons on the doctrine of each of the four Churches, which adopt the Thirty-Nine Articles, together with the Book of Common Prayer 1662 and its Ordinal, as a statement of doctrine incorporating by reference Articles VI, XX and XXI and the supremacy of Holy Scripture in conciliar decision-making.[204] In Nigeria and South East Asia, the Thirty-Nine Articles are the conduit for the reception of the "Historic Faith, Doctrine, Sacrament and Discipline of the One, Holy, Catholic and Apostolic Church as the Lord has commanded in his holy word.[205] Such contextualization

---

[203] *Lambeth Resolution 11* (1888): That, in the opinion of this Conference, the following articles supply a basis on which approach may be by God's blessing made towards home reunion: a. The Holy Scriptures of the Old and New Testaments, as "containing all things necessary to salvation," ***and as being the rule and ultimate standard of faith.***" (Emphasis added) <http://www.anglicancommunion.org/resources/document-library/lambeth-conference/1888/resolution-11?author=Lambeth+Conference&year=1888> Accessed 20 November 2015.

[204] Australia [n99], Constit. II.4 "Ruling Principles"; South East Asia [n99], Constit. Can. A5 "The Doctrine of the Church in the Province"; Nigeria [n99], Constit. I.3(1) and Can. I.1; Ireland [n99], Constit. Preamble and Declaration II.

[205] Nigeria [n99] I.3 (1) and Can. I.1; See also *PCLCCAC,* [n17], Principle 49.1: "The faith of Our Lord Jesus Christ is taught in the Holy Scriptures..." and South East Asia [n99], Constit. Can. A5: "The doctrine of the Church in the

emphasizes the "catholicity" of Scripture as the ultimate rule and standard in all things, a biblical consensus that extends over both time and place. Not surprisingly, Australia places the Thirty-Nine Articles in the context of its roots in the Reformation and the Church of England.[206] Such contextualization thus emphasizes Reformational Anglican ecclesiology: where councils are subject to the Holy Scriptures, where their role is to interpret them, and where they are always tested by them.[207] Either way, these fundamental declarations and principles of doctrine recognizing the Thirty-nine Articles implicitly place conciliar governance under the scrutiny of the Scriptures that are interpreted with both catholic and Reformational authority.

Secondly, in their constitutions, Australia and Ireland declare the Holy Scriptures as the ultimate standard and rule of faith for the Church "given by inspiration of God," apart from any mention of the Thirty-nine Articles.[208]

Province is grounded in the Holy Scriptures and in such teachings of the ancient Fathers and Councils of the Church as are agreeable to the said Scriptures. In particular such doctrine is to be found in the Thirty-Nine Articles of Religion, the Book of Common Prayer, and the Ordinal." Can. A5 is almost verbatim a citation of *PCLCCAC* Principles 49.4-5.

[206] Australia [n99], Constit. II.4: "This Church, being derived from the Church of England, retains and approves the doctrines and principles of the Church of England embodied in the Book of Common Prayer with [the Ordinal] and in the Articles of Religion sometimes called the Thirty-nine Articles..."

[207] See Chapter 5. See also South East Asia [n99], Constit. Can A2, which also expresses the Reformational Anglican view that the Thirty-nine Articles are authoritative precisely because they are agreeable to the word of God.

[208] Australia [n99], Constit. I "Fundamental Declarations" 1: The canonical scriptures of the Old and New Testaments are "the ultimate rule and standard of faith"; Ireland [n99], Constit. Preamble and Declaration I.1: The Church of Ireland accepts "and unfeignedly believes all the Canonical Scriptures of the Old and New Testament." See also Nigeria: *Diocese of Ogbia* [n112], Constit. II, "Fundamental Principles" 2 and 3: Defines the Holy

With regard to disputes over the interpretation of the Scriptures, South East Asia provides for a conciliar process of appeal to authorities beyond the church for guidance and definitions,[209] while Nigeria reserves such guidance and definitions to its own "Ecclesiastical tribunals".[210] With such robust definitions of the authority of Holy Scripture, Nigeria understands its plenary power to "banish and drive away all erroneous and strange doctrines which are contrary to God's word as understood and interpreted in the aforementioned formularies" (emphasis added).[211]

In short, in the declarations of doctrine in all four Churches, the Holy Scriptures stand with ultimate

---

Scriptures as "the record of God's revelation of himself to man, and as being the rule and ultimate standard of faith...the whole hearted acceptance of [which]" is the basis for unity with other Churches; see also *Diocese of Etsako* [n113], Constit." Fundamental Aims and Declarations" 7(a) (b). See also *PCLCCAC,* [n17], Principle 49.2.

[209] South East Asia [n99], Constit. III: When House of Bishops cannot reach consensus, Archbishop may refer the matter to Canterbury or other Primates of the Anglican Communion for "guidance"; see also *Diocese of Singapore* [n112], Constit. Fundamental Declarations 1 and 2: Where Christians differ as to interpretations, the Diocese accepts the interpretations and practices according to the 1662 Book of Common Prayer and Ordinal and the 39 Articles. If there is any dispute about these historical interpretations, appeal to the Provincial House of Bishops for final decision. See also *PCLCCAC,* [n17], Principle 53.10: Appeal for guidance in interpretation both within and beyond the Church.

[210] Nigeria [n99], Constit. I.3 (2).

[211] Ibid., Can. I.2. See also *PCLCCAC,* [n17], Principle 51.2: "Ministers are to ensure that biblical texts are treated respectfully and coherently, building on tradition and scholarship, so that scriptural revelation may continue to illuminate, challenge and transform cultures, structures, thinking and doing," and Principle 55.6: "Liturgical adaptation and innovation must not be inconsistent with the Word of God and the spirit and teaching of the Book of Common Prayer 1662."

authority over conciliar decision making as a fundamental principal of faith or as an expression of the doctrine of the Church in the Thirty-nine Articles. Whether the provenance is Catholic or Reformational Anglican, the authority of the Scriptures is final.

There is overwhelming evidence in the laws of these four representative Churches that Conciliarism is indeed an organizing principle for other Churches in the Anglican Communion. Despite the vast geographical and cultural differences between Australia, Asia, Africa and Europe, the truth of that old proverb remains true – the apple has not fallen-far-from-tree.

FOUR

The Medieval Church, The Great Schism, and the Development of "Strict Conciliarism"

In Beyond the Reformation, Paul Avis uses the Great Schism (1378-1417) both to make the case for the appropriation of a "modified catholic" conciliarism by Reformational

Anglicans, and to suggest that this historical development may have some principles Anglicans could use to address current schism within the Communion. He paints a picture of the impact the election of two rival Popes had, by the same College of Cardinals, within a few months' time:

> "For the first time in the Church's history, two popes, each with his own hierarchical structure, demanded the allegiance of Christendom. The schism produced a dual system of popes, cardinals, curia and ecclesiastical allegiances, right down to the parochial clergy. It could mean that people did not know who was their rightful parish priest, bishop, religious superior or dean of cathedral. They could not tell whose sacraments were valid. Rival candidates were appointed to important

offices, such as the headship of religious houses. Each side denounced and excommunicated the other."[212]

Avis goes on elsewhere to explain how this crisis produced a movement in the two centuries immediately preceding the Reformation, a conciliar movement that aimed to reform the Church, expunge heresy, and unite the Church – healing the breach in the papacy by "calling together bishops, lay rules and theologians in a free general council that would ultimately be above the popes."[213]

In developing the distinctive stages and characteristic of this Catholic conciliar movement, Avis draws heavily upon the works of Francis Oakley[214] and Brian Tierney.[215] Oakley lays the foundation for the Anglican maxim that conciliar governance is "episcopally led and synodically governed," through his citation of the works of the great Dominican theologian and canonist John of Paris (1255-1306). According to Oakley, it was John who most accurately drew together all of the pre-Schism teaching of medieval canonists into the principle that, while Papal authority is conferred by God, the particular person called to exercise that authority was to be decided by *the whole Church* in the corporate person of the College of Cardinals. Moreover, the Pope so called was to exercise that authority for the common good of the whole Church.[216] This is the

[212] Avis, *Beyond the Reformation: Authority, Primacy and Unity in the Conciliar Tradition* [n5], at 72-73.

[213] Avis, *The Identity of Anglicanism: Essentials of Anglican Ecclesiology* [n12], at 9.

[214] Francis Oakley, *The Conciliarist Tradition: Constitutionalism in the Catholic Church 1300-1870* [n13]

[215] Brian Tierney, *Foundations of the Conciliar Theory* (Cambridge: CUP,1955, reprinted 1968)[n13]

[216] Oakley, [n13] at 105-106.

heart of episcopal leadership. With regards to the governing role of synods, Oakley goes on to cite Tierney for the observation that:

> "The strict conciliar theory, far from being a reaction against canonistic teaching or an alien importation onto ecclesial soil of secular constitutional notions, had instead deep (and impeccably orthodox) roots in the ecclesiological traditions of the pre-Marsiglian era. It unquestionable drew a great deal of inspiration from the *communio* ecclesiology and synodal practice of the first millennium of Christian life, and especially from the essentially conciliar mode of governance that had characterized the ancient church for long centuries after the Council of Nicaea (325)."[217]

In other words, during this time and all the way to the Great Schism, there existed side by side within the Medieval Catholic Church two separate doctrines for the unity of the Church: (1) subordination of all members under a single head or "papal monarchy," and (2) the theory that stressed the corporate association of the members of the Church as the true principle of its ecclesiastical unity [see Acts 11-15, I Corinthians 12 and Ephesians 4] and which envisaged "*the exercise of corporate authority by the members of the church even in the absence of an effective head* (emphasis added).[218] Conciliarists like Juan de Segovia (d. 1458) used St. Paul's analogy between the Christian community and the human body (Romans 12:4-8; I Corinthians 12:12-14, 18-21; Ephesians 4:12-16; Colossians 2:19) as further proof that power belongs to the whole rather than to any one part. They also argued that

---

[217] Ibid. at 106.

[218] Ibid, at 107.

the passage from Ephesians 4:11-12 on different gifts within the body justified "the inclusion of other clergy, in particular university doctors, in the council on equal terms with bishops.[219] Opponents like Cardinal Cajetan (1468-1534) retorted that a body was imperfect without a head, and that without the Pope convening and presiding over any Council – to use the Pauline analogy – it was like a headless body and therefore had no legislative authority.[220] Other conciliarists including Segovia argued that authority in the Church must not be understood as dominatio – as it was exercised "among the Gentiles" and condemned by Jesus in Matthew 20:25-28 and Luke 22:26-27 – but rather as humble service.[221] And so the controversy raged.

But the authority of the whole over any one person or party also derives from the maxim championed by Marsilius of Padua (1250-1306) in *Defensor Pacem,* "The whole is greater than any of its parts."[222] Marsilius describes the procedure for gathering such dispersed authority into a council: at a place and time convenient to the majority, by election of faithful representatives (clerical and lay), by "proportionate representation" according to quality and quantity, from every province and community of the church, "to settle those matters pertaining to divine law which seem doubtful…and necessary to define."[223] Nicholas of Cusa (1401-1464) argues that in such councils

---

[219] Anthony Black, *Council and Commune* (London: Burns and Oats, 1979) at 130. See especially n.18 for citations to other conciliarists.

[220] Cajetan: "On the Comparison of the authority of pope and council," Ch. XII "That, without the Pope, there is no legislative power in the Church," in J.H. Burns and Thomas Izbicki, eds., *Conciliarism and Papalism* (Cambridge: Cambridge University Press, 1997), at 60: "…the Church is not a perfect community without the pope, because it would be without a head."

[221] Black, *Council and Commune,* [n219] at 130.

[222] Avis, *Beyond the Reformation* [n5], at 52.

[223] Ibid, 52-53, citing *Defensor Pacis, II, xx, 2.*

there must be "freedom of speech" for all participants and that the whole church has a right to know what happens in the proceedings.[224]

Within this Catholic conciliar tradition there emerged in turn three strands. The first strand is what Oakley defines as "episcopal reforming conciliarism." This is the simple practice, of ancient and apostolic provenance, of frequent and regular councils as a necessary precedent for ongoing reform and holiness of the church, by councils acting in concert with and not apart from Bishops, especially the Pope.[225] The second strand or expression is "quasi-oligarchic conciliarism," in which the corporate nature of the Church is constituted in a Pope whose powers were somewhat limited by the College of Cardinals, with whose "advice, consent, direction and remembrance" he had to rule.[226] Some viewed it as a kind of "mixed monarchy," others as a constitutionally limited executive (the Pope) whose powers were limited by an Apostolic Senate (the Cardinals).

But there were weaknesses in this quasi-oligarchic model, in principle and in practice. In principle, it left unanswered the question "where is the authority of the corporate nature of the whole Church beyond the executive (the Pope) and the senate (the Cardinals)"? This

---

[224]Valliere [n8] 154; See also Paul Sigmund, ed. *Nicholas of Cusa: The Catholic Concordance* (Cambridge: Cambridge University Press, 1996) 54-56 (2.3.75-76) where Nicholas of Cusa cites a letter from a pope to an emperor on the eve of a council: "Give permission to speak freely to everyone who wishes to speak on the faith that he believes...so that all may recognize clearly that no one who wished to speak about the truth was in any way impeded or dissuaded by fear, power, threats or rejection."

[225] Oakley, [n13], at 66-67.

[226] Ibid, at 68-71.

ambiguity also led to questions of whether there were now two competing ultimate authorities within the Church, the Pope or the Cardinals. Secondly, in practice it not only failed to heal the Great Schism – it exacerbated it by the College of Cardinals electing *a third Pope* to replace the other two, at the Council of Pisa (1409).[227]

This failure set the stage for the Council of Constance (1414-1418) where the great conciliarist Jean Gerson and the proclamation *Haec Sancta* declared the third strand of strict constitutional conciliarism – namely, that there are exigent circumstances under which a free and general council of the whole Church must assemble to correct erring bishops, including a Pope and the Cardinals, and must take action to heal the schism and restore the doctrine, discipline and order of the Church. Such a free and general council derives its authority immediately from Christ himself as representative of the universal church on the basis of the Holy Scriptures, and that therefore all Christians, including the Pope and bishops, are bound to obey its decrees in settling controversies of faith, ending schism, and reforming the church.[228] Moreover, only the whole Church gathered together as "community of the faithful" is indefectible as a "mystical body animated and directed by the Holy Spirit."[229]

Therefore it is the General Council that provides checks and balances against erring popes when necessary – but meeting even apart from these exigent circumstances of heresy, ungodly leadership, schism and reform. The whole Church does not exhaust its corporate authority by electing a Pope, but retains residual power "to preserve the truths

---

[227] Ibid, at 11-12, 37-38.
[228] Ibid, at 39-40.
[229] Ibid, at 76, 80.

of the Christian faith, to prevent its own subversion or ruin…exercise that power through its representatives assembled in a General Council… and in certain cases act alone and against the wishes of the Pope – and in such cases if need be to judge, punish and even depose the Pope."[230] This *communio* ecclesiology understands the headship of the Pope in a secondary and ministerial way as subordinated to the headship of Christ (from whom the Council derives its authority directly).[231] The power of the Pope is also restrained or "checked" by the institution of the Cardinals who also have authority to call a council if the Pope will not.[232]

Understandably, the medieval conciliarists were more ambiguous about the composition of a general council beyond the bishops. Around the Roman maxim "what touches all must be decided by all," Oakley notes that Cardinal d'Ailly (1351-1420) retranslated the maxim to "What touches all must be approved at least by many and by the most notable ones,"[233] William of Ockham (1287-1347) who said that "all" includes laity and women[234] and Marsiglio of Padua (1275-1342) who defined "all" as "more than just the clerical order alone."[235]

The corporate *communio* ecclesiology that emerged fully in strict Catholic constitutional conciliarism gave birth to many of the principles of synodal government in the Church – the constitutional checks and balances between

---

230 Ibid, at 72.

231 Ibid, at 78.

232 Ibid, at 71, 81.

233 Ibid, at 81.

234 Ibid, at 102.

235 Ibid, at 103.

bishops, clergy and laity, the composition of synods and their representative nature of the whole Church, a focus on "exigent circumstances" which justify special procedures for settling matters of faith and avoiding schism, and more. Even the conciliar principle that synods are a necessary and regular feature of the life and governance of the Church may be traced back to the proclamation in *Frequens* from the Council of Constance that General Councils shall assemble at "stated and regular intervals" to ensure the ongoing reform of the Church.[236]

In short, Strict Catholic constitutional conciliarism is not some radical intrusion upon the Catholic nature of the Church – or in the words of Tierney, "something accidental and external, thrust upon the Church from the outside." It was instead, "a logical culmination of ideas that were [deeply] embedded in the law and doctrines of the Church itself."[237] Indeed, even among canonists within the Roman Catholic Church today, it lives on in part through the doctrine of "episcopal collegiality" in *Lumen Gentium,* a mustard seed that is growing quietly alongside the doctrine of unity grounded in the Pope alone.[238]

---

[236] Ibid, at 98.

[237] Tierney, [n13] at 13.

[238] Orsy, "Episcopal Collegiality Revisited" in Alberto Melloni, Silvia Scatena, Eds. *Synod and Synodality*: *Theology, History, Canon Law and Ecumenism in new contact,, International Colloquium Bruges 2003* (Piscataway NJ:Transaction Publishers, 2005) at 32.

FIVE

The Ecclesiology of Reformational Anglicanism: Modified Conciliarisn Under the Supreme Authority of Holy Scripture

Bishop John Jewell's *Apology for The Church of England* (1562)[239] amounts to the first sustained vindication of Reformational Anglican's ecclesiology.[240] In it, he seems to embrace strict Catholic constitutional conciliarism. In Part I he cites the Council of Carthage (365 AD) that no bishop should be called the highest or chief priest – for the principle of episcopal collegiality.[241] He cites the strict conciliarist Jean Gerson with approval in documenting the canonical and doctrinal excesses and errors in the evolution of papal sovereignty.[242] "Yet truly we do not despise councils, assemblies and conference of bishops and

[239] John Jewell's 1562 work, *The Apology of the Church of England: An Apology, or answer, in Defense of the Church of England, With a Brief and Plain Declaration of the True Religion Professed and Used in the same* (London: Cassell and Company, Limited, 1888) republished at < http://www.anglicanlibrary.org/jewel/apology/2.htm > Accessed 20 August 2015.

[240] Avis, *The Identity of Anglicanism* [n12], at 185.

[241] Jewell [n239] at 12-13.

[242] Ibid, at 38.

learned men, neither have we done that we have done altogether without bishops or without a council," he writes in Part VI, noting both the long consultations in Parliament (including the laity) and "before a notable synod and convocation."[243] He goes on to point out the absurdity and uselessness of councils if the Pope is the final authority, cites the ancient Canons and Councils of Nicaea (325 AD), Carthage (365 AD) and Chalcedon (452 AD) for the proposition that local/provincial councils can and should meet regularly, and not just in emergencies, but to "speedily meet with and cut short those heretics" without delay, and notes that such "provincial synods" have been the practice in the Church of England from the very beginning.[244]

But Anglican Reformed ecclesiology does not accept strict Catholic conciliarism without qualification. Jewell also declared that the truth of the gospel "dependeth not upon councils," thereby placing Holy Scripture as the ultimate and final authority within the Church.[245] He also pointed out that for at least 500 years "the Christian emperors of old called the councils" and not bishops, for the proposition that Christian rulers are the ones to legitimately call a council.[246] The execution of reformers Jan Hus and Jerome of Prague at the "great" Council of Constance – despite assurances of safe conduct – stood for the English Reformers' demand that councils be free and fair.[247] All these qualifications became enshrined in the three central propositions of Article XXI of the Thirty-Nine Articles of Religion: (1) General Councils may not be

[243] Ibid, at 54-55.
[244] Ibid, at 66.
[245] Ibid.
[246] Ibid, at 61-62.
[247] Avis, *Beyond the Reformation* [n5], at 136-137.

called except by the civil ruler or "magistrates", (2) councils are not infallible: "they can and do err," and (3) whatever a council may ordain with regard to salvation is valid only if it is found in Holy Scripture.[248]

For all these reason Avis concludes that Anglicans have adopted a rather modest version of strict Catholic conciliarism. In addition to the three qualifications above in Article XXI, the English Reformers would not wait for a General Council in order to reform the Church. *Semper reformanda* means that there must be regular and ongoing councils to ensure reformation of the Church always and at all times. Secondly, councils are always subject to the word of God and their role was and is merely to interpret the Scriptures. Where the scriptures do not touch directly on a subject before the council, the matter may be left to the discretion of the Church so long as the council does not ordain anything contrary to God's word.[249] Richard Hooker (1554-1600) reaffirmed this liberty in his ***Laws of Ecclesiastical Polity*** where he argued that the abuse of the counsels should inspire people to "reduce them to that first perfection" of the Early Church, not abandon them.[250]

But Hooker also did not envisage that return "to first perfection" in the Jerusalem Council of Acts 15 as a static pattern to be replicated in successive generations. He does indeed suggest that Acts 15 establishes a precedent – but it is a hermeneutical precedent and not merely a fixed model.

---

[248] Ibid, at 137-138.

[249] Ibid, at 139-140. See Article XXXIV which affirms this liberty.

[250] John Keble, Ed. *The Works of That Learned and Judicious Divine, Mr. Richard Hooker: Of the Laws of Ecclesiastical Polity, Vol. 1* (Books One through Four) (Oxford: Oxford University Press, 1836), Book 1, Chapter X.14 at 316

In Book III of the *Lawes of Ecclesiastical Polity*, Hooker carefully unpacks the passage. He notes first that in Acts 15:28, "what seems good to us" is not of the same order as what seems good to the Holy Spirit, and that the apostles were simply giving their approbation to what they discerned from the Holy Spirit.[251] Secondly, discernment involved asking whether the end for which the Jewish ceremonial laws were written was still existent. He concluded from the passage and its larger context in the New Testament that those ceremonial laws had an end which was fulfilled through the death of Jesus Christ as the perfect sacrifice for all sins. Therefore the Apostles concluded in Council that the ceremonial law could no longer apply to the Gentile converts as a condition of salvation.[252] That the "moral law" in the Bible has an end that is never extinguished sets such laws apart from the ceremonial.[253] But he then goes on to say that even when

[251] Ibid., Book III, Chapter X.2 at 487: "'To the Holy Ghost and to us it hath seemed good' which style they [the Apostles] did not use as matching themselves in power with the Holy Ghost, but as testifying the Holy Ghost to be the author, and themselves but only utterers of that decree." See also Book VIII, Chapter 6.7, where Hooker argues that the Jerusalem Council is unique in its precedence, "not as the canons of other ecclesiastical assemblies, human, but very divine ordinances" due to the unique "enlightenment" of the Apostles directly from Christ through the Holy Spirit, and "wherein no such kind of persons" in councils will ever be so. For this reason he also disclaims the Jerusalem Council as precedent for episcopal conciliarism alone.

[252] Ibid, at 486-487: "But (that which they [the Jews] in the blindness of their obdurate hearts are not able to discern) sith the end for which that law was ordained is now fulfilled, past and gone; how should it but cease any longer to be, which hath no longer any cause of being in force as before?"

[253] Ibid., at Book III, Chapter X.4 at 489: "In a word, we plainly perceive by the difference of those three laws which the Jews received at the hands of God, the moral, ceremonial and judicial, that if the end for which and the matter according whereunto God maketh his laws continue always one and

the end of a law continues, its means may become ineffective due to change in time and circumstances – citing for example the judicial law of "bridling theft" (whose end is never extinguished) by "means" of quadruple restitution (a Biblical law, but one which might presumably be altered if it can be shown to be ineffective in achieving its end.)[254] Lest this open a door to doctrinal innovations as a means to an end, Hooker says that while "matters of regiment" or government within the Church may be adaptable, matters touching faith and doctrine are "immoveable and impossible to be framed or cast anew."[255]

In the tradition of Reformational Anglicanism, Hooker is taking the scriptures seriously – by allowing his exegesis of Acts 15 to raise at least three important questions that must be asked to discern the mind of Christ in the midst of controversy, and in council. First, if there is a Biblical law that applies, is the end for which the law is cited as authority still in existence? Secondly, even if the ends of that Biblical law are permanent, is there some "unfitness in

---

the same, his laws also do the like; *for which cause the moral law cannot be altered.*"(emphasis added)

[254] Ibid, at 488-489: "The end wherefore laws were made may be permanent and those laws nevertheless require some alteration, if there be any unfitness in the means which they prescribe as tending unto that end and purpose... Theft will always, and will always need to be bridled. But that the mean which this law provideth for that end (citing Ex. 22:1 and 2 Sam. 12:6), namely the punishment of quadruple restitution, that this will always be sufficient to bridle and restrain that kind of enormity no man can warrant."

[255] Ibid., at Book III, Chapter X.7 at 491: "To make new articles of faith and doctrine no man thinketh it lawful..."The rule of faith,' saith Tertullian, 'is but one and that alone immoveable and impossible to be framed or cast anew.'"

the means which they prescribe" unto that end and purpose? If so, what adjustments in the means could be accomplished without compromising the end? Thirdly, does the controversy before the church "touch" points of faith and doctrine that may not change under any circumstance? As some have observed, Hooker is creating here a hermeneutical precedent and not merely a static model for replication – a Biblical hermeneutic that seems to have gone missing from many of the Anglican "Instruments" in the last 50 years (see Chapter 6). In short, Hooker is creating a dynamic Biblical framework for discerning the mind of Christ in the councils of the Church:

> One of Hooker's intentions in writing the *Lawes* was to tie spiritual discernment to conciliar judgement amidst controversy… namely, the connection between I Corinthians 14:33 and Acts 15, that God is a God of order and peace, and has been faithful to the continuity of the visible Church throughout history through conciliar authority.[256]

Likewise, in the spirit of the Reformers, Hooker argues that proof based on human authority is not as weighty as that which comes from a stronger proof, therefore "one word from the mouth of God will bear more weight than 10,000 General Councils."[257]

---

[256] Matthew Thollander, "The conciliar intent of Richard Hooker's theological hermeneutic," *Reformation and Renaissance Review,* Vol. 16, No. 1 April 2014, 52-67 at 53.

[257] Hooker, *Laws of Ecclesiastical Polity*, [n250] at Book 2 Chapter VII.5 at 407-408: "and therefore although ten thousand general councils would set down one and the same definitive sentence concerning any point of religion whatsoever, yet one demonstrative reason alleged, or one manifest testimony cited from the mouth of God himself to the contrary. Could not choose but overweigh them all."

For the Reformers, only Holy Scripture is inerrant. Therefore it is the Biblical substance and content of any council that gives it authority – not the number of bishops present or the authority of their office.[258] So councils are to be held in honor and studied with reverence, but always tested by Scripture.[259]

Finally, unlike Catholic conciliarism Reformed Anglican ecclesiology has no place for a Pope – not in council or otherwise. True, Catholic conciliarists inspired the English Reformers:

> "The conciliar movement aimed to reform the Church, expunge heresy and unite the Church by healing the breach within the papacy. It attempted this by calling together bishops, lay rulers and theologians in a free and general council that would ultimately be above the popes."[260]

But unlike Catholic conciliarists, Anglican ecclesiology seems to have no place for a central legislative and

---

[258] Avis, *Beyond the Reformation* [n5] at 141: "Finally, the English Reformers insisted that the authority of councils should not be measured by their size. Neither numbers nor unanimity were necessarily a guide to truth. Those ancient Israelites who worshipped the golden calf were very much of one mind, as Jewell pointed out, not to mention the crowds who urged Pilate to have Jesus crucified [citing *Parker Society Edition of the Works of the English Reformers,* Vol. III at 69]..."

[259] Gerald Bray, ed. *Tudor Church Reform: The Henrician Canons of 1535 and the Reformatio Legum Ecclesiasticarum* (Woodbridge: Suffolk: Boydell Press and the Church of England Record Society, 2008) at 183. See also Avis, *Beyond the Reformation* [n5] at 141: "But as Greenslade points out, this tactic demands a doctrine of reception, which the English Reformers did not elaborate," citing Greenslade, S.L. "The English Reformers and the Councils of the Church," *Oecumenica: An Annual Symposium of Ecumenical Research* (1967), 95-115 at 108.

[260] Avis, *Identity* [n12] at 9.

executive authority. Citing Lambeth Resolutions 48 and 49 (1930), Avis argues that at the global level of governance, the Churches of the Anglican Communion are held together "by mutual loyalty sustained by the common counsel of the bishops in *conference*," (emphasis added) and affirms that the Lambeth Conference of Bishops, meetings of the Primates and the Anglican Consultative Council and structures of synodical government at local, diocesan and provincial or national levels" are a striking example of conciliar ecclesiology.[261] But in fact, this one word concession by Avis to "conference" rather than "council" illustrates the problem in his own definition of conciliarism. For a conference is not a council. And from that fact one may rightly question whether Anglican Communion governance has *ever* truly practiced conciliar governance at the global level?

In any case, it is clear from our next section (Chapter Six) that for quite some time Anglicans have not taken seriously the legacy of Hooker's Biblical framework for dealing with controversies on matters touching faith and doctrine at the Communion level. As a result, these considerations have harkened us back to the times of the Great Schism and the Reformation. When the structures of the Church can no longer resolve controversies touching the faith and order of the Church do we have the exigent circumstances present to replace those structures with ones that are faithful to the Reformer's intent and faithful to Catholic conciliarism.

---

[261] Ibid, at 9-10.

Part III

Loss and Recovery of Conciliarism

SIX

Beyond the Breaking Point – The Loss of Conciliarism in Principle and Practice Within Anglican Governance

Paul Avis provides us with a real but limited definition of conciliarism at the global level of Anglican Communion governance:

> "[Anglicanism] believes that provinces gathered into communions should act in a conciliar fashion within the limits imposed by the divisions in the Church. It [Anglicanism] sets out to extend conciliarity as far and wide as it can until it runs up against the barriers erected by broken communion, rival claims to jurisdiction or serious differences in doctrine or order."[262]

This belief and practice is a far cry from the robust definition of conciliarism by Gerson and Catholic Conciliarists of the 14th and 15th centuries (See Chapter Four), Reformational Anglicans (see ChapterFive), and an equally far cry from the principles and practice of conciliarism at all levels within such Churches as Australia, South East Asia, Nigeria and Ireland (see Chapter 3). Avis alludes to the limits imposed on conciliarism by the current crisis within the Anglican Communion, which includes

[262] Avis, *"Anglican Conciliarity: History, Theology and Practice"* [n1], at 11.

serious differences in doctrine and order, broken communion between Churches, and rival claims to jurisdiction. This crisis has been characterized as a "deficit of authority" within the polity or governing structures (The Instruments of Communion) of Anglicanism, a crisis which threatens both the theological coherence and political cohesion of the Communion.[263]

Although the ordination of women to the presbyterate and a few consecrations of women to the episcopate strained the existing Instruments of Communion, the breaking point came in North America in 2002-2003 when the Diocese of New Westminster, Anglican Church of Canada (ACoC) unilaterally authorized public rites for the blessing of same sex unions[264], followed by the election and subsequent consecration of a priest who was living publicly in a same-sex relationship as bishop-coadjutor in the Diocese of New Hampshire, The Episcopal Church, USA

---

[263] Avis, *Beyond the Reformation* [n5]. *See also* Norman Doe, "The Instruments of Unity and Communion in Global Anglicanism "in Ian Markham, J Hawkins, Justyn Terry and Leslie Steffensen, eds. *The Wiley-Blackwell Companion to the Anglican Communion* (Chichester, West Sussex: John Wiley & Sons, Ltd., 2013, 48-53, where he describes the Archbishop of Canterbury , the Lambeth Conference of Bishops, the Anglican Consultative Council and the periodic Primates Meetings as the authoritative Instruments of Unity and Communion.

[264] In direct contradiction of Lambeth Conference (1998) Resolution 1.10 which provides in part, "... *(b)* in view of the teaching of Scripture, upholds faithfulness in marriage between a man and a woman in lifelong union, and believes that abstinence is right for those who are not called to marriage...*(e)* cannot advise the legitimising or blessing of same sex unions nor ordaining those involved in same gender unions." ." The Lambeth Conference Official Website: Resolutions of 1998 <http://www.lambethconference.org/resolutions/1998/1998-1-10.cfm> Accessed 3 November 2015.

(TEC).[265] Both Valliere and Avis describes the anti-conciliar nature of these acts,[266] their unacceptability to many Anglicans in TEC and most Anglicans throughout the Communion,[267] Avis describing the consecration in particular as "a brutal and unavoidable new fact in the Anglican ecclesiastical landscape" that has placed a question mark over the viability of Anglican polity and the cohesion of the Anglican Communion."[268]

The "Preamble to the Letter of Accession" from the Church of the Province of South East Asia to the proposed Anglican Covenant (2009, Final Text)[269] is a recitation of both the roots and the fruit of this crisis. Step by step, it documents the inability of the existing "Instruments of Communion" to deal with the unilateral actions of TEC and ACoC, thereby demonstrating the need to establish new conciliar structures within the Anglican Communion – or at the very least, to radically reinforce the existing

---

[265] Avis, *Beyond the Reformation* [n5] 171.

[266] Ibid. and Paul Valliere, *Conciliarism* [n8], at 199-200.

[267] "The episcopal ministry of a person living in a same-sex relationship is not acceptable to the majority of the Communion," *and* reaffirming Lambeth Conference (1998) Resolution 1.10 as "the standard of teaching on human sexuality accepted by the [Anglican] Communion. " *The Communiqué of the Primates Meeting in Dar es Salaam 19th February 2007,* Para. 17 Anglican Communion-Instruments of Communion-Primates Meetings-Resources <http://www.anglicancommunion.org/communion/primates/resources/downloads/communique2007_english.pdf > Accessed 7 January 2014.

[268] Avis, *Beyond the Reformation* [n5] at xv: "It is because that consecration or ordination was, like all ordinations, a sacramental act, an ecclesial sign with universal intention, of what is true of the Church and of the values that the Church stands for and of the message that it proclaims...that at the time of writing it has placed a question mark over the viability of Anglican polity and the cohesion of the Anglican Communion."

[269] "Preamble to the Letter of Accession- Province of South East Asia" 07 May 2011, <http://www.anglicanwestmalaysia.org.my/images/articles/Preamble%20to%20the%20Letter%20of%20Accession.pdf> Accessed 4 November 2015

structures with a doctrinal and disciplinary "Covenant" . It is worth citing, step by step, to understand the depth of this crisis and its trajectory.

First, the Province of South East Asia took note that the words in Section 4.2.1 of the Covenant expressing "common commitments and mutual accountability which hold each Church in the relationship of communion one with another" bear a strong resemblance to the closing appeal in the Second South-to-South Encounter Kuala Lumpur Statement (1997) where the need for mutual accountability was also noted.[270]

Secondly, this resemblance was not accidental. While the Covenant was seen as the culmination of a decade long struggle over ethical teaching and church order within the Communion, it was the Kuala Lumpur Statement (1997) which marked the beginning of a united effort by Anglican Churches largely in the Global South to contend "for the faith that was once delivered to the saints across the Communion."[271] This prompted the appeal in the Kuala Lumpur Statement to uphold the authority of Scripture in every aspect life, including the family and human sexuality[272] which was embraced one year later at Lambeth Conference 1998 in Resolution 1.10.[273]

---

[270] Ibid, Paras. 2 and 3;

[271] Ibid, Para. 4.

[272] Preamble, [n269], para. 5, citing sections 6 and 9 of the Kuala Lumpur Statement (1997): "6. We believe that the clear and unambiguous teaching of the Holy Scriptures about human sexuality is of great help to Christians as it provides clear boundaries," and "9. We are deeply concerned that the setting aside of biblical teaching in such actions as the ordination of practicing homosexuals and the blessing of same-sex unions calls into question the authority of the Holy Scriptures. This is totally unacceptable to us,"
<http://www.globalsouthanglican.org/index.php/comments/the_kuala_lum

Thirdly, despite these Communion-wide pleas, the Diocese of New Westminster decided to authorize services for same-sex unions in 2002. In 2003, the Episcopal Church (USA) appointed Gene Robinson, a priest in a committed same-sex relationship, as one of its bishops.[274] In October 2003, the Primates of the Anglican Communion issued a unanimous and strong warning in an extraordinary meeting that the consecration of Robinson would "tear the fabric of our Communion at its deepest level, and may lead to further division on this and further issues."[275]

---

pur_statement_on_human_sexuality_2nd_encounter_in_the_south_10/> Accessed 4 November 2015.

[273]Compare Lambeth Conference (1998) Resolution 1.10 [n264], which provides in pertinent part, "in view of the teaching of Scripture, upholds faithfulness in marriage between a man and a woman in lifelong union, and believes that abstinence is right for those who are not called to marriage; (Resolution 1.10b)" and "notes the significance of the Kuala Lumpur Statement on Human Sexuality and the concerns expressed...on the authority of Scripture in matters of marriage and sexuality and asks the Primates and the ACC to include them in their monitoring Process (Resolution 1.10g)."

[274] Preamble, [n269], para. 6.

[275] Ibid, Para. 7 citing "A Statement by the Primates of the Anglican Communion, Meeting at Lambeth Palace 16 October 2003," <http://www.globalsouthanglican.org/index.php/blog/comments/a_statement_by_the_primates_of_the_anglican_communion_meeting_in_lambeth_pa> Accessed 4 November 2015: "If [Gene Robinson's] consecration proceeds, we recognise that we have reached a crucial and critical point in the life of the Anglican Communion and we have had to conclude that the future of the Communion itself will be put in jeopardy. In this case, the ministry of this one bishop will not be recognised by most of the Anglican world, and many provinces are likely to consider themselves to be out of Communion with the Episcopal Church (USA). This will tear the fabric of our Communion at its deepest level, and may lead to further division on this and further issues as provinces have to decide in consequence whether they can remain in communion with provinces that choose not to break communion with the Episcopal Church (USA)."

Although the Presiding Bishop of TEC was present at that meeting and signed the extraordinary Primates Communique, he took order of the consecration and proceeded in November 2003. The response of the working group of the Global South Primates was swift:

> "A state of impaired communion now exists both within a significant part of ECUSA and between ECUSA and most of the provinces within the Communion. By its actions, ECUSA is held solely responsible for this division….
>
> "As Primates who represent over fifty million Anglicans, we have a solemn stewardship to steadfastly uphold and promote the historic and universal Apostolic Faith and Order of the Church throughout the ages as well as to protect those who are one with us in this same. We therefore affirm the ministry of the bishops, clergy and laity in ECUSA who have, as a matter of principle, and in fidelity to the historic teaching of the Church, opposed the actions taken at General Convention and objected to the consecration. We will continue to recognize and support their membership within the worldwide Communion fellowship and promise them our solidarity and episcopal support."[276]

This twofold response would set off a chain of events that is still unfolding: the development of parallel structures, cross-boundary intervention and litigation.

In response to the request of the Primates in their extraordinary 2003 meeting, the Archbishop of Canterbury appointed the Lambeth Commission on Communion (2004) to report on the legal and

---

[276] Preamble, [n269], para. 8, citing "Statement of the Primates of the Global South in the Anglican Communion, 2 November 2003," <http://www.globalsouthanglican.org/index.php/blog/comments/statement_of_the_primates_of_the_global_south_2_Nov_2003> Accessed 4 November 2015.

ecclesiological issues raised by the North American innovations. The resulting ***Windsor Process and Windsor Report*** recommended a draft "Anglican Covenant" as a means to resolve trans-provincial conflicts and establish a common statement of doctrine, discipline and worship that would hold Anglican churches together.[277]

The Primates met again in 2005 to respond to the innovations in the North American churches. The Communique of their 2005 meeting (Dromantine, Ireland) underlined the serious nature of the innovations of TEC and ACoC that threatened to undermine and obscure communion, and asked them to voluntarily withdraw from the Anglican Consultative Council.[278]

In 2005 The Anglican Consultative Council (ACC-13) – arguably the most representative of the whole church among the Instruments[279] – requested TEC and ACoC to

---

[277] Avis, *Beyond the Reformation* [n5], at 171; the exact remit for the Windsor Report, the Windsor Process and the Covenant Design Group came from the Archbishop of Canterbury to report "on the legal and theological implications flowing from the decisions of the Episcopal Church USA to appoint a priest in a committed same sex relationship as one of its bishops, and of the Diocese of New Westminster to authorize services for use in connection with same sex unions," and "to include practical recommendations...for maintaining the highest degree of communion that may be possible in the circumstances resulting from these decisions, both within and between the churches of the Anglican Communion" (Lambeth Commission on Communion 2004, 13). See also Andrew Goddard , "The Anglican Communion Covenant" in Ian Markham, J Hawkins, Justyn Terry and Leslie Steffensen, eds. *The Wiley-Blackwell Companion to the Anglican Communion* (Chichester, West Sussex: John Wiley & Sons, Ltd., 2013) 119-120.

[278] "The Primates Meeting Communique, February 2005 (Dromantine), <http://www.globalsouthanglican.org/index.php/blog/comments/the_anglican_communion_primates_meeting_communique_february_2005_dromantine> Accessed 4 November 2015.

[279] Samuel Van Cullin and Andrew Terry "Anglican Consultative Councils" in Ian Markham, J Hawkins, Justyn Terry and Leslie Steffensen, Eds. *The Wiley-*

voluntarily withdraw their members in response to the request of the Primates to do so "for the period leading up to the next Lambeth Conference [2008]." [280] This action was the closest the Instruments ever came to following the proposals for "enhanced Primatial responsibility" in *To Mend the Net.*[281] Nevertheless, representatives from TEC and ACoC were seated as observers and invited to make a presentation on the theological basis for their actions.[282]

The Primates met again at Dar es Salaam, Tanzania in 2007 and issued a communiqué with concrete conditions and an ultimate sanction of exclusion for TEC and ACoC from Communion bodies altogether. The Dar es Salaam Communique reiterated:

> "Since the controversial events of 2003, we have faced the reality of increased tension in the life of the Anglican Communion – tension so deep that the fabric of our common life together has been torn. The Windsor Report of 2004 described the Communion as suffering from an "illness." This "illness" arises from a breakdown in

---

Blackwell Companion to the Anglican Communion (Chichester, West Sussex: John Wiley & Sons, Ltd., 2013) 105,107.

[280]This request from the Primates was the consequence of their reaffirming Lambeth Resolution 1.10 (1998) as the standard of Christian teaching on matters of human sexuality "which should command respect as the position overwhelmingly adopted by the bishops of the Anglican Communion, and the consequent decisions of the Episcopal Church and the Anglican Church in Canada in 2003 to disrespect those norms and hence the "integrity of all parties." *Anglican Consultative Council (ACC-13) 2005: Resolution 10 Response to the Primates' Statement at Dromantine,* The Anglican Communion official website-Instruments of Communion-ACC-13 Resolutions <http://www.anglicancommunion.org/communion/acc/meetings/acc13/resolutions.cfm#s10 > Accessed 10 January 2014.

[281]Gomez and Sinclair, [n11].

[282] ACC-13 Resolutions, [n280], *Resolution 11: Supplementary Resolution of Thanks*

the trust and mutual recognition of one another as faithful disciples of Christ, which should be among the first fruits of our Communion in Christ with one another."[283]

The Primates faithfully rooted their conditions in the Windsor Report. The Windsor Report identified two threats to our common life: first, certain developments in the life and ministry of the Episcopal Church and the Anglican Church of Canada which challenged the standard of teaching on human sexuality articulated in the 1998 Lambeth Resolution 1.10; and second, interventions in the life of those Provinces which arose as reactions to the urgent pastoral needs that certain primates perceived. The Windsor Report did not see a "moral equivalence" between these events, since the cross-boundary interventions arose from a deep concern for the welfare of Anglicans in the face of innovation. Nevertheless both innovation and intervention are central factors placing strains on our common life. The Windsor Report

---

[283] "In particular, the Primates request, through the Presiding Bishop, that the House of Bishops of The Episcopal Church 1. make an unequivocal common covenant that the bishops will not authorise any Rite of Blessing for same-sex unions in their dioceses or through General Convention (cf TWR, §143, 144); and 2. confirm that the passing of Resolution B033 of the 75th General Convention means that a candidate for episcopal orders living in a same-sex union shall not receive the necessary consent (cf. TWR, §134); **unless** some new consensus on these matters emerges across the Communion (cf. TWR, §134). The Primates request that the answer of the House of Bishops is conveyed to the Primates by the Presiding Bishop by 30th September 2007. If the reassurances requested of the House of Bishops cannot in good conscience be given, the relationship between The Episcopal Church and the Anglican Communion as a whole remains damaged at best, and this has consequences for the full participation of the Church in the life of the Communion." Schedule of The Key Recommendations of the Primates, "On clarifying the response to Windsor" in *The Communiqué of the Primates Meeting in Dar es Salaam* [n267].

recognised this (TWR Section D) and invited the Instruments of Communion to call for a moratorium of such actions."[284]

The Archbishop of Canterbury did not apply the sanctions recommended by the Primates at their 2007 meeting in Dar es Salaam.[285] Instead, he proceeded to invite all the TEC bishops (except New Hampshire) to attend Lambeth 2008 as full members - and this in spite of warnings from Global South churches as early as 2006 that they would boycott the meeting if he did so.[286] He also announced in advance that the business of Lambeth 2008 was discussion by "Indaba" only and not action on the crisis and the proposed Covenant. "Not to decide" was a decision that the once-every-ten-year Lambeth Conference would *not* play a major role in resolving the crisis.[287] As a result almost 300 bishops, mostly from the majority global south, boycotted Lambeth 2008 and went instead to the 2008 Global Anglican Future Conference (GAFCON) in Jerusalem.

---

[284] Ibid, paras. 9 and 10.

[285] Stephen Noll, "Sea Change in the Anglican Communion," (November 11, 2013) Anglican Mainstream <http://www.anglican-mainstream.net/2013/11/11/sea-change-in-the-anglican-communion-2/ > Accessed 11 January 2014.

[286] "We have concluded that we must receive assurances from the Primates and the Archbishop of Canterbury that this crisis will be resolved *before* a Lambeth Conference is convened. There is no point, in our view, in meeting and meeting and not resolving the fundamental crisis of Anglican identity. We will definitely not attend any Lambeth Conference to which the violators of the Lambeth Resolution are also invited as participants or observers." *The Road to Lambeth: A Statement from the Primates of the Council of Anglican Provinces in Africa (CAPA) 23 September 2006, Kigali Rwanda,* <http://www.globalsouthanglican.org/index.php/blog/printing/the_road_to_lambeth_presented_at_capa> Accessed 10 January 2014.

[287] Valliere [n8] 206-207.

When the Archbishop of Canterbury called a meeting of the Primates in 2011 in Dublin, its final documents defined the purpose of the Primates meetings as largely for fellowship, study, prayer and reflection, "acknowledging diversity and giving space for difference [and] being open to the prophetic spirit" – purposes that seemed tailor made for Communion innovators rather than conciliar centrists.[288] As a result only 23 of the 38 Primates showed up to the meeting – with seven boycotting in protest against the presence of the Primates of the innovating North American churches.[289] This performance has caused other global Anglican leaders to question the office of the Archbishop of Canterbury as an "Instrument of Communion."[290] But the Archbishop of Canterbury is not the only "Instrument" whose legitimacy has been

---

[288]"Towards an Understanding of the Purpose and Scope of The Primates' Meeting: A Working Document Approved by The Primates Meeting January 29, 2011" The Anglican Communion website-Instruments of Communion-Primates Meetings <http://www.aco.org/communion/primates/resources/downloads/prim_sc_purpose.pdf> *Accessed* 12 January 2014.

[289]"Anglican Communion Primates Meeting, January 2011" Wikipedia, <http://en.wikipedia.org/wiki/Anglican_Communion_Primates'_Meeting#January_2011_meeting> Accessed 12 January 2014.

[290]See *GAFCON 2013*: *The Nairobi Communique* (26 October 2013) 2, The Gobal Fellowship of Confessing Anglicans Anglicans <http://gafcon.org/images/uploads/Nairobi_Communique_Final.pdf> Accessed 13 November 2015. In the context of a declaration of itself as an Instrument of Communion, the Nairobi Communique speaks volumes in what it does *not* affirm about Canterbury: "In our gathering, we reaffirmed our view that we are a global fellowship of confessing Anglicans, engaged in a movement of the Holy Spirit which is both personal and *ecclesial.* We appreciated that the Archbishop of Canterbury sent personal greetings via video and gave us the assurance of his prayers, and we likewise pray for him. We believe we have acted *as an important and effective instrument of Communion during a period in which other Instruments of Communion have failed both to uphold gospel priorities in the Church, and to heal the divisions among us."* (Emphasis added)

questioned.[291] – Overall it seems that none of the Instruments are fully functioning at this time according to the principles and practice of conciliarism that we see at other levels of the Churches of the Communion.

While the warnings have been clear and unambiguous since the Kuala Lumpur Statement of 1997, the official Instruments of Communion have not been able to slow the divisions within the Anglican communion between those who accept the innovations of the churches in North America, and those in the largely Global South provinces who reject these innovations. In fact those innovations and resulting divisions have actually accelerated since 2003[292]

---

[291]At ACC-13 TEC failed in its presentation *To Set our Hope in Christ* to make a case for changing the standards for human sexuality set forth in Lambeth Resolution 1.10 (1998) by any appeal to evidence from the conciliar and catholic history of the universal Church. See Valliere [n8] 208-209. Nevertheless, the ACC reinststed TEC and ACoC as full participating members of the ACC when it met three years later (May 1-13, 2009) in Kingston, Jamaica. ACC-14 did not give a ringing endorsement of the proposed Anglican Covenant. Instead, it resolved that the Covenant *"may* provide an effective means to strengthen and promote our common life together as a Communion," and in the face of a narrow vote on the section on conflict resolution (section 4 of the Ridley-Cambridge draft) sent the Covenant out for further review and redrafting by yet another committee to be appointed by the Archbishop of Canterbury. Ibid, 203-204. ACC-15 (2012) took no action on the Final Text Covenant (2009), deferring it to ACC-16 in 2015.

[292]**In 2010**, The Episcopal Church consecrated a second partnered same sex person as a suffragan bishop in the Diocese of Los Angeles. See Valliere [n8] 205 *noting* "The moratorium, if it was one, was over." Following the Diocese of New Westminster, ten more ACoC dioceses (Edmonton, Nova Scotia and Prince Edward Island, Rupert's Land, Ottawa, Toronto, London-based Huron, Quebec, Hamilton-based Niagara, Montreal and Victoria-based British Columbia) have also offered public rites for the blessing of same-sex unions. The Anglican Parishes of the Central Interior (formerly the Diocese of Cariboo) also permit such rites" in "Blessing of same-sex unions in Christian churches," *Wikipedia: The Online Encyclopedia* <

---

http://en.wikipedia.org/wiki/Blessing_of_same-sex_unions_in_Christian_churches > Accessed 11 January 2014.

In March 2012, following rejection of the Covenant by the GAFCON Primates Council, The General Synod of the Church of England failed by diocese to approve the proposed Anglican Covenant "Half of the Church of England's dioceses reject unity covenant," *BBC News UK Website (12 March 2012)* <http://www.bbc.co.uk/news/uk-17500144> Accessed 11 January 2014.

In July 2012 the 77th General Convention of TEC passed Resolution A049 to "Authorize Liturgical Resources for Blessing Same-Gender Relationships" for study and use in congregations and dioceses of TEC *Resolutions of the 77th General Convention of The Episcopal Church: Resolution A049 "Authorize Liturgical Resources for Blessing Same-Gender Relationships" (2012)* in The Archives of The Episcopal Church website <http://www.episcopalarchives.org/SCLM/2012-A049/dioceses/2012-A049.pdf> Accessed 10 January 2014; To date at least ten TEC dioceses have published such resources: Atlanta:<https://www.episcopalatlanta.org/Content/Same_Sex_Blessings.asp> Accessed 10 January 2014 Olympia - <http://www.ecww.org/marriage-and-same-sex-blessings> Accessed 10 January 2014 Southern Ohio - <http://www.diosohio.org/How%20we%20work/blessing-of-same-gender-unions.html > Accessed 10 January 2014; Northern California - <http://www.norcalepiscopal.org/marriage-and-same-sex-blessings > Accessed 10 January 2014; Western Massachusetts - <http://www.diocesewma.org/diocesan-policy-on-blessing-same-sex-marriages/> Accessed 10 January 2014; Pittsburgh - <http://www.goerie.com/article/20131127/NEWS06/311279952/Pittsburgh-Episcopal-bishop-OKs-same-sex-blessings> Accessed 10 January 2014; East Tennessee - <http://archive.wbir.com/news/article/245014/2/episcopal-church-approves-same-sex-blessings-in-east-tn > Accessed 10 January 2014: Upper South Carolina <http://www.kendallharmon.net/t19/media/dioceseofuppersouthcarolinasamesexblessingsltr.pdf> Accessed 10 January 2014; Rio Grande - <http://www.dioceserg.org/app/webroot/files/uploaded/files/Our%20Covenant%20of%20Understanding.pdf > Accessed 10 January 2014; Diocese of Virginia - <http://www.episcopalcafe.com/lead/dioceses/diocese_of_virginia_and_samese.html > Accessed 10 January 2014.

In November 2012 the 15th meeting of the ACC (Auckland NZ) offered no resolutions on the proposed Anglican Covenant, thereby deferring any action until ACC-16 in 2015. http://www.anglicancommunion.org/communion/acc/meetings/acc15/resolutions.cfm ACC-15 members from Nigeria and Kenya , representing over 30 million Anglicans, published a "minority" report declaring that those controlling the agenda at ACC-15 had failed to address the crisis within the Anglican Communion—the departure by some western provinces from historic, biblical faith – and alleged that the failure of the Instruments of Communion was in part due to a "subversion of leadership at the highest levels." "What Really Happened in Auckland NZ at ACC-15?" para's 3 and 4. *Anglican Ink,* 8 November 2012, <http://anglicanink.com/article/what-really-happened-auckland-nz-acc-15> Accessed 21 November 2015

From 21st to 26th October 2013 1358 delegates (331 bishops, 482 other clergy and 545 laity) from 38 countries met in Nairobi, Kenya for the second Global Anglican Future Conference (GAFCON). Their "Nairobi Communiqué" stated among other things "We want to make clear that any civil partnership of a sexual nature does not receive the blessing of God." *GAFCON 2013: The Nairobi Communiqué* [n290], at 2.

One month later, the Church of England released "The Pilling Report" which recommended "public services" by priests (with the agreement of the relevant PCC) "to mark the formation of a permanent same-sex relationship." *The House of Bishops Working Group on human sexuality: The Pilling Report (28 November 2013),* para, 490.16, page 151. The Church of England <http://www.churchofengland.org/media/1890818/pilling%20report.docx.pdf> Accessed 12 January 2014.

Almost within a week, the Primate of Kenya and Chairman of the Global Fellowship of Confessing Anglicans wrote in his Advent letter: "If this [Pilling Report] is accepted I have no doubt that the Church of England, the Mother Church of the Communion, will have made a fateful decision. It will have chosen the same path as The Episcopal Church of the United States and the Anglican Church of Canada with all the heartbreak and division that will bring." *GAFCON Chairman's Advent Letter (7 December 2013)* <http://gafcon.org/news/chairmans-advent-letter> Accessed 12 January 2014.

On July 1, 2015, The Episcopal Church through its General Convention made a full marriage right available to all same-sex couples (Resolution A054).

under the conciliar practice of the Instruments of Communion.

These facts are proof that Avis' definition of conciliarism as a practice "as far and as wide as possible" is insufficient to meet the divisions within the Communion over Biblical authority, human sexuality, marriage, holy orders, the clarity of Scripture and its authority in decision making – and the deeper issue of the authority needed to resolve such divisions. It also suggests that Avis' definition is insufficient to deal with the deeper issue and challenge facing conciliar governance in the Anglican Communion – namely, "how, in the midst of the pressures of time, do the churches both remain faithful to the teaching and practice of the apostles and yet witness relevantly and in context to the truth of the Gospel amongst these changes and chances of history?"[293]

As Norman Doe observes, the "Instruments of Communion" are points at which Anglicans take common counsel and encouragement, but the authority they exercise is at best moral and not juridical.[294] In some ways it is possible to affirm the existing Instruments of Unity in their practice of conciliarism "as far and as wide as possible" (Avis). Nevertheless history suggests that the Anglican Communion has never embraced classic conciliarism as a governing principle. In 1867, when faced with doctrinal and disciplinary disputes between bishops in South Africa, and the deficit of higher authority to resolve

<http://www.generalconvention.org/gc/2015-resolutions/A054/current_english_text> Accessed 21 November 2015.

[293]Gomez and Sinclair [n11], at 28. Paul Avis has framed this as "the tension inherent in a polity that seeks to do justice, in terms of the Church, to the integrity of the local and the demands of the universal." [n5] 171.

[294] Doe, *Instruments of Unity* [n263], at 64.

issues of litigation and ecclesiastical discipline ("the Colenso affair") the Archbishop of Canterbury offered a *conference* rather than a council. He organized it as far as possible not to be a council – for reasons that were driven in part by the internal politics within the Church of England.[295] It failed to enact a proposal for a central tribunal to adjudicate inter-provincial disputes on doctrine and discipline. "Idealists who hoped that the Conference would evolve into a worldwide Anglican council were outmaneuvered in the beginning," notes Valliere, "and their vision has made no comeback."[296]

Although Primates meetings have an inherent authority to address such issues by virtue of the office that Primates hold as chief pastors,[297] such meetings are a relatively recent development. Moreover, the proposals for "enhanced Primatial responsibility" in *To Mend The Net* (Gomez and Sinclair) were sidelined during the Anglican Covenant process[298] The proposals included juridical authority – not just moral – to request innovators to refrain from further "facts on the ground" in the face of objections

---

[295]See Graham James, "Resolving to Confer and Conferring to Resolve: the Anglican way," in Kenneth Stevenson, ed., *A Fallible Church: Lambeth Essays* (London: Dartman, Longman & Todd, 2008), at 70-71, who notes that invitations even to a "Lambeth Conference" would imply a superior authority in Canterbury over York and London, a superiority which was not then self-evident.

[296] Valliere [n8] 195-196.

[297] *The Report of the Inter-Anglican Theological and Doctrinal Commission*: *The Virginia Report* (London: The Anglican Consultative Council, 1997) , sec. 61.

[298]Gomez and Sinclair, eds. [n11]. The failure to take up the proposals was viewed in partisan terms by some Global South Anglican primates: "The ecclesiastical politicians, seeking to avoid such discipline, managed to get this proposal sidelined." "The Road to Lambeth: A Statement from the Primates of the Council of Anglican Provinces in Africa (CAPA) 23 September 2006, Kigali Rwanda," [n286].

from other provinces, to issue "Godly admonitions" to innovating provinces, to reduce continuing innovating provinces to observer status within the Anglican Communion, and to re-order and even provide for the formation of a new province in the case of Churches that continue to innovate and willfully ignore such Godly admonitions.[299] Even though such "Primatial conciliarism" would not have been a council of the whole church, the proposals would have honored the conciliar principles of legitimate authority preserving the spiritual unity (the common good) of the Communion and its *consensus fidelium* within the limits of subsidiarity.[300]

Having turned to a conference rather than a council, the Anglican Communion turned in similar circumstances to a new surrogate: a covenant. The Anglican Covenant Design Group produced four Drafts which removed authority from the Primates and proposed instead the organizing principles of "[Provincial] autonomy-in-communion" and that "the Communion guides, each [national, Provincial] church decides," with principles for conflict resolution[301] to

---

[299] Gomez and Sinclair [n11] 20-23, 127-128.

[300] Gomez and Sinclair reject the notion that The Archbishop of Canterbury and The Primates can exercise only moral authority above the Provinces. The Archbishop of Canterbury's authority to invite has a corresponding political authority to withhold invitation. Secondly, The Archbishop "in fellowship with the other bishops of the Communion, has power to break communion with a Province or diocese that threatens the peace and unity of the Communion by rejection of a godly admonition." This exercise of juridical power, as a last resort and after a conciliar process of moral persuasion would honor the principle of subsidiarity without committing Anglicans to a more centralized form of global polity. Ibid, 87-89.

[301] See Andrew Goddard, "The Anglican Communion Covenant" [n277], at 122-127, who notes the significant position of the Primates Meeting in overseeing and resolving conflict in the first Nassau Draft (2007) their removal and replacement by the Archbishop of Canterbury and the ACC in the St. Andrew's Draft (2008) and the removal and replacement of the Instruments of Canterbury and the ACC by a committee (the Joint Standing

be administered ultimately (but without specific guidance) by the joint Standing Committee of the Primates and the Anglican Consultative Council[302] – both of which included representatives from the innovating North American churches! This latter fact alone was viewed as a fatal flaw in overcoming the "ecclesial deficit" identified in the Report of the Windsor Continuation Group.[303]

By placing "autonomy" before "Communion," and submitting the Covenant to Provincial ratification, the Covenant Design Group virtually ensured a default to mere "provincialism."[304] In light of this and the lack of Provincial ratification, the process promises to drag on for years, as Valliere notes, "years during which there nothing

---

Committee of the Anglican Communion, elected by the ACC and the Primates) to resolve conflicts under section 4 of the Ridley Cambridge Draft (April 2009) and the Final Text (December 2009)—an evolution reflecting increasing authority concentrated in ever smaller circles.

[302]Valliere [n8] at 234: "Discussions that have taken place since finalization have shown that there is still no agreement on how the Standing Committee [of the Anglican Communion] would actually resolve Communion conflicts. The composition of the committee is also a matter of contention, as is the degree to which the committee would in fact depend on its parent bodies. Its allegiance to two parent bodies, which might disagree with each other, is also problematic."

[303] Preamble, [n269] at paras. 12 and 16: The consecration of Mary Glasspool, a partnered lesbian, on 15 May 2010, as a bishop in Los Angeles, further underscores The Episcopal Church's total disregard for the mind of the Communion in matters of unity, faith and order," and "We recognise at the same time that the overcoming of "ecclesial deficit� that the Windsor Continuation Group (Report of March 2008, Section D i, ii) identified is a longer term undertaking... Implicit to this is the deeper need to review and develop the canonical basis on which inter-Anglican bodies and officers interpret their tasks and make executive decisions (Windsor Report, 113-120). The recent controversy on Standing Committee membership underscores this concern. We regret the decisions of the Archbishop of Canterbury and the Secretary General to include TEC members in the Standing Committee, despite Mary Glasspool�s consecration (para 12)."

[304]Valliere [n8] 201-202.

to prevent the Anglican Communion from continuing to disintegrate."[305]

And so from the original call for an Anglican Council came a conference, and from a conference consultative "instruments," and from such instruments a covenant, and finally from a covenant came a committee.[306] This is the exact reverse of both the practice and the ideal of conciliarism – from councils which are representative of the whole church and its *consensus fidelium* to an ever smaller group of decision makers.[307] In fact, there has been an ever-diminishing practice of conciliarism under the stress of the North American innovations. One could say that the 20th and 21st centuries have seen the *devolution* of Anglican conciliarism.

And so we are left with the question: in the context of the growing division between those who affirm and those who reject the North American innovations, and the failure of the Instruments to live up to the practice of conciliarism at other levels of governance within the Churches of the Communion, is there any prospect for the renewal of conciliarism as a principle of governance *among* the Churches of the Anglican Communion?

---

305 Ibid, at 202.
306 Ibid, at 234.
307 Avis, *Beyond the Reformation* [n5], at 18.

SEVEN

The Loss of Conciliarism and Deficit of Authority in the Anglican Communion: And the North American Revitalization

The 1930 Lambeth Conference of Bishops defined the universal and particular nature of the Communion of Anglican Churches in its Resolution 49:[308] *Universal* in the upholding and propagation of the Catholic and Apostolic faith as set forth in the Book of Common Prayer, and *particular* in the national expression of Christian faith and life within each national or territorial Church. But the enduring question is how to balance the universal and the particular nature of communion? Resolution 49 suggested two ways to keep that balance. First, communion is defined historically and geographically as relationship with the See of Canterbury. Secondly, the Churches in the Communion are not bound together by a central legislative and executive authority, but by "mutual loyalty sustained

[308] *Resolutions of the Lambeth Conference of Bishops 1930,* Resolution 49: "The Anglican Communion," <http://www.anglicancommunion.org/resources/document-library/lambeth-conference/1930/resolution-49-the-anglican-communion?author=Lambeth+Conference&year=1930> Accessed 10 November 2015

through the common counsel of the bishops in conference."[309]

This balance of the "universal" and the "particular" on the basis of geography (communion with the See of Canterbury) and relationships ("common counsel of bishops") seemed to work so long as there was a doctrinal consensus among the Churches of the Anglican Communion. But already in 1930 the Communion was showing the incipient strains of doctrinal and ethical differences that would bloom in the latter half of the 20th century. Doctrinal consensus collapsed under the weight of challenges from the Churches in North America to the biblical limits on human sexual expression, followed by innovations in the doctrine of marriage, blessing same-sex relationships and ordaining, and even consecrating as Bishops those in such relationships.

Contrasting Ecclesiologies in North America

The decline and devolution of conciliarism in global Communion governance has permitted the emergence of two different *ecclesiologies* in North America, one in The Episcopal Church (TEC) and the other in the Anglican Church in North America (ACNA).

Colin Podmore has argued that the ecclesiology of TEC is essentially egalitarian and democratic in its historical origins, shaped more by Locke and the American Revolution than by the traditions of the Church. Its congregations pre-dated its dioceses, so that "in terms of church order (though not, of course, of ordination) episcopacy was 'bolted on' to a system which was in

[309] Ibid, para. (c).

practice essentially congregational."[310] Or, as he wrote later in *A Tale of Two Ecclesiologies*,[311] unlike the Church of England, TEC is "a church which has 'taken episcopacy into its system' but perhaps not fully digested it." He concluded that there is currently a "mismatch" between the historic ecclesiology and the current "working ecclesiology" of TEC, the latter being more centralizing in its governance.[312] Based on the founding documents of TEC, especially William White's 1782 ***The Case of the Episcopal Churches in the United States Considered***, bishops were originally conceived to serve principally as administrators or "Presiding ministers" within the dioceses, with special powers to confirm and ordain, and Podmore argues that this historical framework lives on in the limited powers of bishops under TEC canons.[313]

---

[310] Podmore, [n16] at 27-28.

[311] C. Podmore, "A Tale of Two Churches: The Ecclesiologies of The Episcopal Church and the Church of England Compared," [n81] at 143. First published in *Ecclesiastical Law Journal* (2008), 10 Ecc. LJ 34-70.

[312] Ibid., at 133, where Podmore notes the litigation over congregations departing TEC for ACNA and elsewhere as an example of this mismatch: "This is another example of the mismatch between The Episcopal Church's historical ecclesiology still deeply ingrained in the thinking of many of its members and still reflected in many aspects of its structure—that of a church created from below in which the parishes and congregations are the original and fundamental units—and the more centralist ecclesiology reflected in some aspects of the Constitution and canons [citing the Dennis canon on property ownership]. This mismatch has arisen because, although the Episcopal Church is highly decentralized and its polity has many features that are confederal in character, as we have already seen it is ultimately a unitary body, in that the Constitution places no limits on the decisions that the General Convention may take and those decisions do not require the consent of individual dioceses or indeed congregations. The Episcopal Church's nature as a church constructed from below, whose fundamental units are its parishes and congregations, is in tension with its constitution as a unitary church, in which the conventions have unlimited power."

[313] Ibid, at 128, 135 and 142. This is especially evident in his discussion of the TEC canons pointing to the administrative role of bishops without any

In reply,[314] TEC Bishop Pierre Whalon vigorously disputes the mismatch that has been alleged by Podmore. First, while conceding the egalitarian-democratic nature of congregations that pre-dated the dioceses, he declares categorically that White's *Case for the Episcopal Churches* is not a founding document of the church and therefore is not an authority for the assertion that TEC is a church created from below.[315] Secondly, he argues that TEC reflects "episcopal leadership in synodal government" in its historic choice to reestablish the election of bishops, as in the earliest stages of Christianity, "consonant both with the new democratic ideals being tried and the Reformation pattern of looking to the sources of the Church ('*ad fontes*') for inspiration for reforming its life," and thereby linking the nascent church with antiquity.[316] Thirdly, he argues that TEC has modeled the principle of subsidiarity from its very beginning, preserving the rights of the local communities (dioceses and congregations) as "the locus of all human flourishing" within "a necessary larger framework" (the Constitution and Canons).[317] Fourthly, he argues that under the canons TEC bishops are chief pastors, priests and teachers of the diocese and its congregations, not unlike bishops in the Church of England.[318]

---

mention of propagating and guarding faith, doctrine and worship of the Church.

314 P Whalon, "The Tale Needs Retelling: A Reply to Colin Podmore's 'A Tale of Two Churches," *Theology (SPCK Sage Journals online)* January/February 2011, no. 1 at 3-12. Available for download at <http://www.collegeforbishops.org/assets/1145/the_tale_needs_finalrevision.pdf> Accessed 6 November 2015.

315 Ibid, at 4.

316 Ibid.

317 Ibid, at 8.

318 Ibid, at 6.

Whalon's reply is not very convincing. Podmore cites a number of authorities in addition to White, and who agree with White, that TEC was a church historically created from below.[319] Whalon cites only one for his categorical exclusion of White (presumably an omission among other documents cited in that one source).[320]

Secondly, Whalon cites no authority for the proposition that the election of bishops was principally a matter of linking the nascent church to ancient principles of conciliar governance. By contrast, Podmore demonstrates that this is one strand in the development of the role of bishops in TEC, but was also shaped by such political factors as the "high church" movement in New England and the rival claims of Bishop Samuel Seabury and his party, and the missional needs in the 19th century to build dioceses around missionary bishops like Jackson Kemper.[321]

Thirdly, in regard to the principle of subsidiarity, Whalon ignores entirely the radical revisions TEC made just two years earlier when it overhauled the Title IV Disciplinary Canons with a new disciplinary strategy which places all clergy at the mercy of three member panels dominated by the bishop and at least one appointee, bishops who are now under the direct discipline of a Presiding Bishop with metro political authority to discipline them along the same lines, and all of which weaken diocesan independence.[322] It is astonishing that Whalon

[319] Podmore, [n81], fns. 20-30 at 128-129.

[320] Whalon, [n314], fn. 4 at 4, 10.

[321] Podmore, [n81], at 134-140.

[322] C. Alan Runyon and M. McCall, "Title IV Revisions: Unmasked," *The Anglican Communion Institute,* September 12, 2010 at <http://www.anglicancommunioninstitute.com/wp-content/uploads/2010/09/title_iv.pdf> Accessed 6 November 2015. Runyon and McCall document by comparing the changes in the text of new Title V with replaced Title IV to demonstrate that the changes have

can assert that in TEC "The Presiding Bishop is not a metropolitan to whom the Episcopal bishops swear obedience."[323] In practice, at the very time he wrote and up to the present, under revised Title IV the Presiding Bishop of TEC now functions in the trial of a Bishop with the same control over the intake and trial process as a Diocesan Bishop has over clergy. He or she may place a Bishop on "restricted ministry" (formerly inhibition) "at any time" and without prior notice or hearing. This can be based solely on the presiding Bishop's determination that the Bishop in question "may have committed any Offense."

The Presiding Bishop may also restrict the ministry of a bishop whenever she or he determines that "the good order, welfare or safety of the Church or any person or Community may be threatened" by that bishop, and may do so without the consent of the Standing Committee of the Diocese or senior Bishops in the House.[324] One can only imagine the chilling effect this has on the independence, or freedom of speech, that bishops might otherwise choose to exercise.

---

removed procedural safeguards for clergy (including the right to a speedy trial, exclusion of hearsay evidence, attorney-client privilege and right against self-incrimination), expanded greatly the number and nature of clergy offenses, broadened the reach of existing offenses, dramatically increased the authority of the bishop in both the decision to charge the clergy, to sit as a judge on a three person panel to try the case with a power to appoint one of the two remaining judges, and to direct the process of discipline, and thereby removing the allocation of clergy discipline from the authority of the dioceses, in violation of Article IX of the Constitution.

[323] Whalon, [314] at 7.

[324] Runyan and McCall, [n322] at 16-18: "However, what the new Title IV gives the Bishop Diocesan with the one hand, it effectively (and stealthily) takes away from him [or her] with the other."

The 2009 revisions to Title IV, combined with the implied trust TEC has as a national body on all personal and real property held by congregations, have effected a dramatic centralization of power in the Presiding Bishop, the Bishops and the General Conventions that has no limits, and reflects a centralizing ecclesiology far beyond any such tendencies in the Church of England, the Churches that are the subject of this study, or the *PCLCCAC*.

Fourthly, while Whalon argues that TEC Bishops play the same role that bishops do in the Church of England, he also concedes that the teaching office of the Bishop has a voice that has grown faint, much less a robust scholarship among its bishops.[325] This is a tacit admission of what is clear from the Constitution and Canons of TEC: that its bishops are not in fact guardians of faith, doctrine and liturgy. In Principles and Practice, such ancient and traditional guardianship is *not* as an essential role of their office. In practice, their role does not reflect this principle of governance among the Churches of the Anglican Communion.[326] The most recent example of this is in the passage of Resolution A054 at General Convention 2015, a Trial Rite for Same Sex Marriage, where this fundamental change to the Book of Common Prayer and its definition of marriage was passed in the House of Bishops without a roll call vote and without a majority of all the Bishops entitled to vote, as prescribed by the Constitution.[327] Of course, this

---

[325] Whalon, [n314], at 7.

[326] *PCLCCAC,* [n17], Principle 37.4: "The bishop must teach, uphold and safeguard the faith and doctrine of the Church."

[327] "The New Episcopal Church: What Hath General Convention 2015 Wrought?" *The Anglican Communion Institute*, July 27, 2015, <http://www.anglicancommunioninstitute.com/2015/07/the-new-episcopal-church-what-hath-general-convention-2015-wrought/> Accessed 6 November 2015, citing TEC, Constit. X: Adoption of any alterations and

is not the first time that bishops and other leaders of TEC have done this. In fact, it is part of a disturbing pattern of ignoring and even violating the black letter law found in its Constitution and Canons for the sake of the very doctrinal innovations that have stretched the Instruments of Communion to the breaking point.[328]

Such actions have cast doubt on whether TEC currently observes principles of conciliar governance like discerning the mind of the whole Church (the *consensus fidelium*), episcopal leadership within synodical government and more:

> "Given the latitude with which the BCP and the [Constitution and Canons] are being treated, and given that The Episcopal Church has no Historical Confessions, supreme Ecclesiastical Court, Book of Discipline, Barrier Act or other mechanisms for ordering its common life, how are we to understand the future of this church body? And how are we to understand the role of a Bishop and a Diocese, itself governed by constitution and canons?"[329]

In the absence of bishops actually propagating and guarding the faith of the Church, much less coherent doctrine, within TEC, the wholesale revision of Title IV is

---

additions to the BCP requires "a majority of all Bishops, excluding retired Bishops not present, of the whole number of Bishops entitled to vote in the House of Bishops."

[328] "The Episcopal Church: Overbearing and Unjust Episcopal Acts." *The American Anglican Council,* February 2, 2010 < https://americananglican.org/wp-content/uploads/2014/02/TEC-Overbearing-and-Unjust-Episcopal-Acts-Feb-2010.pdf > Accessed 10 November 2015: Citing abuse of former Title IV Disciplinary Canons in the depositions of 12 bishops and 404 clergy and the unconstitutional assumption of power by the Presiding Bishop in dissolving a lawfully constituted diocesan Standing Committee in order to substitute another of her choice, at 3-22.

[329] "The New Episcopal Church," [n327), at p. 1.

the ecclesiastical equivalent of the imposition of martial law, with depositions and litigation as the exercise of such martial powers. In TEC, bishops are guardians of order alone. This is not the Anglican way, much less any conciliar expression of governance by any Anglican standards:

> "We must acknowledge that TEC as a national body is no longer recognizably "Anglican" in an Anglican Communion sense. A broad range of commonly defining features of Anglican Communion churches, e.g. the Lambeth Quadrilateral, which makes Scripture the "rule and ultimate standard of faith"; the definition of Anglicanism specified in TEC's own constitution and in 1930 Lambeth Resolution 49 (i.e. "upholding and propagating he historic Faith and Order as set forth in the Book of Common Prayer"); other Lambeth Resolutions including 1998 I.10; the Windsor Report and its moratoria that were subsequently adopted by all the Instruments of Communion; the framework of an Anglican Communion "Common Law" (as N. Doe and others have identified it), etc. no longer exists in TEC." [330]

Instead, there is a new Anglican Church in North America. It is a Church that was organized with the help of other Churches in the Anglican Communion. Its Constitution and Canons were shaped by the Constitution and Canons of those "rescuing" Churches. It has a set of Fundamental Declarations that describe the essential

[330] Ibid, at 2. The reference to the violation of the *PCLCCAC* [n17] seems to be to Principles 70.1: "Marriage, an honourable estate instituted by God, is an exclusive life-long union, signifying the mystical union that is between Christ and his Church, effected on the free exchange of consents *between one man and one woman joined together by God as husband and wife and lasting until the death of one spouse,"* and 71.1: "Ministers must comply with the civil law as to the formation of marriage *and with church law as to the solemnization of marriage according to ecclesiastical rites."* (Emphasis added).

principles of "The Anglican Way," including the Lambeth Quadrilateral which makes Scripture "the rule and ultimate standard of faith," as well as many other declarations to that effect. It has a statement of mission which consciously paraphrases the definition of the Archbishops of Canterbury and York's 1945 Commission on evangelism, *Toward the Conversion of England*. Its governance frequently expresses those principles of Anglican "Common Law" found in the *PCLCCAC*. And it boldly and repeatedly describes its Bishops as guardians of faith, doctrine, liturgy *and* order, in keeping with those Principles of Anglican Common Law.

The Anglican Church in North America is recognizably "Anglican" – not by default, and not simply because it is in contrast to TEC, but because it reflects the very principles of Anglican governance and conciliarism which are at the heart of the Churches of the Anglican Communion.

CONCLUSION

It is that rejection of higher synodal authority – the substitution of a "Conference of Bishops" for a "Council" – that has dogged the implementation of conciliar principles and practices at the level of global Communion governance. It is the substitution of other structures (such as the Anglican Consultative Council (ACC)) for the conciliar principles and practices that are otherwise present at every other level of Anglican polity, from the PCC (Vestry) to General Synod, that has made the Communion of Anglican Churches vulnerable to doctrinal division and disorder. On the one hand, Avis sees this "common counsel in conference" as a great expression of the conciliar nature of Anglicanism:

> "The conciliar nature of Anglicanism is certainly implicit in the Lambeth 1930 statement...The Anglican Communion, with its Lambeth Conference, its Anglican Consultative Council, its Primates Meeting and its structures of synodical government at local, diocesan and provincial or national levels, is a striking example of conciliar ecclesiology."[331]

But the same facts cause Podmore to see "common counsel in conference as mere "episcopal collegiality" in place of coherent decision making by councils. The deficit of authority in the Communion to deal with doctrinal division and disorder is the prime example of the discontinuity between conciliar principles and practices at other levels of the Churches of the Communion and the global level of governance.[332]

If one concedes this reality, as Avis does, one choice is to redefine the meaning of conciliarism at the global level of governance:

> "[Anglicanism] believes that provinces gathered into communions should act in a conciliar fashion within the limits imposed by the divisions in the Church. It [Anglicanism] sets out to extend conciliarity as far and wide as it can until it runs up against the barriers erected by broken communion, rival claims to jurisdiction or serious differences in doctrine or order."[333]

---

[331] Avis, [n12], at 9.

[332] Podmore, [n16], at 120-121: "At present, it is not possible for the Church of England to be represented at a Synod with any binding authority at any level above the national level," he writes, precisely because those Instruments of Communion like the Lambeth Conference and the Primates Meetings are merely expressions of "episcopal collegiality," while the Anglican Consultative Council lacks the legislative or governing authority of a Synod.

[333] Avis,"Anglican Conciliarity" [n1] at 8.

But this is far from the robust definition of conciliarism by Gerson and others, as we have already observed in principle from Chapters 2, 4 and 5, and noted in ***practice*** in Chapters 2 and 3. What happens when the common counsel of Bishops in conference fails to address within *communion* "serious differences in doctrine and order"? What is left to an Anglican *Communion* but relationship with the See of Canterbury, or the art of practiced ambiguity? Is conciliarism as Avis and others have defined it enough to hold a global Communion together?

No, it is not. In 2003, the working definition of conciliarism at the global level revealed a deficit of authority within the dispersed authorities of the Anglican Communion, the "Instruments of Unity" – the Archbishop of Canterbury, The Lambeth Conference of Bishops, the Primates' Meetings and the Anglican Consultative Council.

The breaking point came in North America when a diocese in the Anglican Church of Canada (ACoC) authorized Rites for the Blessing of same-sex unions, while TEC elected and consecrated a partnered homosexual as Bishop of New Hampshire, in both cases contradicting received Biblical, apostolic, catholic and Anglican Communion teaching on the subjects.[334]

---

[334] In direct contradiction of Lambeth Conference (1998) Resolution I.10 which provides in part, "... *(b)* in view of the teaching of Scripture, upholds faithfulness in marriage between a man and a woman in lifelong union, and believes that abstinence is right for those who are not called to marriage...*(e)* cannot advise the legitimising or blessing of same sex unions nor ordaining those involved in same gender unions." The Lambeth Conference Official Website: Resolutions of 1998 <http://www.lambethconference.org/resolutions/1998/1998-1-10.cfm> Accessed 3 November 2015. See also Avis, *Beyond the Reformation* [n5] at xv: "It is because that consecration or ordination was, like all ordinations, a sacramental act, an ecclesial sign with universal intention, of what is true of

Since then the supposed "conciliar" structures of the Anglican Communion – the "Instruments of Communion" – have not been able to heal the wounds to communion. Instead, those wounds have deepened; serious doctrinal divisions and disagreements have accelerated, revealing an increasing "devolution" of conciliar principles and practices at the level of Communion governance.

Like the broken cisterns in Jeremiah 2:13, the existing Instruments of Communion seem to be irreparably broken. (See Chapter Six).

The North American Fruit of Lost Conciliarism

In reaction to the unilateral innovations of TEC and ACoC, many Biblically faithful Anglicans sought refuge in other Churches of the Anglican Communion until they formed in 2009 a new Anglican Church in North America (ACNA). If we use the same principles from Podmore and the *Principles of Canon Law Common to the Churches of the Anglican Communion* to compare and contrast conciliar principles and practices within these different expressions of Anglicanism in North America we see the following similarities and differences between TEC and ACNA (and two of their dioceses.)[335]

---

the Church and of the values that the Church stands for and of the message that it proclaims...that at the time of writing it has placed a question mark over the viability of Anglican polity and the cohesion of the Anglican Communion."

[335] *Constitution and Canons for The Episcopal Church, Adopted in General Conventions 1789-2012. Together with the Rules of Order, Revised by the 77th General Convention* (New York: General Convention Office, 2012); and *The Anglican Church in North America Constitution and Canons, as ratified by the inaugural Provincial Assembly 2009 and revised 2014*, < https://c119b78671d19b8aee34-1ab073aa91389396dfc8b6aabc9b141e.ssl.cf2.rackcdn.com/Constitution-

TEC and ACNA: The Similarities

In both Churches, synodical government is necessary, regular and permanent at the Provincial, diocesan and congregational level. Both "central church assemblies"[336] propose and enact legislation, form or suppress dioceses, and establish the processes for electing bishops. In both Churches the business of the Convention or Synod is carried on between meetings by a delegated executive body. In both Churches bishops, clergy and laity are represented within Convention or Synod, with greater representation for laity at the diocesan level. Both Churches provide for episcopal leadership within synodical government, especially in the gathering and presiding

---

and-Canons-CURRENT-9-5-14.pdf> Accessed 24 October 2015. From each of these Churches two dioceses were chosen covering two metropolitan areas: (1) Atlanta, as represented by TEC, *The Constitution of the Diocese of Atlanta, as Adopted by the Council of the Diocese 1987 and amended 2011,* <*https://www.episcopalatlanta.org/Diocese/Governance/Diocesan-Canons-and-Constitution/The-Constitution-of-the-Diocese/*> Accessed 24 October 2015, *The Canons of the Diocese of Atlanta* <https://www.episcopalatlanta.org/Diocese/Governance/Diocesan-Canons-and-Constitution/The-Canons-of-the-Diocese/> Accessed 24 October 2015, and as represented by ACNA, *Constitution and Canons of the Anglican Diocese of the South,* <http://adots.org/?s=Constitution+and+Canons&submit= > Accessed 24 October 2015; and (2) Los Angeles, as represented by TEC, *The Constitution and Canons of the Church in the Diocese of Los Angeles, adopted 1896 and revised 2012,* <http://s3.amazonaws.com/dfc_attachments/public/documents/3168510/The_Constitution_and_Canons_through_2012.pdf > Accessed 24 October 2015, and as represented by the ACNA, *The Constitution and Canons of the Diocese of Western Anglicans,* <http://www.westernanglicans.org/sites/default/files/attachments/c_cs_dwa_feb_2015_0.pdf > Accessed 24 October 2015.

[336] See *PCLCCAC* [n17], "Definitions" of "central church assembly" would include the General Convention of TEC and the Provincial Synod and Assembly of ACNA.

authority of the TEC Presiding Bishop and the ACNA Archbishop. The Conventions or Synods of both Churches express, in practice, a commitment to synodal life as a spiritual event of the Church, through daily worship, prayer and Holy Communion.

But beneath these superficial similarities there are significant differences.

TEC and ACNA: The Differences

Broadly speaking, the differences can be summed up under at least five categories:

1. ***Subsidiarity.*** In TEC centralized power and property ownership flow from the top down. It seems that TEC changed some of its governing principles – especially with regard to centralization of property ownership (i.e., the "Dennis canon"[337]), mandatory accession to the Constitution and Canons of the Church, and revisions of its ecclesiastical discipline – as individuals, congregations and even whole dioceses left to join the ACNA. By contrast, in ACNA property ownership rests in the congregation and all authority flows from the bottom up from reserved powers in the diocese to enumerated powers in the Province;

2. ***Discerning the Mind of the Church.*** (The *Consensus Fidelium*) There are many differences

[337] TEC, [n335], Can. I.7.4, II.6.4: "The Dennis canon": "All real or personal property held by or for the benefit of any parish, Mission or Congregation is held in trust for this Church and the Diocese thereof in which such parish, Mission or Congregation is located, The existence of this trust, however, shall in no way limit the power and authority of the Parish, Mission or Congregation otherwise existing over such property *so long as the particular Parish, Mission or Congregation remains a part of, and subject to, this Church and its Constitution and Canons."* (Emphasis added)

between TEC and ACNA including the posture, thresholds and subject matter for such discernment;

3. *The Role of Bishops.* Bishops are guardians of order in TEC, whereas bishops are guardians of faith, doctrine, liturgy ***and*** order in ACNA;

4. *The Emphasis and Focus on Mission*: Very brief and general in TEC; specific, intentionally Anglican and repeated in ACNA; and

5. *The Supremacy of the Holy Scriptures for Faith and Life, Including Church Governance.* Almost absent in TEC. Repeated in a variety of ways in ACNA, including a statement ("Fundamental Declarations") of doctrine, discipline and order as a prerequisite for membership in the Church.

You can find a comprehensive examination of the similarities and differences between the Constitution and Canons of TEC and ACNA with respect to the eleven principles of conciliar governance the Appendix. The study includes the Constitution and Canons of the dioceses of Atlanta and Los Angeles in *both* TEC *and* ACNA.

CONCLUSION

In short, the loss of conciliarism in global Communion Governance has permitted the emergence of two different ecclesiologies in North America, one in TEC and the other in ACNA.

The bottom line is that there is a "mismatch" in TEC between its historical ecclesiology of a church created from below and its working ecclesiology of increasingly centralized power in the Presiding Bishop, Bishops and General Conventions of the Church exercised from the top down, and without many limits. Revisions of its Title IV Disciplinary Canons, depositions, litigation, and Prayer

Book revisions resemble the ecclesiastical equivalent of imposing martial law. These "centralizing" developments in turn resemble the decline and "devolution" of conciliar principles and practice in global Anglican governance.[338] This has led some to conclude that, in its centralizing of governance and its assignment of bishops as guardians of order but not of faith, TEC is no longer recognizably "Anglican." Instead, it is ACNA that is recognizably more "Anglican" in its governance, and by any measure of Anglican conciliarism that is practiced at all levels of the Church (See the Appendix).

The fact that there are two different "Anglican" ecclesiologies in North America highlights the very divisions that stretched the Instruments of Communion beyond the breaking point. As Avis concedes, the practice of conciliarism within the current scheme of global Anglican governance is limited precisely because it cannot withstand "the barriers erected by broken communion, rival claims to jurisdiction or serious differences in doctrine or order," whose "Exhibit A" is North America. North America presents the choice facing the Anglican Communion today – will the Communion move toward the practice of conciliarism within global Communion governance – especially the role of Bishops in settling conflicts over doctrine and order? Or will its Churches embrace the same moral and doctrinal innovations pioneered by TEC and ACoC – and with them authority that flows increasingly from a top-down "bureaucracy," with ever diminishing circles of decision-making? This is

[338] This "mismatch" mirrors almost exactly the same devolution of conciliar principle and practice in the history of the Anglican Communion Covenant (see Chapter 9) and the divisions over the definition of "Communion" (see Chapter 10).

exactly what the GAFCON Primates understood to be at stake in the January 2016 gathering of the Primates.[339]

[339] "Chairman's October Pastoral Letter 2015: Archbishop Eliud Wabukala, Primate of Kenya and Chairman of the GAFCON Primate's Council," *GAFCON NEWS,* October 24, 2015, <http://gafcon.org/news/chairmans-october-pastoral-letter-2015> Accessed 11 November 2015. In reflecting upon a visit to an ACNA congregation which bought a disused factory and turned it into a large church with growing outreach to the community of Wheaton IL and its college, he writes: "My experience of this new wineskin in North America brought home to me just how much is at stake when the Primates of the Communion meet in Canterbury at the invitation of the Archbishop of Canterbury next January. I believe this will be an historic meeting unlike anything that has gone before. *There is now a shared realization that the time for dialogue is over and there must be a decision which will settle the future direction of the Communion and free us from being dragged down by controversy and confusion."* He went on to note the critical role that Archbishops and Bishops must play going forward: "In recent days the Lord has put on my heart the seriousness of the call to be a faithful watchman. In a time of crisis and confusion in ancient Israel, God appointed Ezekiel to be a watchman over his exiled people (Ezekiel 33:1-9). This is one of the set readings in the Anglican Church of Kenya's service for the ordination of priests and for those of us who are bishops and archbishops, this responsibility to watch is even greater." (Emphasis added)

Part IV

A Way Forward

EIGHT

Recovering Conciliarism within the Anglican Communion

Conciliarism is how we live together, how we are shaped by the whole, how we give expression to the whole, how we make decisions as a whole *together*.[340] Of course, there is a difference between the ideal and the practice of conciliarism. One might describe the ideal as the "ontology" and the practice as the "phenomenology" of councils. The approach of Anglican conciliarists like Avis and Podmore is to focus on the practice or phenomenology of councils and to let the definition or reality of conciliarism emerge from that.

The laws of the Churches of the Anglican Communion are the evidence from which we may deduce whether conciliarism remains an organizing principle and practice within Anglicanism. In Chapter Three (also in the Appendix) we have demonstrated how the Churches of Australia, South East Asia, Nigeria, Ireland, TEC and ACNA are conciliar in their governance – how they are being shaped at a national, regional or provincial level "by the whole," or not.

[340] Humphrey, "The nature of the Church: Apostolic, conciliar and concrete" [n6] at 2.

We also have the failure of those conciliar structures currently in place at the global level of Communion governance (see Chapter 6). We have the multiplication of overlapping jurisdictions in North America, diverging from each other in their principles and practices of conciliarism (see the Appendix). We have no effective structures at present to prevent the multiplication of such crises and confusion elsewhere in the Communion. Currently, we have a deficit of authority within dispersed authorities, Instruments that are beyond repair.

How might we overcome this deficit of authority and recover the practice of conciliarism within Communion governance? The answer lies in extrapolating those principles (from Podmore and the *PCLCCAC*), practices and synodal structures of the Churches and their dioceses in Chapter 3, and to deeply reform, if not altogether replace, the current Instruments of Anglican Communion along the following lines:

1. FUNDANMENTAL DECLARATIONS OF FAITH, WORSHIP AND ORDER AS THE BASIS FOR COMMUNION:

Australia, South East Asia, Nigeria and Ireland each have a set of "Fundamental Declarations" at the beginning of their constitution and/or canons containing similar points of faith, worship and order around which the church is formed.[341] In North America, the ACNA has exactly

[341] The church is **part of the "One, Holy Catholic and Apostolic Church,"** see Australia, [n99], Constit. Fundamental Declaration 1; South East Asia, [n100], Can. A1 ("true and apostolic Church of Christ"), Nigeria, [n99], Fundamental Declaration 1, Can.1.1, Ireland, [n99], Constit. Preamble. See also *The Canons of the Church of England, Seventh Edition,* [n42], Can. C15 "Preface"; **the church "holds the Christian faith as professed by the Church**

such a set of "Fundamental Declarations" around which

---

of Christ from primitive times and in particular as set forth in the Nicene and Apostles Creed," Australia, [n99], Constit. Fundamental Declaration 1, see also South East Asia, [n99], Constit. Fundamental Declarations 1: "in the Holy Scriptures, preached by the Apostles and summed up in the catholic Creeds ***and confirmed by the Councils of the undivided Holy Catholic Church***," (emphasis added), Nigeria, [n99], Constit. Fundamental Declaration 1 and Can. I.1, Ireland [n99], Constit. Decla. I.1,3: "continues to profess the faith of Christ as professed by the Primitive Church" and "reaffirms its constant witness against all those innovations in doctrine and worship, whereby the Primitive faith hath been from time to time defaced or overlaid..," see also *Canons of the Church of England,* [n42], Can. C15: "in the catholic creeds"; the church "**worships the one true God, Father, Son and Holy Spirit,"** *Canons of the Church of England,* [n42], Can. C15, Ireland, [n99], Constit. Preamble; the church **"receives all the canonical scriptures of the Old and New Testaments as being the ultimate rule and standard of faith given by inspiration of God and containing all things necessary for salvation,"** Australia, [n99], Constit. Fundamental Declaration 2, South East Asia, [n99], Canons, Cans. A2, A3.1 and A5 affirming 39 Articles, Book of Common Prayer 1662 and Ordinal as "agreeable to the Word of God" as the highest authority, Nigeria, [n99], Can. I.2, Fundamental Declaration 1.2: "therefore banish and drive away all erroneous and strange doctrines which are contrary to God's word as understood and interpreted in the aforementioned formularies." Ireland, [n99], Constit. Decla. I.1: Holy Scriptures "given by inspiration of God"; the church "**bears witness" to the historic formularies of Anglicanism**: **the 39 Articles, Book of Common Prayer 1662 and Ordinal**: *Canons of the Church of England,* [n42], Can. C15, Australia, [n99], Constit. Ruling Principle 4: "retains and approves the doctrine and principles of the Church of England embodied in the historic formularies," South East Asia, [n99], Cans. A2, A3.1, A5: Doctrine of the Church is in the 39 Articles, Book of Common Prayer 1662 and Ordinal because they are "agreeable to the Word of God," Nigeria, [n99], Can. I.1, Fundamental Declaration I.1, Ireland, [n99], Constit. Decla. II: "receives and approves" the historic formularies; the church further **declares the Book of Common Prayer 1662 as authorized standard of worship and doctrine**, Australia, [n99], Constit. Ruling Principle 4; and **pledges to ever obey the commands of Christ, teach his doctrine, administer His sacraments of Holy Baptism and Holy Communion, follow and uphold his discipline and preserve the historic threefold orders of Bishops, Priests and Deacons,** Australia, [n99], Constit. Fundamental Declaration 3 and Ireland, [n99], Constit. Decla. I.2.

the Church is formed, while TEC does not.[342] The law of the Church of England is ambiguous on matters of assent to declarations of faith.[343]

The GAFCON Jerusalem Declaration (2008) is a current model for a set of Fundamental Declarations around which a Communion of Anglican Churches could form. The Jerusalem Declaration includes almost all of the declarations of faith and order found in the churches in this study,[344] while adding necessary theological clarity on essentials of the Christian faith,[345] the priority of mission,[346]

---

[342] Compare *The Anglican Church in North America, Constitution and Canons,* [n335], Constit. Preamble and Art. I, Fundamental Declarations of the Province, with TEC, [n335], Can. IV.2: Doctrine defined within canons on "Ecclesiastical Discipline" as "the basic and essential teachings of the Church and is to be found in the Canon of Holy Scripture as understood in the Apostles and Nicene Creed and in the sacramental rites, the Ordinal and catechism in the Book of Common Prayer."

[343] On the one hand, The Church of England is established according to the laws of the realm and "belongs to the true and apostolic Church of Christ," so that "no member thereof shall be at liberty to maintain or hold to the contrary," *Canons of the Church of England,* [n42], Can. A1. On the other hand, the Thirty-Nine Articles "*may* be assented unto with a good conscience by all members, ibid, at Can.A2. As Doe notes in *The Legal Framework of the Church of England,* [n42], at 263 n.66: "It is uncertain whether this canonical right is repugnant to the royal prerogatival declaration preceding the Thirty-Nine Articles and therefore what its effect is in light of *SGM* 1969, s. 1(3)(b); see also Cans. 3-5 [permissive assent only]."

[344] "The Jerusalem Declaration (2008)," *GAFCON: Global Anglican Future Conference* <http://gafcon.org/images/uploads/jerusalemdeclaration.pdf> Accessed 13 November 2015. But see, e.g., ACNA, [n335], Constit. I.5, Fundamental Declarations, "Concerning the seven Councils of the undivided Church," where ACNA also recognizes the Christological clarifications of the fifth, sixth and seventh Councils, "in so far as they are agreeable to the Holy Scriptures."

[345] "Jerusalem Declaration," [n344], at Para. 1: Salvation is by grace through faith in Jesus Christ by the power of the Holy Spirit; Para. 5: Jesus Christ is the unique and universal savior and Lord of all, by his substitutionary death

the nature of ecclesial communion,[347] and the issues currently dividing the Communion.[348] Where it fails to capture the declarations of faith of the Anglican churches in this study, or others, such areas could be the subject for discussion and further drafting of a set of Fundamental Declaration for the Anglican Communion.

It may be argued that both the Windsor Report (2004)[349] and the proposed Anglican Covenant (Final Draft)[350] sought to establish such fundamental declarations

---

on the cross and resurrection from the dead; and Para. 13: Repudiation of the authority of those Anglican churches that have denied the orthodox faith in word or deed.

[346] Ibid, at Para. 9: The mission of Anglicans is to fulfill Christ's Great Commission to make disciples; Para. 10: Mission includes justice, empowerment of the poor and needy, and stewardship of God's creation; and Para. 14: Participate in Spirit's work of building his church by miraculously transforming lives as we await Christ's coming in glory.

[347] Ibid, at Para. 11: Authentic communion is based on orthodox faith and practice.

[348] Ibid, at Para. Para. 8: God's creation of humankind as male and female and the unchangeable standard of Christian marriage between one man and one woman as the proper place for sexual intimacy and the basis of the family, and repentance for failure to keep this Biblical standard; and Para. 12: Celebrating diversity, freedom in secondary matters, and pledging to seek the mind of Christ on matters that divide.

[349] *The Lambeth Commission on Communion: The Windsor Report 2004* (London: The Anglican Communion Office, 2004), Paras. 52-70: The authority of Scripture, Scripture and interpretation, the Episcopate, Discernment in Communion and Reception, and paras. 87-96: Adiaphora. See, e.g., para. 94 at p. 40: "The two notions of 'adiaphora' and 'subsidiarity' work together like this: the clearer it is that something is 'indifferent' in terms of the Church's central doctrine and ethics, the closer to the local level it can be decided,; whereas the clearer it is that something is central, the wider must be the circle of consultation."

[350] *The Anglican Communion Covenant (Final Text)* <http://www.anglicancommunion.org/media/99905/The_Anglican_Covenant.pdf> Accessed 13 November 2015, Sections 1-3, Affirmations and Commitments by each covenanting church to a common inheritance of faith (section 1), The life we share with others: Our Anglican vocation (section 2)

as a basis for Communion. Fundamental Declarations are the foundations around churches practice conciliarism. But for both theological and political reasons, the Covenant could not provide such foundations (See Chapter 9).

Currently Communion is defined in terms of relationship with Canterbury.[351] This definition has outlived its usefulness and is in tension with the Anglican *ius commune* which holds a common faith as essential to ecclesial communion.[352] Moreover, Anglican Churches need the articulation of a "common good" more meaningful than geography, and around which they can enjoy genuine ecclesial communion. (See Chapter 9). The harbinger of this change came from the Primate and the Church of Nigeria who in 2005 changed the definition of ecclesial communion from Canterbury to a shared confession of faith.[353]

---

and Our Unity and Common Life (section 3). See also s. 4.1.2: "In adopting the Covenant for itself, each Church recognizes in the preceding sections a statement of faith, mission and interdependence of life which is consistent with its own life and with the doctrine and practice of the Christian faith as it has received them." The section goes on to note that such a statement of common faith is a "foundational element" for the life of the Anglican Communion and the covenanting Churches.

[351] *Resolutions of the Lambeth Conference of Bishops 1930,* [n308], Resolution 49(c).

[352] *PCLCCAC,* [n17], Principle 94.1: "Ecclesial communion between two or more churches exists when a relationship is established in which each church believes the other to hold the essentials of the Christian faith and recognizes the apostolicity of the other."

[353] Nigeria, [n99], Constit. Art. 3: "The Church of Nigeria (Anglican Communion) hereinafter called "The Church of Nigeria" or "This Church" shall be in full communion with all Anglican Churches Dioceses and Provinces that hold and maintain the Historic Faith, Doctrine, Sacrament and Discipline of the one Holy, Catholic, and Apostolic Church as the Lord has commanded in His holy word and as the same are received as taught in

If such a set of fundamental declarations were to be created as the basis for Communion, they would function in a very conciliar way as a "constitution" of the Anglican Communion. Under this constitutional conciliarism those acceding to the Declarations would submit themselves to the review and adjudication of any conflicts or controversies touching their accession, by the Primates (in their executive capacity), the General Synod (in their legislative capacity), or a Court of Final review (in their judicial capacity).[354]

2. A COUNCIL OF PRIMATIAL BISHOPS WITH ENHANCED RESPONSIBILITY FOR DOCTRINE, DISCIPLINE AND ORDER OF THE COMMUNION:

the Book of Common Prayer and the ordinal of 1662and in the Thirty-Nine Article of Religion. In the interpretation of the aforementioned formularies and in all questions of Faith, Doctrine and Discipline, the decisions of the Ecclesiastical tribunals of the Church of Nigeria shall be final." It is significant that Article 3 of the Constitution, where the change was made, is titled "See of Canterbury," thereby underscoring the change in the definition of membership from Lambeth Conference Resolution 49(c) (1930). See also "Nigerian Church New Constitution Redefines Relationship with Canterbury," *Christianity Today (19 September 2005)* <http://www.christiantoday.com/article/nigerian.church.new.constitution.redefines.relationship.with.canterbury/3994.htm> Accessed 13 November 2015. As if to drive home the point, the then Archbishop and Primate of all Nigeria, Peter Akinola, was quoted in the BBC 18 October 2004 as saying "You don't need to go through Canterbury to get to Jesus." < http://news.bbc.co.uk/2/hi/uk_news/3752412.stm> Accessed 13 November 2015.

[354] *PCLCCAC*, [n17], Principle 53.5: Doctrinal discipline and the width of permissible theological opinion in a church. The role of the courts is simply to state what the law is with regard to doctrine—and not to declare true doctrine or develop new doctrine. Ibid, Principle 53.9. But see N Doe *Legal Framework of the Church of England,* [n42], at 259-260, who suggests that this classic view has been expanded in the courts of the Church of England to include clarification of doctrine in resolving a legal question.

If there is anything close to unanimous agreement within the Anglican *ius commune* and the conciliar practice of the churches in this study, it is that bishops have a special responsibility to guard the faith and order of the Church at every possible level.[355] And what better body to guard the faith and order at the highest level of governance within the Anglican Communion than those bishops who exercise archiepiscopal and metro political power – the Primates.[356] This is certainly the recommendation of Lambeth Resolution III.6 (1998)[357] that was subsequently

---

[355] *PCLCCAC,* [n17], Principles 37.4, 48.3, 56.7-8 and 60.1.

[356] This would include the Archbishop, Presiding Bishop, Moderator or other bishop who holds the "principal episcopal office in the Province," Ibid., at Principle 39.1.

[357] Lambeth Resolution III.6 (1998), *Anglican Communion Archives, Lambeth 1998,* <http://www.anglicancommunion.org/resources/document-library/lambeth-conference/1998/section-iii-called-to-be-faithful-in-a-plural-world/section-iii6-instruments-of-the-anglican-communion?author=Lambeth+Conference&year=1998> Accessed 14 November 2015: **"Instruments of the Anglican Communion"**: "This Conference, noting the need to strengthen mutual accountability and interdependence among the Provinces of the Anglican Communion,

a. reaffirms Resolution 18.2(a) of Lambeth 1988 which "urges that encouragement be given to a developing collegial role for the Primates' Meeting under the presidency of the Archbishop of Canterbury, so that the Primates' Meeting is able to exercise an enhanced responsibility in offering guidance on doctrinal, moral and pastoral matters";
b. asks that the Primates' Meeting, under the presidency of the Archbishop of Canterbury, include among its responsibilities positive encouragement to mission, intervention in cases of exceptional emergency which are incapable of internal resolution within provinces, and giving of guidelines on the limits of Anglican diversity in submission to the sovereign authority of Holy Scripture and in loyalty to our Anglican tradition and formularies;
c. recommends that these responsibilities should be exercised in sensitive consultation with the relevant provinces and with the Anglican Consultative Council (ACC) or in cases of emergency the

developed into a working proposal in *To Mend the Net* (2001)[358] on how such a Primatial Council could take order of the controversies diving the Anglican Communion. This would include juridical authority (not just moral) to request innovators to refrain from further "facts on the ground" in the face of objections from other provinces, to issue "Godly admonitions" to innovating provinces, reduce continuing innovating provinces to observer status within the Communion, re-order and even provide for the formation of a replacement province for Churches that continue to innovate and willfully ignore such Godly admonitions.[359] On the other hand, it would be within the authority of the Primates to review the matter and submit it for "reception" on the terms proposed by both *The Virginia Report* and *The Windsor Report*.[360] Even though such "Primatial

---

> Executive of the ACC and that, while not interfering with the juridical authority of the provinces, the exercise of these responsibilities by the Primates' Meeting should carry moral authority calling for ready acceptance throughout the Communion, and to this end it is further recommended that the Primates should meet more frequently than the ACC.

It should be noted that Resolution III.6 followed the *The Report of the Inter-Anglican Theological and Doctrinal Commission*: *The Virginia Report* [n297] which, at paras. 3.50 and 6.33, raised the question why serious consideration had not yet been given to Lambeth Resolution 18.2(a) (1988), nor the resources set aside for the Primates to exercise such an enhanced responsibility for doctrine, discipline and order. Resolution III.6 (1998) is the answer to that question.

[358] Gomez and Sinclair, *To Mend the Net* [n11].

[359] Gomez and Sinclair [n 11] 20-23, 127-128.

[360] *The Virginia Report (1997),* [n297], at paras. 5.21-5.26. Among the parameters for discernment and reception of doctrinal changes are the following: the burden of responsibility lies on the local church to consider the implications of its decisions upon the wider Communion, whether the doctrinal change it wishes other churches to receive and recognize expresses "the truth of the Gospel," providing adequate space "for clearly

conciliarism" is not a council of the whole church, it honors the conciliar principles and practice of episcopal authority ultimately preserving the spiritual unity (a common good) of the Church and its *consensus fidelium* within the limits of subsidiarity.[361]

This is not a radical departure from Anglican norms. In fact, it is merely a logical extension of an existing Anglican Principle of Canon Law.[362] For example, one could take

---

expressed dissent in testing and refining the truth," relationships within the fellowship of the church must be maintained so that "there is opportunity for correcting one-sidedness or ignorance," and the preparation of appropriate study materials for conversations between those "on both sides of the particular issue." *The Windsor Report (2004),* [n349] cites the history of the reception of the ordination of women to the priesthood in Paras. 4.14-4.21 of *The Virginia Report* as an example of these parameters. But it adds this significant caution at para. 69: "We should note, however, that the doctrine of reception only makes sense *if the proposals concern matters on which the Church has not made up its mind. It cannot be applied in the case of actions which are explicitly against the current teaching of the Anglican Communion as a whole, and/or of individual Provinces. No province, diocese or parish has the right to introduce a novelty which goes against such teaching and excuse it on the grounds that it has simply been put forward for reception."* (Emphasis added). In other words, "facts on the ground" do not establish reception.

[361]Gomez and Sinclair [n11] at 87-89 reject the notion that The Archbishop of Canterbury and The Primates can exercise only moral authority above the Provinces. The Archbishop of Canterbury's authority to invite has a corresponding political authority to withhold invitation. Secondly, The Archbishop "in fellowship with the other bishops of the Communion, has power to break communion with a Province or diocese that threatens the peace and unity of the Communion by rejection of a godly admonition." This exercise of juridical power, as a last resort and after a conciliar process of moral persuasion would honor the principle of subsidiarity without committing Anglicans to a more centralized form of global polity.

[362] *PCLCCAC,* [n17], Principle 50.5, which provides that "No new doctrinal formulae may be approved by a central church assembly without the consent of the House of Bishops or equivalent collegial body." Better to have this consent at the beginning of the process rather than the end, and hence the consent of the Council of Primates to any new doctrinal formulae

this Principle as it is applied to matters of faith and order in the Church of Nigeria and, with some adjustments to the five levels of review in Nigeria, extend that process of discernment to the global level.[363] This would include review and ratification by a Council or Synod of the Communion (see next section). Finally, if such a Council ratified the actions of the Primates, there could remain a right of appeal to whatever Court of the Anglican Communion might be reserved for such "ecclesiastical causes."[364] With its limited jurisdiction under the *ius commune* to simply declare the law of the Church on the doctrine at issue,[365] it could either affirm the decision of the

---

at the beginning of any process of discerning the mind of the Communion on matters touching the Fundamental Declarations.

[363] See nn. 149-151 , *infra*, for the process of discerning the mind of the Church in Nigeria to the limits of faith and order. By extension, if there were a decision or practice of a Church with doctrinal ramifications that seemed to violate the Fundamental Declarations of the Anglican Communion, it would be referred as a matter of first order to the Council of Primates. It would come first to whatever Theological or Doctrinal Commission the Council of Primates has appointed to review such matters and make recommendations (in keeping with *PCLCCAC Principle 50.6*). Secondly, the Commission could seek in a timely manner the review and recommendations of all those Churches acceding to the Fundamental Declarations. Thirdly, with such input from the Churches the Commission could then make its recommendation to the Primates, who would then take action in a timely manner. During this time, the Primates would have the juridical authority to take such interim steps as necessary to protect those dissenting from the decisions and practices of the alleged innovating Church, and as outlined above from *To Mend the Net*. Fourthly, the Primates might be required to submit their actions to review by the Standing Committee (see 4. Below) for recommendation to and ratification by the Anglican Communion Council (see 3. Below), or not. Fifthly, the Anglican Communion Council could either ratify the actions of the Primates, or not, in which case the matter would be referred back to the Primates for reconsideration and modification by the Primates *"and not otherwise."*

[364] *PCLCCAC [n17],* Principles 16.4, 55.3

[365] Ibid, Principle 53.9: In this case, if provided, the function of the court would be to simply review whether the recommendation or action of the

Anglican Communion Council or remand to the Council of Primates for reconsideration and action in light of the correct statement of law on the doctrine at issue. Such a framework preserves both the special responsibility of bishops to guard the faith and order of the Church and their leadership in synodical government. But it also preserves the representation of the clergy and the laity in conciliar governance while honoring the ancient canonical maxim that what touches all must be decided by all.

And who will chair, convene and preside over this Council of Primates? Even the Archbishop of Canterbury recognizes that it is time to heed the call for the Primates themselves to elect a Chair – a practice that itself would be more conciliar and less "colonial."[366]

3. A GENERAL SYNOD OR COUNCIL OF THE GLOBAL COMMUNION OF ANGLICAN CHURCHES:

From 21st to 26th October 2013 1358 *delegates* (331 bishops, 482 other clergy and 545 laity) from 38 countries representing millions of Anglicans in all orders of the

---

Primates, and its review and ratification by the Council, was based upon an accurate description of the Fundamental Declarations. This might dampen the appetite for such a court, as it would be most difficult to draw a line between statement, interpretation and declaration. See Doe, *op. cit.*, n.237.

366 "Anglican Structures need updating, says Archbishop," *Christianity Today*, 13 October 2013, <http://www.christiantoday.com/article/anglican.structures.need.updating.says.archbishop/34431.htm> Accessed 13 November 2015. See also "Primates Meet as Conference Opens," *GAFCON Media Release, Leaders Conference, London, 23 April 2012*, <http://gafcon.org/news/primates-meet-as-conference-opens> Accessed 13 November 2015: "We believe that in the future development of the Anglican Communion the Chair of the Primates meeting should be elected by the Primates themselves."

worldwide Communion of Anglican Churches, met in Nairobi, Kenya for the second Global Anglican Future Conference (GAFCON). In publishing *The Nairobi Communique*, they met in part to share in synodical government.[367] As ***delegates*** they gathered to represent "the whole church" to serve the common good, the spiritual unity of the Communion, which they defined as faithfulness to the truth and power of the Bible over and against a "false gospel"[368] They did so according to the conciliar principle and practice of daily worship, bible study and prayer.[369] They addressed controversies over essentials of the Christian faith that presented themselves as disciplinary issues,[370] just as such conflicts over doctrine and discipline drove and shaped the great Ecumenical

---

[367] "Bishops, clergy and laity of a church share authority in synodical government," *PCLCCAC,* [n17], Principles 15.9 and 18.1-3. See *GAFCON 2013: The Nairobi Communiqué* (26 October 2013)[n290] at 2.

[368] "Our willingness to submit to the written Word of God and our unwillingness to be in Christian fellowship with those who will not, is clearly expressed in The Jerusalem Statement and Declaration. This means that the divisions in the Anglican Communion will not be healed without a change of heart from those promoting the false gospel, and to that end we pray" Ibid., The GFCA and the Future of The Anglican Communion, 2..

[369] "We gathered each day for prayer and praise, studied Paul's letter to the Ephesians and shared in the Holy Communion at the beginning and end of our conference." Ibid, Introduction, 1. See discussion, *infra,* at 26, 55-56 and 84-85.

[370]"In 2008, the first GAFCON was convened in order to counter a false gospel which was spreading throughout the Communion. This false gospel questioned the uniqueness of Christ and his substitutionary death, despite the Bible's clear revelation that he is the only way to the Father (John 14:6). It undermined the authority of God's Word written. It sought to mask sinful behaviour with the language of human rights. It promoted homosexual practice as consistent with holiness, despite the fact that the Bible clearly identifies it as sinful. A crisis point was reached in 2003 when a man in an active same-sex relationship was consecrated bishop in the USA." Ibid, "The Formation of the Global Fellowship of Confessing Anglicans," 1.

Councils of the undivided Church.[371] They placed the authority to define the width of permissible theological opinion under the ultimate authority of the Scriptures rather than any institutions.[372] They reaffirmed Lambeth Resolution I.10 (1998) as "an authoritative statement" for Anglicans on human sexuality.[373] They reaffirmed the traditional definition of marriage as grounded in the Biblical doctrine of creation, and its implications for the

---

[371] Valliere, *Conciliarism,* [n8] at 58-62: For instance, the quarrels in Carthage in the 250's over the rebaptism of repenting heretics (a disciplinary issue, or so it seemed) grew into a doctrinal debate about the very nature of the church in the Council of Carthage 256 AD. Likewise, the Seven Ecumenical councils were called to deal with heresies that often presented themselves as disciplinary issues, and to ensure the unity of doctrine and discipline in the Church. The first call for a Pan-Anglican Council was precipitated by theological differences between bishops in South Africa (the "Colenso affair") over the interpretation and authority of Scripture—with a deficit of authority to resolve the differences, litigation and ecclesiastical discipline. This was the context of the first Lambeth Conference (1867).

[372] *The Nairobi Communique,* [n290] at 2: "*The character and boundaries of our fellowship are not determined by institutions but by the Word of God.* The church is a place where the truth matters, where it is guarded and promoted and where alternatives are exposed for what they are — an exchange of the truth of God for a lie (Romans 1:25). Our willingness to submit to the written Word of God and our unwillingness to be in Christian fellowship with those who will not, is clearly expressed in The Jerusalem Statement and Declaration. This means that the divisions in the Anglican Communion will not be healed without a change of heart from those promoting the false gospel, and to that end we pray." (Emphasis added). Compare *PCLCCAC,* [n17], Principle 53.5 which provides an institutional answer to the question.

[373] Ibid, at 2: "The 1998 Lambeth Resolution I.10 on Human Sexuality states that sexual activity is to be exclusive to marriage and that abstinence is right for those who are single. We still hold to that authoritative statement."

Church facing countervailing claims based on human rights.[374]

In Nairobi, they declared themselves to be a reforming council of the church, a new "Instrument of Unity" in the face of the failure of the existing Instruments of Communion/Unity.[375] They pledged to set in order Anglican provinces and dioceses that upset the spiritual unity of the Communion through doctrinal innovations, and pledged to do so through the enhanced responsibility of bishops in a Primates' Council.[376] They went beyond the internal life of the Anglican Communion to define the mission of all Anglicans in terms of evangelism, discipleship

---

[374] Ibid, "We grieve that several national governments, aided by some church leaders, have claimed to redefine marriage and have turned same-sex marriage into a human rights issue. Human rights, we believe, are founded on a true understanding of human nature, which is that we are created in God's image, male and female such that a man shall leave his father and mother and be joined to his wife (Matthew 19:6; Ephesians 5:31). We want to make clear that any civil partnership of a sexual nature does not receive the blessing of God. We continue to pray for and offer pastoral support to Christians struggling with same-sex temptation who remain celibate in obedience to Christ and affirm them in their faithfulness."

[375] Ibid., 1: "We believe we have acted as an important and effective instrument of Communion during a period in which other instruments of Communion have failed both to uphold gospel priorities in the Church, and to heal the divisions among us," Ibid., Introduction, 1.

[376]Ibid, 3, 4: "Authorising and affirming faithful Anglicans who have been excluded by their diocese or province. The main thrust of work here would be devoted to discerning the need for new provinces, dioceses and churches — and then authenticating their ministries and orders as Anglican," and "For this reason, the bishops at GAFCON 2013 resolved 'to affirm and endorse the position of the Primates' Council in providing oversight in cases where provinces and dioceses compromise biblical faith, including the affirmation of a duly discerned call to ministry. This may involve ordination and consecration if the situation requires." Ibid, 3, 4. These resolves bear a striking resemblance to the proposals by Gomez and Sinclair for "enhanced primatial responsibility" in *To Mend the Net* [n 11].

and the transformation of communities, with specific commitments.[377] Having met in 2008 and 2013, they pledged to meet again in council implying, perhaps a regularity and frequency of every five years.[378] The delegates came to one mind in approving this Nairobi Communiqué, in the ancient conciliar tradition of doing so by near unanimity rather than seeking decisions by majoritarian rule.[379] In short, they did almost everything we would expect a Council to do operating at this level of governance.

Three years later, in October 2016, Archbishops, bishops, clergy, theologians and lay leaders from 16 Provinces of the Global South met in their capacity as delegates in council in Cairo Egypt for the Sixth Global South Encounter. They were following the example of previous Global South encounters meeting in council. These 16 Provinces included Churches both aligned with GAFCON, and those who were not. From this meeting they issued a statement in which they recognized the Anglican Church in North America as "the Province of North America" with whom they are 'in communion," declared that Anglican Churches which depart from

---

[377] Ibid, at 3-5 and Nairobi Commitments 2 and 7.

[378] Ibid, at 5, Commitment 9. See discussion of conciliar principle of synodal government as permanent, necessary and *regular, infra* at Principle 1 in Chapters Two and Three. In contrast to the Lambeth Conferences which require ten years to plan, the GACON Provinces managed to plan approximately one year in advance, and without incurring any debt.

[379] Valliere, *Conciliarism,* [n8] at 108-109: In the many councils of the undivided Church, nowhere is there a close vote. In virtually every council there was an overwhelming majority bordering on unanimity, and those who dissented later (for the most part) conformed to that consensus. Decisions were reached instead by patient negotiation over scripture, precedent, under the leading of the Holy Spirit, consensus building, and discernment rather than by simple majority vote—with the goal of developing a *consensus fidelium*.

Biblical and historic Christian doctrine "sever themselves form their roots and compromise their mission," declared that the exiting Instruments of the Communion are "broken cisterns" (Jeremiah 2:13) beyond repair, warned the Church of England of "serious consequences" should its bishops and Synod permit the blessing of same-sex unions in any way and claimed "enhanced ecclesial responsibility" among its own bishops to order the 16 Anglican Churches represented in Cairo.[380]

The GAFCON 2013 *Nairobi Communique*, the Communique from the Sixth Global South Encounter, Cairo 2016, demonstrates that in a global Communion of Churches a pan-Anglican Council is not only possible, it is imperative. Why should such a global Communion resort to half-measures such as a Lambeth Conference of *Bishops only* – an admitted concession to the internal politics shaping the Church of England at that time[381] – with doctrinal controversies and missional challenges touching the whole Church within the whole Communion? As Gerald Bray observed, it is time to replace the Lambeth Conference of Bishops with a "Council of the Anglican Communion" building on this very GAFCON and Global South model:

> "One date that must concentrate everyone's minds is 2018—the year that the next Lambeth Conference is due and that another GAFCON might conceivably be held. The leaders of GAFCON II should be getting together with Canterbury *now* (not in four years' time) in order to prepare for that conjunction. The best outcome for everyone would be to turn the next Lambeth Conference

[380] P. Ashey, "The Global South Statement from Cairo Egypt: Seven Takeaways," <https://americananglican.org/current-news/global-south-statement-cairo-egypt-takeaways/ > Accessed 24 January 2017

[381]See Chapter 6 at n.295.

into GAFCON III, using the Jerusalem Declaration and its successors as the new charter for the whole Anglican Communion."[382] (Emphasis added)

Bray goes on to make the point that it is time to scrap the idea of a "conference of Bishops" in favor of the GAFCON/Global South conciliar model of representation of the whole Church, through all orders of ministry (bishops, clergy and laity together).[383] If we continue to extrapolate from existing models of conciliar representation at the diocesan and national or provincial synods of the churches in this study, composition of such a global synod or council would need to be on the basis of a higher ratio of laity to clergy and/or the size of the Province.[384]

Clearly this would require a constitution of some kind (not unlike the Constitution of the General Synod of the

---

[382] G. Bray, "Editorial: A Canterbury Tale," *The Churchman: Journal of the Church Society,* <http://archive.churchsociety.org/churchman/documents/Cman_127_4_Editorial.pdf> Accessed 15 November 2015, at 294

[383] Ibid, at 296: "Another important aspect of GAFCON that is easily overlooked is that it is not a movement confined to bishops and clergy. The fact that the Lambeth Conference is exclusively episcopal is now a real weakness, and this lopsidedness needs to be challenged. Why should only bishops attend a worldwide gathering of Anglicans? Instead of inviting them (and having to decide which ones to recognise) could the Archbishop of Canterbury not issue an open invitation to the different provinces to send whomever they want? The presence of delegates from their clergy, and especially from their laity, might have a sobering effect on first-world prelates that nobody from the majority world could match. What bishop would want to be embarrassed by members of his own diocese who appear to be more in tune with the renewal agenda than he is? Some of them might well be renewed themselves if presented with such a challenge, and that would be the best outcome of all."

[384] See discussion of representation at diocesan and national or provincial synods, *infra,* Principle 2 in Chapter Three. See also *PCLCCAC,* [n17], Principle 22.3-4. This leaves unanswered the question of whether the size of a Province would be measured by membership rolls, numbers of communicants in good-standing, or average Sunday attendance—and how such measures would be verified.

Church of England found in Schedule 2 of the *SGM 1969*). As a matter of subsidiarity such a Council or General Synod of the Anglican Communion[385] would have a jurisdiction that is limited and with enumerated powers, honoring the autonomy of national and provincial Churches by reserving to their Synods those matters that do not otherwise touch the Fundamental Declarations of the Anglican Communion.[386] This would also be in keeping with the historic purpose of more general and "Ecumenical" Councils of the Church being purposed to

---

[385]What would the name be for this "central church assembly" of Communion governance? We might expect it to be the Council of the Anglican Communion, or the General Synod of the Anglican Communion, or the Anglican Communion General Synod or Council, or perhaps simply the Council of wherever it meets every five years (as in ancient times). For purposes of this discussion we will call it simply The Council.

[386] See *PCLCCAC,* [n17], Principle 12.7: Respecting the greatest possible liberty in each autonomous Church to order its own life and affairs. See also principle within subsidiarity of reserving powers not otherwise specifically delegated to the higher governing body lower bodies. See, e.g., discussion in Appendix, ACNA, Constit. VIII.1. The warrant for a "central church assembly" of the Anglican Communion to address matters touching doctrine in its Fundamental Declarations would be an extension of that same principle in *PCLCCAC,* [n17], Principle 53.5(a). Other enumerated powers would include (1) any legislation to alter, amend or add to the Fundamental Declarations—in which case we would expect to see rigorous procedures to discern the *consensus fidelium,* with approval of any changes by supermajorities that would include near unanimity (see n.379 citing Valliere [n8] at 108-109) at successive meetings of the Council and the Provinces; (2) as the "central church assembly" adding and/or approving Churches who accede to the Fundamental Declarations and the authority of the Council, in keeping with the principle in *PCLCCAC,* [n17], Principle 13.4; (3) authority to establish a supreme judicial court of appeal on matters of faith and order, not unlike a Court of Ecclesiastical Causes Reserved, with limited jurisdiction to declare the law of the Church on any matter of doctrine in keeping with *PCLCCAC,* [n17], Principles 53.5(c) and 53.9; and (4) celebration and strengthen the mission of the Communion. See e.g. ACNA [n335], Constit. VI the Provincial Assembly.

resolve conflicts and controversies around the faith and order of the Church universal.[387]

4. A STANDING COMMITTEE THAT SERVES AS AN EXECUTIVE COMMITTEE OF THE COUNCIL OR GENERAL SYNOD OF THE ANGLICAN COMMUNION:

If such a Council of the Anglican Communion were to meet every five years, this would imply a duration or "session" of five years for all those participating. It might be necessary for members to meet in between those five-year gatherings around mission, and perhaps in regions, to develop the kind of corporate "identity" or "life together along the way" that is intrinsic to synodality. But at the very least it would require an Executive Committee to meet between meetings of the Council to execute its decisions and such other enumerated duties carefully delegated to the Executive Committee.[388]

Typically we would call such a body The Standing Committee of the Council, with its members elected from that body.[389] It might also include a number appointed from outside for their expertise or representation of committees and missionary bodies touching matters of

---

[387] See Valliere, *Conciliarism* [n8] at 58-62. See also Francis Oakley, *The Conciliarist Tradition: Constitutionalism in the Catholic Church* [n13] on strict catholic constitutional conciliarism and the priorities in *Haec Sancta* and Council of Constance *on resolving* matters pertaining to the faith, ending schism and reforming the Church.

[388]See *PCLCCAC,* [n17], Principle 17.4. This would obviously also be a replacement of the current Anglican Consultative Council (ACC) and Standing Committee of the Anglican Communion (SCAC), and their powers under the constitution of the ACC.

[389] See discussion of this in Chapter 3, *infra*.

concern to the whole Communion.[390] A good model for the powers of such a Standing Committee might include the Archbishops' Council in the Church of England, which coordinates, promotes, aid and further the work and mission of the Church of England. But as with the Standing Committees of the Churches surveyed in Chapters Two and Three it would also have delegated powers and responsibilities specific and appropriate to the work of the Council or General Synod.[391]

This proposed model for conciliar governance within the Communion is classically Anglican because it builds from the ground up on the basis of existing principles of an Anglican *ius commune* and the conciliar practices already embedded in the structures of its Churches at every level up to the and including Provincial.

In contrast to Anglican conciliarism, the Orthodox theology of conciliarism places ontology *before* phenomenology. According to Schmemann, we see the Church herself as a council revealing and reflecting the

---

[390] Ibid.

[391] Such powers might also include a review of the decisions of the Primates Council with regards to actions and controversies touching the Fundamental Declarations (with recommendations to the Council or General Synod to ratify, or not), review and recommendations of applications of Churches wishing to join the Communion through accession to the Fundamental Declarations, regular consultation with the Primates Council with regards to developing the mission of the Communion, and an accountability review of its actions by the Council or General Synod. See *PCLCCAC,* [n17], Principle 13.4: "It is within the jurisdiction of the central assembly of a church to regulate relationships between that church and other churches of the Anglican Communion." See also Principle 16.4: "Leadership and authority should be exercised in an accountable manner, within the episcopal and synodical structures of a church, with respect for others in authority, and with regard for the common good and the dignity, rights, needs and gifts of all."

"perfect council" within the godhead of the Blessed Trinity:

> "In the Orthodox perspective, however, the 'validity' of the institution or "form" comes to it from its ontological adequacy to the reality which it truly "represents," makes present and therefore can communicate and fulfill…"[392]

Moreover, New Testament passages like Peter's sermon on Pentecost day (Acts 2:14-41) and the description of the expression of the life of the Church in Acts 2:42-47 are like icons, revealing the role of the Blessed Trinity in the birth and early life of the Church, before orders of ministry (Acts 6) councils (Acts 11-15) and other forms or institutions ever appeared.[393]

But the Anglican conciliarism outlined above is not only practical. It also reflects an ontological understanding of councils as essential to Communion. If, as Valliere hints in *Conciliarism*,[394] Philippians 2:5-11 is a Biblical template for both the ontology and phenomenology of councils, then we have both in this proposed model. In practice, we have a kenotic "self-emptying" of Provinces who consider not their autonomy in communion something to be grasped, but empty themselves *for the sake of Communion*[395] through

---

[392] Alexander Schmemann, *Church, World, Mission: Reflections on Orthodoxy in the West* (New York: St. Vladimir's Seminary Press, 1979), p. 163.

[393] Humphrey, [n6]: "Conciliarism is how we live together, how we are shaped by the whole, how we give expression to the whole, how we make decisions as a whole together…Church implies 'synaxis': simply the need for the church to come together for worship, if nothing else. And if the church is expressed by its coming together for worship, then gathering together is at the very center of its being."

[394] Valliere, [n8] at 48, 68.

[395] And for a "communion" that has a focused definition, which brings together a shared faith and order, relational commitments and a common good (the mind of Christ in the mind of the Church). See Chapter 10.

acceding and submitting to a Council of the Anglican Communion, with Fundamental Declarations, enhanced responsibility of a Council of Primates to guard the faith and order of the Communion, and a Council of the Anglican Communion representative of the whole Church that serves the confession of its Christological center in ways that are both loyal to scripture and the *consensus fidelium*, and intelligible to the people we are seeking to reach with the transforming love of Jesus Christ. Around the authority of the Fundamental Declarations we have the interaction of the Council of Primates, the General Synod of the Communion, and its Standing Committee reflecting the active life of loving and self-giving (*perichoresis*)[396] that already exists within Blessed Trinity. And we have the mission of the Communion flowing out of both – that every knee should bow, and every tongue confess, that Jesus Christ is Lord, to the glory of God the Father (Phil. 2:10-11) (Chapter 10) "Communion and the Common Good")).

The Orthodox perspective reminds us at the very least that there is a creative tension between the priorities of ontology and phenomenology, of ideal and practice. It is this creative tension that enables us to explore possibilities Anglicans might not otherwise consider to recover conciliarism as both ideal and practice – as well as a deeper recovery of *communion*. It also enables us to imagine, in

[396] Alister McGrath, *Christian Theology: An Introduction, Third Edition* (London: Blackwell, 2001) at 325. Perichoresis is a Greek term used by Basil of Caesarea and other Eastern Fathers to describe the triune relationship within each person of the Godhead. It can be defined as co-indwelling, co-inhering, and mutual interpenetration. McGrath writes that "it allows the individuality of the persons to be maintained, while insisting that each person shares in the life of the other two." It is therefore a fitting analogy for the interdependent relationships between the Council of Primates, the Council of the Anglican Communion, and the Standing Committee.

retrospect, how different an outcome there might have been in North America had these conciliar structures been in place.

Of course "the devil is in the details." Lest we idealize Councils, we have a record of how "messy" they may be, and how bishops behave during them.[397] Nevertheless, this proposed model seeks to provide the same checks and balances on errant bishops (and others) that one would find in the synodical government of the Churches in Chapter 3. It provides an ongoing role for the *Principles of Canon Law Common to the Churches of the Anglican Communion* as an Anglican *ius commune* to help shape and guide this model as it adapts to new challenges, perhaps even as a silent "fifth instrument." It also expresses at the same time both the "episcopal conciliarism" Roman Catholic canonists like Orsy view as latent and growing silently as a mustard seed out of *Lumen Gentium*, and the Orthodox view of councils as reflecting the life of the Blessed Trinity itself.[398] There is

[397] M Whitby, "An unholy crew? Bishops behaving badly at Church Councils," in R Price and M Whitby, eds., *Chalcedon in Context: Church Councils 400-700* (Liverpool: Liverpool University Press, 2009), at 178-195. See also the commentary of St. Gregory Nazianzen from his *Epistle CXXX:* "For my part, if I am to write the truth, my inclination is to avoid all assemblies of bishops, because I have never seen any Council come to a good end, nor turn out to be a solution of evils. On the contrary, it usually increases them. You always find their love of contention and love of power… which beggar description; and, while sitting in judgment on others, a man might well be convicted of ill-doing himself long before he should put down the ill-doings of his opponents. So I retired into myself; and came to the conclusion that the only security for one's soul lies in keeping quiet."

[398] Ladislas Orsy, "Episcopal Collegiality Revisited" [n238], at 32: "in the practical order the 'immense changes' are still to come. But then, I would remind the students of the parable of the mustard seed. Has anyone ever seen a mustard tree grow instantly? The seed has been sown, and is striking roots slowly and painfully; some tender shoots already are appearing (yes, the episcopal conferences and synods already exist), but their internal energies (power given by the Spirit) are latent and hardly

common ground here for Anglicans, Roman Catholics and Orthodox Churches to come together for recognition of each other's apostolicity and faithfulness to the essentials of Christian faith.

This model for recovering conciliarism in Anglican Communion governance could well be a small but first step in encouraging a return to genuine Ecumenical Councils among these three branches of Christendom—as well as others. And of all the possible common goods and virtues for the Church, would this not please the heart of Christ himself who prayed for his church to the Father "that they may be one as we are one." (John 17:11 NIV)

---

used... The Spirit can preserve and protect the church no less through the corporate operation of the episcopal college (that the pope presides) than through the activities of the pope as a single person. *I would even add that because the church is a reflection of the communion of the three divine persons in one Godhead, to let the church be led and governed by the 'communion of the bishops' (with and under the vicar of Peter, as Vatican II proclaimed) is supremely fitting*" (emphasis added). Despite the qualification of leadership by the Pope, which one would expect, Orsy offers common ground here for both Anglicans and Orthodox.

NINE

Fundamental Declarations: The Sine Qua Non of Conciliarism

The Anglican Communion Covenant was proposed by *The Windsor Report* (2004) as a means of strengthening the Instruments of Communion on matters of doctrine, discipline and order in a more orderly (and hopefully conciliar) way. Although for the theological and political reasons offered below, the Final Text[399] was fatally flawed, it was a positive and hopeful step towards a more conciliar way of mediating conflict within the Communion, in several ways.

First, it was a step forward in defining communion around a statement of shared doctrine, discipline and order. In section 1 there is an affirmation of the Anglican inheritance of faith drawn essentially from the formula in Church of England Canon C15, an inheritance that includes the Holy Scriptures and the catholic creeds to which the historic formularies of the Church of England (the Thirty-Nine Articles and the 1662 Book of Common Prayer and Ordinal) bear witness.[400] It also includes a

---

[399] *The Anglican Communion Covenant* (2009, Final Text) [n350].

[400] John Rees, "Covenant and Communion," *Ecclesiastical Law Journal* (2012) 14 Ecc LJ 235-255 at 242. However, Rees fails to note that by

restatement of the doctrinal affirmations in the Chicago-Lambeth Quadrilateral (1888) at sections 1.1.3-6, shared patterns of "common prayer and liturgy" (section 1.1.7) and participation in "the apostolic mission of the whole people of God" (section 1.1.8). This led at least one bishop to conclude that Section One contains a minimal (if not sufficient) statement of what it means to be an Anglican the absence of which has led to "an unexamined defense of 'comprehensiveness' as a virtue in itself" and an "ecclesiality" that is lacking in integrity.[401] Thus Section 1 of the Covenant does not create any new identity for Anglicans but rather expresses that "distinctive Anglican identity" that has already been received by the Churches of the Anglican Communion through their common life together.[402]

Section Two is completes orthodoxy with *orthopraxis*: a series of strong commitments to Gospel mission ("The Five Marks of Mission") developed in Lambeth Conference 1998 and the AAC meetings in 1996 and 1999. Section Three is likewise commendable for seeking to strike a

---

comparison with the Preface and Declaration in Canon C15, Section 1.1.2 of the Covenant *qualifies* those historic formularies by declaring that they are limited by time and circumstances in their authority, "forged in the context of the European Reformation and acknowledged and appropriated in various ways in the Anglican Communion." This is precisely the qualification and ambiguity that Noll addresses in one of his proposed revisions to the Covenant.

[401] John Hind. "The Idea of an Anglican Covenant: A faith and Order perspective," *International Journal for the Study of the Christian Church*, Vol. 8, No. 2, May 2008, 112-123 at 120. See also Andrew Goddard, "Communion and Covenant: A Theological Exploration." *International Journal for the Study of the Christian Church*, Vol. 8, No. 2, May 2008, 155-170 at 164 who notes from a more Evangelical perspective that such a statement of faith will also "enable the Anglican Communion to enter into communion with other churches."

[402] Goddard, "Communion and Covenant," [n401], ibid.

balance between autonomy and mutual interdependence in communion, and where caution fails and conflicts arise among the Churches, a commitment "to participate in mediated conversations" (section 3.2.6)[403]

On the positive side of Section Four – by far the most controversial part of the Covenant – Rees summarizes it elegantly as simply an orderly process for dispute resolution that facilitates "Anglican self-understanding," respects the autonomy of national and regional Churches, offers recommendations for relational consequences as a last resort, and leaves the imposition of those consequences in the hands of each autonomous Church and each Instrument – who may even decide not to act on such recommendations.[404] This "orderly process" is of first order to Cameron, who notes the order provided in Section Four is essential for mission; it is "the mechanism through which the ardor of the Holy Spirit may be channeled into the mission of the Church. Ardor without order results in chaos, while order without ardor is empty formalism." Section Four facilitates both ardor and order together.[405] From a Biblical/theological perspective "covenant" is also a means by which the people of God are gathered together by God not to focus on their inner life, but to bear witness to God on mission to the world.[406]

Conservative evangelical Anglicans theologians like Stephen Noll were able to find common ground in Sections One and Two of the Covenant – precisely because they overlapped the doctrinal affirmations and commitments

---

[403] Rees, "Covenant and Communion," [n400], at 244.

[404] Ibid, at 246-247, 251

[405] Gregory Cameron, "A Tortoise in a Hurry: The Ordering of the Anglican Communion," *International Journal for the Study of the Christian Church*, Vol. 8, No. 2, May 2008, 69-80 at 78-79.

[406] Goddard, "Communion and Covenant," [n401], at 168.

found in the GAFCON (2008) Jerusalem Declaration[407] – and in Section Three because it reflects Anglican conciliarism with episcopal leadership and "bishops in council" as the "chief organ of rule."[408]

Nevertheless, there are two sets of reasons why the current Anglican Communion Covenant is not able to establish the foundations around which the Churches can practice conciliarism at the global level of governance. The first set of objections are theological, the second political.

There are at least six theological reasons for rejecting the Covenant as a sufficient basis for recovering Anglican conciliarism at the global level of governance. First and foremost, Section Four of the Covenant removes the authority of the Primates together, and the bishops in council, from their special role of guarding the faith and order of the Church and resolving controversies over doctrine discipline and order. The enhanced responsibility of bishops to guard the faith and order of the Church is of biblical and ancient provenance,[409] reaffirmed in both *The*

---

[407] Stephen Noll, "Communion Governance: The Role and Future of the Historic Episcopate and the Anglican Communion Covenant," *Stephen's Witness,* February 2, 2010 <http://www.stephenswitness.org/2012/02/communion-governance-role-and-future-of.html> at 34.

[408] Ibid, at 34-36, citing section 3.1.2 of the Covenant for the conciliar norm of "bishops in synod," section 3.1.3 for the rationale for bishops as guardians and teachers of the faith, and section 3.1.4 for the role of the Anglican Consultative Council as "advisory."

[409] Ibid, at 22: "In terms of ecclesiology, the idea of the church being guided in matters of doctrine and discipline by bishops begins with the Council of Jerusalem in Acts 15." Here Noll is referring to the guidance of the Apostles, But he goes on to cite its continuity with the work of the Nicene Council, citing Peter Huillier, *The Church of the Ancient Councils: The Disciplinary Work of the First Four Ecumenical Councils* (Crestwood NY: St. Vladimir Seminary Press, 1996) at 30: "The fathers of Nicaea took

Virginia Report (1997) and *The Windsor Report* (2004),[410] and a fundamental principle of governance within the Anglican *ius commune*.[411] Instead, Section Four replaces them with a mixed "Standing Committee" of the Anglican Communion. Episcopal governance remained in the first, "Nassau" Draft of the Covenant, with serious disputes submitted to the Primates Meeting for review, guidance and direction. In the second "St Andrew's" Draft, the Primates were no longer specified as the Instruments of oversight. In the third "Ridley-Cambridge" Draft, the authority to adjudicate disputes under the Covenant was given to The Joint Standing Committee of the Anglican Consultative Council and of The Primates Meeting. By the time the Final Draft was published, the Joint Standing Committee was co-opted by a "Standing Committee of the Anglican Communion" which had a minority of Primates participating who were not proportionately representative of the Global South provinces.[412]

Noll observes that throughout Section Four, "The Standing Committee exercises the active role in administering Covenant discipline, and the Anglican Consultative Counsel *and Primates Meetings* are merely

---

advantage of their meeting to discuss a number of points concerning church discipline. Their intention was not to introduce a new law but to recall rules sometimes neglected, indeed contested, to resolve problems arising out of concrete situations."

[410]See *The Virginia Report,* [n297], at sec. 6.32, and *The Windsor Report,* [n349], at sec. 118 et seq: The role of the Primates in reviewing, discussing and finally approving the Covenant by a solemn signing of the Covenant in a liturgical context.

[411] See *PCLCCAC,* [n17], Principles 37, 48.3, 53.5-6, and 56.7-8.

[412] Noll, "Communion Governance, [n407] at 40.

advisory."[413] Moreover, the episcopal members of the Anglican Consultative Council who are not Primates do not have the same authority to speak on behalf of the episcopates of their own churches, thereby leaving the Primates marginalized within this mixed "Standing Committee. For this reason alone Podmore concludes that, from the perspective of the Church of England's ecclesiology, the Standing Committee "cannot be held to have comparable authority" to either the Primates Meeting or the Lambeth Conference of Bishops"[414] In his letter of resignation from the Standing Committee, Presiding Bishop Mouneer Anis of the Province of Jerusalem and the Middle East cited the disregard of the Primates by the Standing Committee as a critical factor in his decision.[415]

Even if the politicized nature of Standing Committee were not suspect, this replacement and marginalization of the Primates is a fundamental error of Anglican Communion governance because it abandons an

[413] Ibid, at 41, citing sections 4.2.4 ("where appropriate" submit to Primates for advice), 4.2.5 and 4.2.6 (on advice from Primates, Standing Committee "may recommend" discipline)

[414] Colin Podmore, "The Governance of the Church of England and the Anglican Communion," General Synod Miscellaneous Paper 910 (January 2009) < https://www.churchofengland.org/media/38963/gsmisc910.pdf> Accessed 21 November 2015, at 19, sec. 4.34.

[415] "A Key Letter from Primate of the Middle East Mouneer Anis explaining his resignation from the JSC," *TitusOneNine*, January 31, 2010,< http://www.kendallharmon.net/t19/index.php/t19/article/28019/#comments> Accessed 21 November 2015: "...I have come to the sad realization that there is no desire within the ACC and the SCAC to follow through on the recommendations that have been taken by the other Instruments of Communion to sort out the problems which face the Anglican Communion and which are tearing its fabric apart. Moreover, the SCAC, formerly known as the join Standing Committee (JSC), has continually questioned the authority of the other Instruments of Communion, especially the Primates Meeting and the Lambeth Conference."

established principle of Anglican and catholic heritage, that bishops in council have a special role in to adjudicating disputes over doctrine and discipline. For all these reasons, Noll encouraged Churches and Provinces not to adopt the Covenant until all references to the "Standing Committee" of the Anglican Communion in Section Four were replaced with "Primates of Churches that have adopted the Covenant."[416]

Secondly, the Covenant adoption process was flawed and led to both an incoherent ecclesiology and meaning of "Communion". The actual language of section 4.1.4 assumes that Churches are "in" the Anglican Communion already by virtue of their being included in the schedule of Churches in the ACC Constitution, and as they are "invited" to enter into the Covenant.[417] Rather than disciplining members or even excommunicating them as a last resort, the Covenant defaults to a voluntary association where Churches may "self-select" their membership status according to whether they adopt or not. At that time, the Archbishop of Canterbury suggested that this would lead to a "two-track" membership within the Communion – one intensifying relationships, the other distancing.[418] But in reality, as Noll observes, this would actually lead to three tracks, with two in the Communion whether they signed the Covenant or not, and one adopting the Covenant as

---

[416] Noll, "Communion Governance, [n407], at 33-34.

[417] *Covenant (Final Text),* [n350] at s. 4.1.4: "Every Church of the Anglican Communion, *as recognized in accordance with the Constitution of the Anglican Consultative Council,* is invited to enter into this Covenant..."

[418] Rowan Williams, "Communion, Covenant and our Anglican Future: Reflections on The Episcopal Church's 2009 General Convention," *Anglican Communion News Service* <http://www.anglicannews.org/news/2009/07/communion,-covenant-and-our-anglican-future.aspx> Accessed 20 November 2015, at Part 4, pars. 23-24.

Anglicans but not included within the Constitution of the ACC. As if this incoherence were not enough, it would lead the churches in broken and impaired communion with TEC over irreconcilable differences in faith and order to pledge to "live into ecclesial communion and interdependence with each other."

In short, the "two-track" model builds into Communion governance an impossible paradox: "that a portion of the Communion agrees to abide by a certain doctrine and discipline and another does not."[419] For all these reasons, Noll encouraged Churches and Provinces not to adopt the Covenant until section 4.1.4 was amended from every Church of the Anglican Communion "*is invited to enter this Covenant*" to "*is expected to enter this Covenant.*"[420]

Thirdly, Section 4.1,5 of the Ridley Cambridge Draft removed the possibility of dissenting minorities who wished to adopt the Covenant (within non-adopting Churches of Provinces) from doing so through the other Instruments of the Communion – such as the Archbishop of Canterbury, the Primates Meeting or the Lambeth Conference.[421] This section of the Ridley-Cambridge Draft of the Covenant as the main source of contention at the ACC-14 (2009) meeting in Kingston Jamaica, precisely because it offered

---

[419] Noll, "Communion Governance, [n407] at 37-38, 44.

[420] Ibid, at 44.

[421] *The Anglican Communion Covenant (Ridley-Cambridge Draft, 2009)*, <http://www.cs.utsa.edu/~wagner/church/gc2009/covenant.pdf> Accessed 21 November 2015, at Sec. 4.1.5: "*It shall be open to other Churches to adopt the Covenant.* Adoption of this Covenant does not bring any right of recognition by, or membership of, the Instruments of Communion. Such recognition and membership are dependent on the satisfaction of those conditions set out by each of the Instruments. *However, adoption of the Covenant by a Church may be accompanied by a formal request to the Instruments for recognition and membership to be acted upon according to each Instrument's procedures.*" (Emphasis added).

theologically orthodox but "dissenting minorities" a legitimate claim to be in full communion with the theologically orthodox and covenanting churches of the Anglican Communion.[422] But in the Final Draft Section 4.1.5 restricted adoption to the Covenant "by invitation only" of the Instruments "using the same procedures as set out by the Anglican Consultative Council for the amendment of its schedule of membership."[423]

Fourthly, the consequences of breaking the Covenant were vague and ambiguous. At the end of the process, the Standing Committee can only propose so-called "relational consequences" for offenders to the Instruments.[424] On the one hand, if such consequences are recommended, how will they be implemented? What if the offenders refuse to withdraw from the Instruments – what then? On the other hand, if the Standing Committee decides not to recommend relational consequences in the case of such a violation (or decides that a violation has not taken place, or decides to wait), and a Church within the Anglican Communion disagrees with the Standing Committee and decides to break or impair communion with what they consider to be an offending Church, would such action bring relational consequences *to them*?[425]

Fifthly, Section 4.2.8 provides that participation in the decision making of the Standing Committee or of the Instruments of Communion in respect to the monitoring of maintenance of the Covenant and dispute resolution under Section 4.2 shall be limited "to...those churches who have adopted the Covenant, *or who are still in the process of adoption.*" (Emphasis added). But as Noll observes, the

[422] Noll, ""Communion Governance," [n407] at 39.
[423] *Covenant (Final Text),* [n350], at Sec. 4.1.5.
[424] Ibid, Sec. 4.2.7.
[425] Noll, "Communion Governance," [n407] at 41.

effect of this is to permit non-Covenanting Churches to operate in all other respects than matters relating to the Covenant within the structures of the Communion, and therefore to operate by a different set of rules than Covenanting Churches, and with no time limit for churches "in the process of adopting," (like TEC) to have at least seat and voice, if not vote, on the Standing Committee with respect even to Section 4.2 matters. Again this displays an ecclesiology that is incomprehensible and incoherent with respect to its order.[426]

Finally, there is an objection that is both theological and political. In light of the politics around the Standing Committee – specifically, its replacement of the Primates as the authority for adjudicating controversies around Communion doctrine and discipline, and giving seat voice and vote on that very Standing Committee to North Americans whose "innovations" have been responsible for the need for the Covenant (see Chapter 6) – Noll suggested five deep and fundamental revisions to the Final Text of the Covenant:

1. In Section. 1.1.3, Strengthen the historic and normative role of the Thirty Nine Articles, the 1662 BCP and Ordinal as authentic witnesses to Anglican with, without any historic or contextual qualifications;[427]
2. Replace the text in Section 1.2.3 with an affirmation of Lambeth Resolution I.10 (1998) as

[426] Ibid, at 42.
[427] Steve Noll, "Communion Governance: A Revised Anglican Covenant," Stephen's *Witness*, August 1, 2010 <http://www.stephenswitness.org/2010/08/communion-governance-revised-anglican_01.html> Accessed 21 November 2015, at 4.

God's standard of marriage and abstinence binding on all Anglicans;[428]

3. Make the following revisions to Section Three: (a) In Section 3.1.2 declare that the Anglican Communion will be constituted by those who adopt the Covenant, and that each Instrument will be constituted only by those who adopt the covenant; (b) In Section 3.1.4, Part I of "The Instruments "declare that the Archbishop of Canterbury presides as *primus inter pares* within a college of bishops which shall now be called the "Lambeth Council" instead of "the Lambeth Conference" conference, omitting his power to gather them, thereby preserving his role as a "focus of unity" while reducing his "executive" role; (c) further in Section 3.1.4, under Part II, also changing the name from Lambeth Conference" to "Council" and substituting "deliberation" (a more conciliar function) for "consultation and encouragement"; (d) delete current Part III, the Anglican Consultative Council, as an Instrument (because it's remit is to be an advisory body only) and renumber Part IV as new Part III with a revised section on the Primates who will now "meet regularly between the Lambeth Council of Bishops" and also "deliberate," to clarify and restore their role as guardians of faith and order;[429]

4. Revise Section 4 by replacing every reference to "Standing Committee" with "The Primates Council" to Restore the Primates Council to their

[428] Ibid.

[429] Ibid, at 5-6.

proper oversight of Communion faith and order;[430] and

5. Revise Section 4 "to bind the Communion into an accountable union," as follows: (a) revise Section 4.1.4 so that every church in Communion, whether already recognized in the schedule of the Constitution of the Anglican Consultative Council, or not, is "*expected*" (replacing "*invited*") to adopt; (b) further, those who reject or fail to adopt in a timely manner are declared vacant by Primates Council and derecognized by the Archbishop of Canterbury; (c) Revise Section 4.1.5 to allow "dioceses, parishes and ecclesial networks in non-adopting national and regional churches" to adopt the Covenant, upon which decision the Primates Council will grant provisional provincial status to such a group until they are ratified as a "replacement" national or regional church by Lambeth Council of Bishops and recognized by the Archbishop of Canterbury; and (d) revise Section 4.3.1 to provide that any covenanting church may decide to withdraw, in which case the Primates Council and Lambeth Council will treat such withdrawal in the same manner as that of non-adopting churches in revised Sections. 4.1.4 and 4.1.5.[431]

---

[430] Ibid, at 10-11.

[431] Ibid, at 6-7. These revisions to Section 4 clearly incorporate many of the proposals of Gomez and Sinclair in *To Mend the Net,* including those proposals that giving theologically dissenting minorities the right of recognition and replacement of those national and regional Churches and Provinces that either reject or withdraw from the shared faith and order of the Anglican Communion.

At the time Noll made these proposals the Anglican Communion Covenant was still the subject and hope of ratification by the Churches of the Anglican Communion. And so he encouraged the Churches of the Global South to insist on those changes.[432]

However, that way forward was overcome by events – namely the rejection by the majority of the dioceses of the Church of England, the "Mother Church of the Anglican Communion," to ratify the Covenant.[433] This places the Church of England in the awkward position of being the subject of a recommendation of the Standing Committee of "relational consequences" which must flow from an action incompatible with the Covenant – on the very terms its members helped to draft in the Covenant.[434]

Those consequences could include an invitation to withdraw from the Instruments of Communion – but that would be difficult for the Archbishop of Canterbury and the members of the Anglican Consultative Council who are required under its governing documents, under UK Charity law, to be members of the Church of England! Or those relational consequences could include declarations of impaired or even broken communion from other Churches within the Communion. So far, nothing like that has happened. But as one prominent opponent of the Covenant within the Church of England said, "The Covenant is now dead in the water in the Church of

[432] Ibid, at 8: "The only feasible political way forward therefore is for the Global South churches to take the authority of revising and adopting a Covenant into their own hands...if a number of Provinces adopt a revised Covenant and begin operating according to it, there is no "Communion law" that would nullify this action."

[433] "Half of the Church of England's dioceses reject unity covenant," *BBC News,* 24 March 2012, <http://www.bbc.com/news/uk-17500144> Accessed 21 November 2015.

[434] *Covenant (Final Text),* [n350] at Section 4.2.7.

England."[435] As Goddard noted following the vote, no Act to reconsider the Covenant could be taken up until the election of a new Synod in 2015.[436] As of this writing those elections have just taken place, but it remains to be seen whether such reconsideration will be brought again before the General Synod and the dioceses.

But it is also true that only fourteen Churches or Provinces have considered the Covenant, and of those fourteen only nine have adopted the Covenant without qualification,[437] and among those who have not yet ratified

---

[435] "Covenant voting continues," *The Living Church,* 26 March 2012, < http://www.livingchurch.org/covenant-voting-continues> Accessed 21 November 2015. "With today's results from the dioceses of Oxford and Lincoln, the proposed Anglican Covenant is now dead in the water in the Church of England," said the Rev. Lesley Crawley, moderator of the No Anglican Covenant Coalition, in a March 24 statement. "This also poses serious problems for the Covenant in other Provinces as it seems nonsensical to have the Archbishop of Canterbury in the second tier of the Anglican Communion and excluded from the central committees."

[436] Ibid, "The Rev. Andrew Goddard, writing at Fulcrum, said further discussion of the Covenant in the Church of England is postponed until 2015. "General Synod cannot reconsider the Act during this Synod. It would be open to the new Synod, elected in 2015, to again request the dioceses to approve a draft Act of Synod adopting the Covenant or consider an alternative way of the Church of England adopting it," Goddard wrote. "However, unless there are significant changes in the text of the covenant or strong evidence of a serious change of mind within the wider church (perhaps if most provinces do adopt it and we are a small minority refusing), both of these paths would appear unwise."

[437] "Responses from Churches of the Anglican Communion to the proposed Anglican Communion Covenant as of 19th January 2015," Anglican *Communion Covenant* <http://www.anglicancommunion.org/identity/doctrine/covenant/responses.aspx> Accessed 21 November 2015. Listing only those churches who have sent official confirmation of their decision to the Secretary General. This represents less than 50% of the Churches and provinces of the Anglican Communion.

the Covenant, fewer are likely to do so following the example of the Mother Church. Although ACC-15 (New Zealand, 2012) received the Report on the Reception of the Anglican Covenant by the Provinces in the Anglican Communion, with some discussion in small groups, there was a lack of serious engagement on the issues surrounding the Covenant.[438] No resolutions were offered on the Anglican Communion Covenant, and it was not revisited at the next meeting of the Anglican Consultative Council (Zambia, 2016). Meanwhile, the divisions within the Communion continue to widen at an accelerating pace (see Chapter Six). For all of these reasons "political," the future of the Anglican Communion Covenant looks bleak indeed.

We must be honest, division has already occurred. The only question is whether the divisions lead to the dissolution of Communion or radical reform. As Noll observes in "Communion Governance," what differentiates conciliarism from a federation of autonomous churches is:

> "(C)ommon consent to an agreed upon deposit of faith and worship in mutual submission of elders in the spirit… a concordant reading of scripture, 'The rule of faith,' epitomized in the ecumenical creeds and historic confessions."[439]

---

[438] See the minority Report of Nigeria and Kenya from ACC-15, "What Really Happened at ACC-15?" *Anglican Ink,* 8 November 2012 [n292]: "In the discussion on the proposed Anglican Covenant, we avoided the serious issues pertaining to discipline in the Church. Instead, we were asked to discuss our feelings about the Covenant-"Why is it a sign of fear for some and a sign of hope for others?" We already have four Instruments of Anglican Communion: the Archbishop of Canterbury, the Primates meetings, the Lambeth Conference of Bishops, and the ACC. If our identity, faith and order as Anglicans cannot be maintained by these Instruments, the Covenant will not solve our problems."

[439] Noll, "Communion Governance," [n407] at 26. See also Ephraim Radner, "Wheels within wheels: The Promise and Scandal of Anglican Particularism,"

That is, *a new set of Fundamental Declarations*. As I noted in the last Chapter, the GAFCON Jerusalem Declaration (2008) is an inspired, Biblical, conciliar model for a set of Fundamental Declarations around which a communion of Anglican Churches could form, *Semper Reformanda*. Such revisions and reforms are what shape the proposal in the last Chapter for extending the conciliarism we find at every other level of Anglican polity to Communion Governance. And there is nothing to prevent those Churches of the Anglican Communion who have such convictions from making it so.

Inaugural Lecture at Wycliffe College, Toronto, October 9 and 10,2007 at <http://www.bing.com/search?q=Ephraim+Radner%2C+%E2%80%9CWheels+within+wheels%3A+The+Promise+and+Scandal+of+Anglican+Particularism%2C%E2%80%9D&form=PRDLCS&pc=MDDCJS&mkt=en-us&refig=809ee50f31b7480495cef1ad2f6cc3f8&pq=ephraim+radner%2C+%E2%80%9Cwheels+within+wheels%3A+the+promise+and+scandal+of+anglican+particularism%2C%E2%80%9D&sc=0-0&sp=-1&qs=n&sk=&cvid=809ee50f31b7480495cef1ad2f6cc3f8> Accessed 21 November 2015.

TEN

Communion and the Common Good

How shall we define the category of "communion" as relating to the principles and the practice of conciliarism?

Is "communion" the proper end of a working Anglican conciliarism, or merely a dream that must give way to the reality of irreconcilable differences of doctrine and discipline among Anglican Churches?

What do we mean by the Anglican *Communion* of Churches?

Is communion defined by the relational "bonds of affection" that have developed over time, as we have gathered to pray together (as good Anglicans do), and to do mission together?

Or is there more content to communion – a shared doctrine discipline and order among Anglican Churches?

Or is it all of the above?

Within the *ius commune* shared by Anglican Churches, there are various categories of "communion."

"Ecclesial communion" between two or more churches exists when each church believes the other holds the essentials of the Christian faith and recognizes the apostolicity of the other.[440]

"Full communion" goes beyond the recognition of unity in faith and includes sacramental sharing, mutual recognition and interchangeability of ministries, and the reciprocal sharing of spiritual, pastoral and collegial resources.[441]

"Inter-Communion" is an ecclesial relationship in which at least one but not all of the elements of full communion is present.[442]

Common to all three categories is that communion "does not require the acceptance of *all* theological opinion, sacramental devotion or liturgical practice of another church."[443] (Emphasis added) Nor does communion require the sacrifice of the autonomy of either church.[444]

The state of impaired communion between the Churches of the Anglican Communion documented in Chapter 6 shares the characteristics of impaired communion of the first two categories (ecclesial and full), precisely because they are around differences of faith and order. This suggests that ***shared faith and order*** is an essential, if not the most essential, characteristic of communion. This is certainly at the heart of the definition of communion in the Bonn Agreement of 1931 that established full communion between the Church of England and the Old Catholic Church of the Union of Utrecht. Paragraph 3 of the Agreement provides, in pertinent part, "Intercommunion does not require from

---

[440] PCLCCAC, [n17], Principle 94.1

[441] Ibid, Principle 94.2

[442] Ibid., Principle 94.3

[443] Ibid., Principle 94.5

[444] Ibid, Principle 95.4: Autonomy with interdependence.

either Communion the acceptance of all doctrinal opinion, sacramental devotion or liturgical practice characteristic of the other, *but implies that each believes the other to hold all the essentials of the Christian Faith.*"[445] (Emphasis added) The Bonn Agreement also spells out what full communion means in practice in the same terms as *PCLCCAC* Principle 94: sacramental sharing, mutual recognition and interchangeability of ministries (including Holy Orders), and the reciprocal sharing of collegial resources.[446]

It is clear from the first Lambeth Conference of Bishops in 1867,[447] and in Resolutions from Lambeth Conferences

---

[445] "The Bonn Agreement of 1931," *Willibrord Society,* <http://www.willibrord.org/bonn_en.html> Accessed 19 November 2015. The Agreement goes on to define the implications of Paragraph 3 specifically: "The third paragraph makes it clear that intercommunion does not affect the independent lives of the churches, *but rather that it affirms their unity in the riches and fullness of Christ.*"(emphasis added) In Paragraph 1 each Communion recognizes the Catholicity and independence of the other, and in Paragraph 2 the sharing of sacraments between each Communion.

[446] Compare The Bonn Agreement, [n557] "What this means in Practice" with *PCLCCAC,* [n17] Principle 94.2. In this case, the Union of Utrecht is represented at the "collegial" Anglican Lambeth Conferences and meetings of the Anglican Consultative Council.

[447] *The Six Lambeth Conferences 1867-1920* (London: SPCK, 1920) at 53-56: Four statements of the nature of Anglicanism by the 76 bishops who attended: (1) Introduction to the Resolutions of Lambeth 1867, in which the Bishops declare themselves "Bishops of the Holy Catholic Church [a greater whole] in visible Communion with the United Church of England and Ireland, professing the Faith delivered to us in Holy Scripture, maintained by the Primitive Church and by the Fathers of the English Reformation; (2) Unity effectively promoted by "maintaining the Faith in its unity and integrity, as taught in the Holy Scriptures, held by the Primitive Church, summed up in the creeds and affirmed by the undisputed General Councils"; (3) Resolution IV, that such unity will be most effectively maintained by the synods of the various churches subordinated to a higher synod of the Anglican Communion, and (4) Resolution VIII, that union with "the Mother Church" of England depends on the other Churches receiving

of 1878,[448] 1888[449] and 1920[450] that a shared confession faith, doctrine and order was an essential condition of communion.

---

and maintaining the "Standards of faith and Doctrine" now in use within the Church of England.

[448] *The Six Lambeth Conferences 1867-1920,* [n447] at 83: No resolutions, but the Report describes "the essential and evident unity in which the Church of England and the Churches in visible communion with her" consisting in a shared faith which includes the faith as revealed in the Scriptures, defined in the Creeds and maintained by the Primitive Church. Also rejected as too difficult the idea of a convening a "Synod of all the Anglican Churches."

[449] Ibid, [n447] at 122, citing Resolution 11, known as "The Chicago Lambeth Quadrilateral," calling for intercommunion with any Christian body on the basis of mutual acceptance and recognition of (1) The Holy Scriptures as containing all things necessary for salvation and as being the rule and ultimate standard of faith; (2) the Apostles Creed as the Baptismal symbol and the Nicene Creed as the sufficient statement of Christian faith; (3) the two sacraments ordained by Christ himself, baptism and Holy Communion, and (4) the historic episcopate, locally adapted. It is significant that, while refusing to impose the Thirty-Nine Articles as a condition for communion, the Conference held that a church seeking communion would need to formulate articles like the Thirty-Nine "in accordance with our own standards of doctrine and worship."

[450] "Resolutions from 1920: Resolution 9: Reunion of Christendom," *Lambeth Conference Archives 1920,* <http://www.anglicancommunion.org/resources/document-library/lambeth-conference/1920/resolution-9-reunion-of-christendom?author=Lambeth+Conference&year=1920> Accessed 19 November 2015: Reaffirming "the wholehearted acceptance" of the Chicago Lambeth Quadrilateral (1888) as the foundation for the visible unity of the Church. See also *The Six Lambeth Conferences 1867-1920,* [n447] at 12 (the record of the 1920 Lambeth Conference has its own numbering within the collection), where by encyclical letter of the bishops the Conference declares that the ideal of the "reunion of Christendom," a priority highlighted by the horrors of World War I, "cannot be fulfilled if these [divided churches] are content to remain in separation from one another or

The 1930 Lambeth Conference expanded the conditions of communion beyond a shared confession of faith, doctrine and order. In Resolution 48, it affirmed the true constitution of the Catholic Church around the principle of "the *autonomy* of particular Churches based upon a common faith and order."[451] The Report of Committee IV went on to explain that such autonomy means that a particular church has no power to change the Creeds or early organization of the universal Church, but it does have the right "to determine the best methods of setting forth to their people the content of the Christian faith."[452] In so doing, the Report acknowledged that the freedom of such autonomy opened the door to "divergence to the point even of disruption," which would ultimately impoverish the life of both the particular church and the Communion.[453] This was quite prophetic in the light of the devolution of conciliar principles and practices in the last 50 years, chronicled in Chapter 6. Nevertheless, the Conference stated that the Lambeth Conference "as such" could take no disciplinary action against a diverging and disrupting church; "Formal action would belong to the

---

to be joined together only in some vague federation." This of course bears on the question at hand – whether it is better to allow the whole of the Anglican Churches to default to such a "vague federation" around the See of Canterbury, or for there to be a smaller but more vigorous number of Anglican Churches united in a visible communion sharing a common faith, doctrine and order?

[451] "Lambeth Conference 1930: Resolution 48: The Anglican Communion,' *Anglican Communion Archives, Lambeth 1930*,< http://www.anglicancommunion.org/resources/document-library/lambeth-conference/1930/resolution-48-the-anglican-communion?author=Lambeth+Conference&year=1930 > Accessed 19 November 2015

[452] *Report of the Lambeth Conference of 1930* (London: SPCK, 1930), at 154.

[453] Ibid, at 155.

several Churches of the Communion individually."[454] Again, this was a prophetic statement in light of the crisis of authority within the Anglican Communion today.

Secondly, in Resolution 49, the Lambeth Conference 1930 added as an essential element of communion relationship to the See of Canterbury and the "mutual loyalty sustained through the common counsel of bishops in conference."[455] This began a trajectory of diminishing the authority of shared faith and order while magnifying "relationships in common counsel" as the essential element of communion. The Report of Lambeth Conference 1948 emphasized "dispersed authority" as essential to the meaning and unity of the Anglican Communion, allowing change as the circumstances warranted and opening the door to the possibility that the "continuing experience of the Holy Spirit through his faithful people" might legitimately take precedence over Scripture.[456] The Report of the Lambeth Conference 1958 argued that the unity of the Anglican Communion does not rest on a shared Prayer Book but rather on the fact that it is a "*federation* of Provinces and dioceses… served and governed by a Catholic and Apostolic ministry and each believing the Catholic faith. *These are the fundamental reasons for our*

---

[454] Ibid, at 154-155.

[455] "Lambeth Conference 1930: Resolution 49: The Anglican Communion," [n308].

[456] *The Lambeth Conference 1948*, (London: SPCK, 1948) at 85: "Authority… is distributed among Scripture, Tradition, Creeds, the Ministry of the Word and Sacraments, the witness of saints and the *consensus fidelium,* which is the continuing experience of the Holy Spirit through his faithful people in the Church. It is thus a dispersed rather than a centralized authority having many elements which combine, interact with and check each other…*the emphasis on one element over the others may and does change with the changing conditions of the Church."* (emphasis added)

unity."[457] (Emphasis added). The Report of the Lambeth Conference 1968 diluted the shared faith even further, accepting the recommendations of the Report by the Doctrine Commission of the Church of England[458] that subscription to the Thirty-Nine Articles no longer be required of any ordinands within the Churches of the Anglican Communion, that each Church should consider whether even to include them with its authorized Book of Common Prayer and, if so "only in the context of a statement which gives the full range of our inheritance of faith and sets the Articles in their historical context."[459]

The net effect of these Conferences was to emphasize the *differences* between Churches in a Communion that functions like a federation, with toleration and comprehensiveness as the principal virtues of such communion within a relational framework that allows discussion on matters touching doctrine to produce a

---

[457] *The Lambeth Conference 1958,* (London and New York: SPCK/Seabury Press, 1958) at para. 2.79.

[458] *Subscription and Assent to the Thirty-nine Articles:* A Report of the Archbishops' Commission on Christian Doctrine (London: SPCK, 1968).

[459] "Lambeth Conference 1968: Resolution 43: The Ministry- The Thirty-Nine Articles," *Anglican Communion Archives, Lambeth 1968* <http://www.anglicancommunion.org/resources/document-library/lambeth-conference/1968/resolution-43-the-ministry-the-thirty-nine-articles?author=Lambeth+Conference&year=1968> Accessed 20 November 2015. Note the unusual reference to the number of dissents: "adopted with 37 dissenting." See also *The Lambeth Conference 1968* (London and New York: SPCK/Seabury Press, 1968) at 82: "We commend the further study of this report which recognizes that the inheritance of faith which characterizes the Anglican Communion is an authority of a multiple kind and that, to the different elements which occur in the different strands of this inheritance different Anglicans attribute different levels of authority. From this foundation arises Anglican tolerance, comprehensiveness, and ordered liberty, though admittedly it makes Anglican theology variegated rather than monolithic, and informal rather than systematically deductive.

consensus fidelium that is "informal rather than systematically deductive."[460] In just over 100 years, the confession of a shared faith, doctrine and order had moved from being an essential element of communion to being one that was barely comprehensible.

The 1978 Lambeth Conference went further by suggesting that Anglican doctrine should be deduced from worship rather than a "confession that will mark us off from other Christian communities."[461] The next blow came from the Report of the Sixth Meeting of the Anglican Consultative Council (ACC-6, Nigeria 1984). In response to the question "What is Anglicanism?" the ACC reported that Anglican identity is no longer shaped by the Thirty-nine Articles.[462] Instead, Anglican identity and communion is shaped by a commitment of loyalty to apostolic faith, Catholic order, reformed by the standards of Scripture and shaped by our Anglican "ethos" – "a way of thinking and feeling which has developed over the centuries which calls for…diversity, an openness, tolerance and mutual respect toward others."[463] This trajectory reached its logical conclusion in the Third Report of the Inter-Anglican Theological and Doctrinal Commission (IATDC) in 2008, *Communion, Conflict and Hope*[464] which argued for the replacement of communion as a common confession of faith, doctrine and order with a "communion from below,"

---

[460] *The Lambeth Conference 1968*, [n459] ibid.

[461] *The Lambeth Conference 1978* (London: CIO, 1978) 99-100.

[462] *Proceedings of the Sixth Meeting of the Anglican Consultative Council,* (London: ACC, 1984), 81: "Whatever place the Thirty-nine Articles have occupied in the life of the Church of England (and even there a shift of emphasis has occurred in recent years) the commitment of other provinces to them has been much less."

[463] Ibid, 82.

[464] *Communion, Conflict and Hope* (London: Anglican Communion Office, 2008)

that is, a communion based on shared relationships in which Anglicans come together to experience the healing and reconciling work of God in Christ.[465]

Even the IATDC admits that the substitution of a "thick" relational ecclesiology in place of a common confession of faith "immeasurably weakens" Anglicanism as a coherent global communion of churches, and its mission.[466] This lack of doctrinal coherence besetting the Anglican Communion is precisely what Avis addresses in his discussion of Anglican identity. He describes two categories of Anglican self-definition. The first is content based and includes those who believe that a shared faith in such doctrines as are set forth in the Thirty-Nine Articles represents the confessional identity of Anglicanism and the basis for communion. The other category is about "spirit and ethos."[467] While Avis might agree that an appeal to a "thick ecclesiology of relationships" will in the short run lower the tensions within the Communion around identity (and authority), to define the identity of Anglicanism in this way is simply "to make a virtue of necessity":

> "The notion of a tacit consensus residing in a common ethos is a *post factum* accommodation to the demise of doctrinal accord within the Church. To say that, however, is by no means to reject the concept of a tacit consensus

---

[465] Ibid, 50: "IATDC has identified theology, canon law, history and culture, communication and voluntary commitment rather than coercion, as essential aspects of communion. Yet real communion can exist in many of the elements separately. The Commission is persuaded that 'thick' ecclesiology, concrete experience of the reconciling and healing work of God in Christ, should take priority over 'thin', abstract and idealized descriptions of the church."

[466] *Communion, Conflict and Hope* [n464] 50-51: "If Anglican fellowship at the level of shared doctrines and ideals of common participation in mission is unable to enjoy the support of coherent global structures, then the Anglican Communion will be immeasurably weakened."

[467] Avis, *Identity* [n12], at 24.

subsisting in the realm of praxis, but simply to make it abundantly clear that what we are talking about is not a supposed timeless essence of Anglicanism, but a conceptual construction, a pragmatic adjustment to the facts of history."[468]

But in its 1997 *Virginia Report*, the IATDC sought to head off the demise of doctrinal accord by defining communion as both shared doctrine *and* shared faith, by analogy of the visible, ordered life of the Anglican Communion to the "life of interdependence and belonging" within the relationships of Father, Son and Holy Spirit within the Trinity.[469] In response to this relational analogy to the Trinity itself, Archbishops Gomez and Sinclair responded in *To Mend the Net* (2001) that there is in fact no human analogy to the life within the Trinity. "Diversity in the Church can just as easily be a matter of human pride and sinful resistance to the truth of the Triune Life."[470] Without the passion and cross of Jesus Christ to balance the picture – a cross and passion which requires humility, sacrifice and even discipline as conciliar practices – the appeal to a Trinitarian "life of interdependence and belonging" will always be too weak in the flesh to overcome doctrinal divergences and differences

---

[468] Ibid, 25.

[469] *The Virginia Report,* [n297], at para. 3.52-3.53: "This complex and still evolving network of structures within Anglicanism has developed a serves to keep Anglicans in a life of belonging together, a life of relationship...This complex network of structures gives expression to the fundamental bond of Anglican life which is that unity given in the life of God, Father, Son and Holy Spirit. *That life of divine communion is made visible in a characteristic way within the ordered life of the Anglican Communion.* The combination of scripture, tradition and reason, the life lived within the gifts of Scripture, creeds, sacraments and ordained ministry, the essential inter-relatedness of lay and ordained and the structured, conciliar life contribute each in their conciliar way to a life of interdependence and belonging." (emphasis added)

[470] Gomez and Sinclair [n 11], at 120-121.

that threaten communion.[471] This suggests as well that the divisions over Lambeth Resolution I.10 (1998) have as much, if not more, to do with the divisions over the definition and meaning of communion than the presenting issues of human sexuality.

The Windsor Report (2004) was silent on the analogy to the life of interdependence and belonging in the Trinity, and made only passing reference to the proposals in *To Mend the Net*.[472] However, it turned again to the need to link the definition of communion to a proper regard "to the common good of the global Anglican community and the Church universal."[473] But by the time the final text of *The Anglican Communion Covenant* was published, and by contrast to the "Proposal for the Anglican Covenant" in *The Windsor Report,* it had only one reference to the common good of the Anglican Communion *alone*, without regard to the common good of the Church universal,[474] and had returned to the analogy to the life within the Trinity as essential to Communion, without any of the

---

[471] Ibid, 31-32.

[472] *The Windsor Report (2004)* [n349], at 44, para. 104.

[473] Ibid, at 36, para. 80: "In our view, therefore, 'autonomy' thus denotes not unlimited freedom but what we might call freedom-in-relation, so it is subject to limits generated by the commitments of communion. Consequently, the very nature of autonomy itself obliges each church to have regard to the common good of the global Anglican community and the Church universal." The commitment to communion as proper regard for the common good is repeated at paras. 51, 82 and 134 of *TWR,* and in "Appendix Two: Proposal for the Anglican Covenant," at Articles 5, 9, 21 and 26.

[474] Compare *The Anglican Communion Covenant (Final Text),* [n350] at Sec. 3.2.1: Each Church commits itself "to have regard for the common good of the Communion in the exercise of its autonomy..." with "Proposal for the Anglican Covenant" in *The Windsor Report (2004),* [n349], at Appendix Two, Article 5: "(3) Every church shares the same concern for good government for the fulfillment of its mission and for the common good of the Anglican Communion *and the Church universal.*" (Emphasis added).

correctives offered by Gomez and Sinclair. For this reason and other reasons theological and political (see Chapter 9), the final *Anglican Communion Covenant* was not able to resolve the divide between the definitions of communion as a shared confession of Christian essentials, and communion as relationship.

This divide lives on as well in the *ius commune* of the Anglican Communion, in the differences between *PCLCCAC* 10 and 94. Whereas Principle 94 defines ecclesial communion as each church recognizing the other to hold the essentials of the Christian faith (echoing almost verbatim the Bonn Agreement 1931),[475] Principle 10 defines ecclesial communion on the same terms as Lambeth Conference 1930, Resolutions 48 and 49: relationship with the See of Canterbury.[476]

However, Principle 10.4 opens the door to ecclesial communion being defined as *both* doctrinal *and* relational on the basis of relationship with any *one or more of the following*:

- The See of Canterbury
- The Church of England
- All the churches of the Anglican Communion
- All churches in communion with the See of Canterbury, **or**
- All churches that profess the apostolic faith as received within the Anglican Communion.[477] (Emphasis added).

Clearly this opens the door to communion as being something more than a federation around one geographic

---

[475] See n445, *infra*.
[476] *PCLCCAC,* [n17], Principle 10.4 (a).
[477] Ibid, Principle 10.4.

point of reference (the See of Canterbury). Under Principle 10.4, shared doctrine alone may be an essential element of communion. But neither Principle defines communion as a proper regard for the common good of the Anglican Communion and the Church universal.[478]

In short, this seems an invitation to reassess and refresh the roots of what communion means. Based on the Bonn Agreement 1931, the Resolutions of Lambeth Conferences, the reports of the IATDC, the limitations on communion as relationship by analogy to the life of belonging and interdependence within the Godhead, and the definition of "autonomy in communion" in *The Windsor Report*, the definition of communion must include at least three essentials:

(1) The recognition that the other holds the essentials of the Christian faith (in accordance with the Bonn Agreement 1931 and *PCLCCAC* 94, that is, a shared confession of faith and doctrine),

(2) Relationships that are comprehensive enough to welcome sacramental sharing, interchangeability of ministries and Holy Orders, and mutual sharing in collegial resources and mission, and

(3) A deeply mutual respect for the "common good" of the Church that each recognizes in the practices of the other.

It is with respect to this third element that we need to ask the question: "What then is the common good of the Church"? The closest the New Testament comes to

[478] Although it could be argued that *PCLCCAC* Principle 12.7 does so very indirectly, by defining "autonomy and interdependence" in terms of a church ordering its life with the greatest possible liberty so long as it is compatible with its belonging to and interdependence with the church universal."

defining "the common good" is I Corinthians 12:7 where the phrase, in context, means "for the building up of the Church."[479] The building up of the Church in turn presumes some kind of unity around the person of Jesus Christ. From the Orthodox perspective, Schmemann observes that the perfect conciliar life of the Trinity expressed in Christ's prayer in John 17:11 "that they [the church] may be one, as we are" is the basis for understanding the "common good of the church" as *communio* – the life of perfect oneness that characterizes the relationships within the Blessed Trinity.[480] In keeping with John 17, Doe defines it as "the deeper unity and communion for which Christ prayed for his church."[481]

Citing the example of the Council of Carthage in 256 A.D., Valliere concludes that "Unity was the first principle of ecclesiology in the ancient church and conciliarism was an expression of it."[482] Among the Medieval canonists Nicholas of Cusa (1401-1464) equates the common good in his *Catholic Concordance* (1433) with *concordantia*, a "beautiful diversified harmony" within the whole church that includes the biblical-prophetic vision of *shalom*, an underlying peace and wholeness often obscured by the discordant.[483] *Concordantia* is not only how the church manages its affairs but intrinsic to what the church is (one, holy, catholic and apostolic), the opposite of schism, and a microcosm of the *concordantia* within the Trinity itself.[484]

---

[479] Avis, *Beyond the Reformation* [n5], at 185.
[480] Schmemann [n392], at 164.
[481] Doe, "The Instruments of Unity and Communion in Global Anglicanism," [n263], at 60.
[482] Valliere, [n8] at 109-11.
[483] Ibid, 150-151.
[484] Ibid, 153.

Within Anglicanism, Avis also reviews the development of the common good in conciliar theory from the New Testament to the present.[485] He cites both *The Windsor Report* (2004) and *The Anglican Communion Covenant* (2014) as witness to the same principles – namely, visible unity as the common good, "common confession of the apostolic faith, common belief in the scripture and creeds," "the highest degree of communion possible," and more.[486] Ultimately Avis concludes that the common good of the church cannot be separated from the vision of God, therefore the common good must be that deeper unity."[487]

But perhaps the best example within the Churches of the Anglican Communion comes from the Constitution of the Church in the Province of South East Asia, which provides that "the common good" is "the unity and good order of the Church in the Province" in consultation with the several dioceses on matters of legislation.[488] The Diocese of Singapore digs a bit deeper, acknowledging the effects of unity, and a common mission of all clergy and laity "to witness to Christ by their lives and by their words."[489] Ever deeper, the Diocese roots this definition of the common good in the New Testament, Pauline language of the church as "the body of Christ": that the Diocesan Synod "may make the Church in the diocese to be ever more and more truly a body, a small living

[485] Avis, *Beyond the Reformations* [n5], at 185-192.

[486] *The Windsor Report 2004* [n349], at *para. 49; The Anglican Communion Covenant (Final Text)* [350], at section 3.2.7.

[487] Avis, *Beyond the Reformation* [n5], at 192. But also that such unity cannot be a confessional matter.

[488] South East Asia, [n99], Constit. Art. XVI

[489] *Diocese of Singapore,* [n112], Constit. "Statement of the Spiritual Background of the Diocesan Synod," at 2.

organism within the body of Christ, working with Him for the salvation of men and for the Kingdom of God."[490]

This may be the best definition of the common good of the Church that we will ever find among the Churches of the Anglican Communion. It points to being in Christ himself as the highest common good of the Church – or to put it simply, to have the mind of Christ fill the mind of the Church, "to have this mind in you, which was in Christ Jesus…" (Phil. 2:5). Valliere hints at Philippians 2:1-11, the great kenotic hymn/confession of Jesus Christ in the early Church as the one text around which we may define that common good. For it is in this text that we find the ontology and the phenomenology (practice) of councils, the doctrinal unity of the Church and its effectiveness in mission, all converging around and guarding the Christological center of the Church.

The common good under the authority of Philippians 2:1-11 includes guarding *the faith and doctrine of the Church.* We find a shared confession of faith, doctrine and order as essential to communion by hearkening back to those earlier Councils of the undivided Church where communion was understood in terms of preserving the unity of the church. For that cause – *the spiritual unity of the church* – Valliere suggests that there *is* in fact a vital role for confession as a basis for unity as the common good. Citing both Raymond Brown and James D.G. Dunn[491], Valliere notes that among the diversity of ecclesiologies among the New Testament churches and early Christian

---

[490] Ibid, at 4.

[491] Raymond Brown, *The Churches the Apostles Left Behind* (New York and Ramsey NJ: Paulist Press, 1984) and James D.G. Dunn, *Unity and Diversity in the New Testament: An Inquiry into the Character of Earliest Christianity,* 2nd ed. (London: SCM Press, 1990)

cosmopolitanism the point of unity was one of *belief*, a confession of the unity between the historical Jesus and the exalted Christ, and a "convergence of all sources upon a Christological center" of the church and its common good, the very outline that we find in Philippians 2:1-11[492]

The common good of the Church under the authority of Philippians 2:1-11 is *ontological.* No "body" can function without a mind. And to "have this mind in you which was in Christ Jesus" (2:5) is to have the mind of the Church (*consensus fidelium*) shaped and filled by the mind of Christ who, in relation to the Father, "considered not equality with God something to be grasped, but made himself nothing." (Phil. 2:6-7) Therefore the life of any Council has the validity of which Schmemann and others speak when the life and the expression of the council bears as close a resemblance as possible to the mind of Jesus Christ which displays the perichoretic life of belonging, giving, mutually submitting and interdependence that we find among the Father, the Son and the Holy Spirit themselves.

The common good of the Church under the authority of Philippians 2:1-11 is also *phenomenological* (practical.) That disagreeing apostles, prophets and teachers in the

---

[492]Valliere [n8] 35-36. The most direct example of this was the Council of Chalcedon (451AD) which focused on the core Christological issue of the divine and human nature of Jesus Christ, the largest representation of any of the seven Ecumenical Council, and seventeen plenary sessions over three weeks to provide ample opportunity for serious debate. Ibid, 84-85. For Philippians 2:5-11 as the earliest extant statement of the whole outline of Christology hailing and confessing Christ as pre-existent, then as incarnate and humiliated, and finally as triumphant, see Ralph Martin, *Carmen Christi: Philippians 2:5-11 in Recent Interpretation and in the setting of early Christian worship* (Grand Rapids, MI: Eerdmans Publishing, 1983) (First published 1967 as Volume 4 in the Society for New Testament Studies Monograph Series by the Syndics of the Cambridge University Press, London)

early Church had to humbly "empty themselves," come together to seek Christ's mind for the church and submit to a common mind indicates that a confession like Philippians 2:5-11 was at the heart of the common good, shaping the very practice of conciliarism,[493] and even leading synods and councils unable to agree among themselves to find that one mind of Christ, to consult with Archbishops and Primates, and the teachings of the wider Church until they find that one mind of Christ.[494]

Finally, the common good of the church under Philippians 2:1-11 is also *missional.* For the end is that "at the name of Jesus every knee should bow… and every tongue confess that Jesus Christ is Lord, to the glory of God the Father." (Phil. 2:10-11).

Given the early provenance of this hymn, its function in guarding the Christological center of the undivided Chuch, its call to have "the mind of Christ" in the mind of the Church, shaped by the very mind and life of Jesus himself in his display of the relationships within the Godhead, and the practical authority this text would have had on the life and expression of those participating in councils, this text seems a kind of "north star" among many texts for the shaping of conciliar governance, the common good and communion together.

---

[493] Valliere [n8], at 48, 68.

[494] See, e.g., South East Asia, [n99], Constit. Fundamental Declarations 4 and 5, at 3: If any questions arises re faith and order or principles of worship herein, Provincial Synod may consult with the Archbishop of Canterbury or the Primates of the Anglican Communion as appropriate, and shall give due weight to the traditions and teachings of the Communion.

Acknowledgements

I freely admit that I am peering from behind the shoulders of giants in the history and development of conciliarism as a model for decision making in the church: Brian Tierney, Francis Oakley, Paul Avis, Gerald Bray, Colin Podmore and Paul Valliere, to name but a few.

I which to thank all those who provided current constitution and canons for primary research into the principles and practices of Anglican conciliarism elsewhere in the Communion. My heatfelt thanks to Registrar Abraham Yisa and Mr. Gbenga Fatoye of the Church of Nigeria; the Right Rev. Rennis Ponniah and Ms. Stephanie Ng of the Province of the Church of Southeast Asia (Diocese of Singapore); and Dr. Catherine Smith, and Ms. Tracey Taggert, of the Church of Ireland.

I am especially indebted to Dr. Steven Noll for all of his recent work on Communion Governance and the proposed Anglican Communion Covenant, and to Dr. Martin Davie for sharing his original research into the history and development of the Lambeth Conferences of Bishops from 1867 to the present.

I give special thanks to Dr. Norman Doe of the Cardiff University Law School and his lectures on Canon Law. Without his inspiration, challenge, humor, encouragement and helpful critique all along the way, this work would not have been possible. Nor would it have been possible without the generous support of the of the Trustees and staff of the American Anglican Council.

Finally, I give great thanks to Bishop David Anderson, my mentor and friend, for his inspiration and wisdom, especially in the hard places.

Ecclesia Semper Reformanda est

About the Author

Phil Ashey grew up in a Christian home, his father a priest in the Episcopal Church and both his father and mother involved in Charismatic renewal and healing ministries within the Church. Phil gave his life to Christ in 1968 at St.James Episcopal Church in Newport Beach, California. In 1981 Phil married Julie Einarsson and they now have four children who have also given their lives to Christ.

Phil leads the American Anglican Council (AAC), a missionary society devoted since 1996 to developing Biblically faithful leaders, equipping local congregations and their leaders to fulfill Christ's Great Commission (Matthew 18:16-20), and the renewal of Anglican Churches at every level within the Church. From 1987 to 2008 he served fulltime as a parish priest and church planter in congregations of all sizes in California, Virginia and Pittsburgh. In 2008 he joined the AAC, but he continues to serve as a pastor, preacher, teacher and discipler in local Anglican congregations and across North America.

Before his ordination Phil was a Deputy District Attorney in Orange County, California. He completed his undergraduate degree at Stanford University, law degree at Loyola Law School (Los Angeles), his Master of Divinity at General Theological Seminary in New York, and received his LLM in Canon Law from Cardiff University (Wales).

APPENDIX

How TEC and ACNA Compare and Contrast in the Principles and Practice of Conciliarism

Out of the ashes of conflict, division, disorder and litigation in the Anglican Communion there have emerged in North America two main expressions of Anglicanism—The Episcopal Church (USA) and the new Anglican Church in North America. One of the conclusions of this study is that the new Anglican Church in North America is organized more faithfully around the principles and practice of Anglican conciliarism than The Episcopal Church USA. But we need to test that hypothesis against the laws of each church in regard to the eleven fundamental principles of conciliarism that we identified in Chapter Two, and that we found evident in other representative Churches of the Anglican Communion in Chapter Three.

So let us examine the laws of each of these Churches, and two of their respective dioceses (Atlanta and Los Angeles), principle by principle, practice by practice.

1. THAT SYNODOL GOVERNMENT IS NECESSARY, REGULAR AND PERMAMENT

Each church, province and diocese has an assembly, namely a synod, council or other body, the function of which is to govern.[495] In the governing documents of both The Episcopal Church (TEC) and the Anglican Church in North America (ACNA), synodical government is a necessary, regular and permanent feature of church governance. In both Churches, the dioceses meet annually – TEC Atlanta in "Council," TEC Los Angeles in "Convention," ACNA Anglican Diocese of the South (ADOTS) in "Synod" and ACNA Western Anglicans in a "House of Delegates."[496] But whereas TEC has its "General Convention" once every three years, ACNA holds its "Provincial Council" annually, and adds a larger gathering called "Provincial Assembly" which meets not less than once every five years to strengthen the Church in its mission and to ratify all constitutional amendments and canons affirmed by Provincial Council.[497]

Both TEC's "General Convention" and ACNA's "Provincial Council" have the authority to propose and enact legislation. But whereas TEC defines either House of Convention has having such power, ACNA makes no such distinction. Rather, it is the Provincial Council as a whole

---

[495] *PCLCCAC,* [n17], Principle 15.6.

[496] *Constitution and Canons for The Episcopal Church, Adopted in General Conventions 1789-2012* [n335], Constit. I.7; *The Constitution of the Diocese of Atlanta, as Adopted by the Council of the Diocese 1987 and amended 2011* [n335], Constit. II.3 ("Council"); *The Constitution and Canons of the Church in the Diocese of Los Angeles, adopted 1896 and 2011* [n335], Constit. V.9-10 ("Convention"); *The Anglican Church in North America Constitution and Canons, as ratified by the inaugural Provincial Assembly 2009 and revised 2014* [n335], Constit. IV.6, VII and Cans.I.1.1, 3; *Constitution and Canons of the Anglican Diocese of the South* [n335], Constit. IV.1 and Can.I.5.1 ("synod"); *The Constitution and Canons of the Diocese of Western Anglicans* [n335], Constit. II and Can.I.2.01 ("House of Delegates")

[497] ACNA, [n335], Constit. VI.1-2 and Can. I.2 "Of the Assembly"

that has such authority, subject to ratification by Provincial Assembly.[498]

Another distinction lies in the powers of each national synodal body. Whereas the ACNA specifically enumerates the "Areas of Provincial Responsibility" in its Constitution, reserving those rights not enumerated to the dioceses as a matter of subsidiarity, there is no comparable provision in the Constitution of TEC.[499] Moreover, any change in those enumerated powers of ACNA are further subject to ratification by Provincial Assembly, and otherwise by canon.[500] Nevertheless, both the TEC General Convention and the ACNA Provincial Council have the authority to approve the formation of dioceses,[501] as well as the

---

[498] See *PCLCCAC,* [n17], Principle 19.1: "The power to legislate is vested in the representative assemblies of a church." Compare TEC, [n335], Constit. I.1 with ACNA. [n335], Constit. VII.1.

[499] See ACNA, [n220], Constit. V, VIII.

[500] Ibid., Can. I.1.1: Such changes subject to majority vote by Provincial Assembly; Council may affirm covenants with other Christians entered into by Archbishop for the Church, and shall consider and report on any matter referred by Assembly, Executive Committee or a Diocese. This enumerated power is also well within the jurisdiction of Provincial Council as the central legislative assembly of the Church, see *PCLCCAC,* [n17], Principle 13.4: "It is within the jurisdiction of the central assembly of a church to regulate relationships between the church and other churches of the Anglican Communion."

[501]See *PCLCCAC,* [n17], Principle 20.3: "Formation, alteration or suppression of a diocese is in the keeping of the central church assembly and may be effected in such cases and manner as are allowed by law." Compare TEC, [n335], Constit. V.1, V.5 and Can. I.10.1-6 with ACNA, [n335], Constit. IV.2 and Can. I.5.1-2, 5. Both Churches include minimum requirements and processes for forming a diocese, and either prior recommendation and/or approval by the Executive Committee. But whereas TEC requires in V.1 "Unqualified accession to the constitution and canons of this Church," ACNA requires only that the Vestry of each congregation forming the diocese has "subscribed to the Constitution and Canons of the Anglican Church in North America." See Constit. "Appendix: Application to the Provincial Council for Recognition as a New Diocese," question 9a.

processes for electing a diocesan bishop, coadjutor or suffragan.[502] With regard to the conciliar principle that neither the bishops nor the synod shall take action without consulting each other, TEC requires that all acts of the Convention shall be adopted by both Houses, that of Bishops and that of Deputies.[503] The dioceses of Atlanta and Los Angeles are silent on the matter. In the ACNA, both Provincial Council and Assembly function as unicameral bodies and therefore require concurrence in the affirmative from all three orders. But the Anglican Diocese of the South and Western Anglicans are as silent on the matter as their TEC counterparts.

In both TEC and ACNA, the permanence of the Church's synodal gatherings at the national and diocesan levels is made manifest through the creation of an Executive body that carries on the work of the synod between its meetings.[504] These executive bodies of the

---

[502] Compare TEC, [n335], Constit. II.1, 9: Bishops are chosen according to rules prescribed by the Convention of that Diocese, no requirement for prior permission from TEC House of Bishops, and compulsory retirement age, and ACNA [n335], Can. III.8.4: Bishops are chosen by rules prescribed by the ACNA canons, requiring prior consent of ACNA College of Bishops to proceed to an election, election in conformance with constitution and canons of both Diocese and the Church, certification of one nominee for consent by ACNA College of Bishops or two to three nominees for choice and consent, and no compulsory retirement age.

[503] TEC, [n335], Constit. I.1.

[504] TEC, [n335], Constit. IV (Standing Committee of the Diocese) and Can. I.4 (Executive Council of General Convention; *Diocese of Atlanta,* [n229], Constit. IV, Can. 3 "Of the Standing Committee," but see *Diocese of Los Angeles* [n335], Cans. XIV (Standing Committee as Council of Advice or Ecclesiastical Authority) and XIX (Diocesan Council carries on work of the Convention between annual meetings); ACNA [n335], Constit. VII.10 and Can. I.1.4 "Concerning the Executive Committee"; *Anglican Diocese of the South,* [n335], Constit. VIII (Standing Committee) and *Diocese of Western Anglicans,* [n335], Constit. Definitions (Executive Committee of the House of Delegates).

synod are the equivalent of the Standing Committees we find in other Anglican Churches. Like them, the powers of the TEC Executive Council and ACNA Executive Committee are broad enough to implement the program, policies and budget decided by General Convention and Provincial Council, respectively.[505] However, in TEC, those powers include the broad right to develop "new work deemed necessary" by the Executive Council, whereas the powers of the ACNA Executive Committee are both enumerated and dispersed throughout the canons.[506] At the diocesan level, in both TEC and ACNA the executive bodies also have broad powers to carry on the work of their respective diocesan synods between meetings—although at least one TEC diocese has the same broad powers as the Executive Council of General Convention.[507]

[505] Compare TEC, [n335], Can. I.4: Executive Council shall carry out the program and policies of General Convention, coordinate, develop and implement ministry and mission of the Church, by members elected from Convention for terms "twice the interval" between Conventions," with ACNA, [n335], Constit. VII.10 and Cans. I.1.4 and I.14: Executive Committee is the Board of Directors for the Church, who serve no more than two consecutive three year terms, and who set the program, agenda and budget for annual Provincial Council.

[506] TEC, [n335], Can.I.4.2 (e). Compare with the enumerated responsibilities of Executive Committee (EC) dispersed throughout the constitution and canons in ACNA [n335], Cans. I.9.2 (Sets financial and accounting standards for the Church), I.5.1 (Prior approval of an application for new diocese before Council may proceed to approve), I.5.7 (review sustainability of existing dioceses and make recommendations to Council), I.11 (Receive annual reports of Special Jurisdiction of Armed Forces and Chaplaincy and approve amendments to its constitution and canons or not), I.12 (Together with Bishops recommend to Council establishing Missionary Districts), and Constit. XIV (Provide warning to a diocese before removal from membership in the Church by a 2/3 majority vote of Council).

[507] TEC, [n335], Constit. IV: Rights and duties of Standing Committees prescribed by Diocesan Constitution and canons; *Diocese of Atlanta,* [n335],

2. THAT THE WHOLE CHURCH IS REPRESENTED IN SYNOD

In both Churches, synodal gatherings are representative of the whole Church, with bishops, clergy and laity participating as full members and sharing authority in synodal government.[508] At the provincial level, clergy and

---

Constit. IV and Can. 3: Standing Committee is the council of advice to the sitting bishop, Ecclesiastical Authority in the absence of a sitting bishop, and reports its activity at annual meeting of Council; and *Diocese of Los Angeles* [n220], Cans. XIV.29-30, 32 and XX.03: Same as Atlanta except powers must be in conformance with the constitution and canons of the Church. But see Can. XIX "Diocesan Council" which gives this executive body similar powers to that of the Executive Council of General Convention—not only the power to initiate new work in areas not addressed by Convention, but even power to cancel the arrears of parishes and missions that would otherwise prevent them from having seat and voice at Convention. Compare with ACNA [n335], Can. I.5.3: Diocesan Standing committee is the council of advice for the bishop, Ecclesiastical Authority in his absence, and with powers otherwise established by Diocesan constitution and canons; *Anglican Diocese of the South,* [n335], Constit., VIII (same powers as ACNA Can. I.5.3) and IX: May establish ad hoc committees upon request of Bishop to study and report on matters assigned by him. See also Cans. I.8, 14: Standing Committee establishes the program and budget of the Diocese; *Diocese of Western Anglicans* [n335], Can. I.3.01 (same powers as ACNA Can. I.5.3). But see Can. I.3.03: May establish committees and task forces upon their own initiative, without bishop's request, because such committees and task forces are "creatures of the Executive Committee." These powers of delegation are also in keeping with *PCLCCAC,* [n17], Principle 17.4: So long as the delegation is not of powers vested in the Standing Committee alone and is "carried out with care, with the consent of those to whom the function is delegated, and in the manner and to the extent prescribed by law."

[508] See *PCLCCAC,* [n17], Principle 15.9, 18.1: "In matters which touch all, all should have a voice." TEC, [n335], Constit. I.1; *Diocese of Atlanta,* [n335], Constit. II.1-2, and *Diocese of Los Angeles,* [n335], Constit. VI.13-15 and Cans. XII-XIII; ACNA, [n335], Cans. I.1.2 and I.1.3 (Representation by diocese, including all three orders, in both Provincial Council and Assembly), *Anglican Diocese of the South,* [n335], Constit. IV.2 (a), and *Diocese of Western Anglicans,* [n335], Cans. I.2.02-03: House of Delegates includes clergy and laity, no mention of bishop.

laity participate in equal numbers in TEC General Convention, and in both ACNA Provincial Council and Assembly.[509] But in both Churches, the dioceses provide greater representation for the laity in diocesan synodal gatherings according to communicant status and/or the size of the congregations.[510]

3. THAT THE MIND OF THE CHURCH IS DISCERNED IN A RIGOROUS SYNODAL PROCESS

The mind of the Church (*consensus fidelium*) on faith, order, worship and other matters important and controversial, manifests through a rigorous synodal process. In the Church of England and the other representative Anglican Churches in this study, there is a

---

[509] See *PCLCCAC,* [n17], Principles 18.2: "The central assembly of a church, and the assembly of a province or diocese, consists of representative bishops, clergy and laity," and 18.3: "Central, provincial and diocesan assemblies consist of houses, orders or other cameral systems which represent their episcopal, clerical and lay character"; TEC, [n335], Constit. I.4: up to four clergy and four laity for each diocese represented at General Convention; ACNA, [n335], Cans. I.1.2 and I.1.3: one bishop, one clergy, and two lay delegates for every diocese represented at Provincial Council. Same for Provincial Assembly with addition of one more clergy and one more lay delegate per diocese for every additional 1,000 ASA. But see Can. I.1.4 which also allows addition of one youth delegate per diocese for every additional 1,000 ASA, which would make lay representation potentially greater in Provincial Assembly.

[510] See *PCLCCAC,* [n17], Principle 22.3-4: "Lay participation in church government is subject to the conditions prescribed in the law of a church as to eligibility, membership, selection and admission. Communicant status is a normal requirement of eligibility." In the TEC *Diocese of Atlanta* [n335], Constit. II.2 and *Diocese of Los Angeles,* [n335], Constit.VI.16, lay delegates are apportioned according to the number of reported communicants in good standing in each congregation. In the ACNA *Anglican Diocese of the South,* [n335], Can. I.2.2 and the *Diocese of Western Anglicans,* [n335], Can. I.2.03, the apportionment of lay delegates is according to the Average Sunday Attendance (ASA) reported 90 days prior to the annual meeting of Synod and the House of Delegates, respectively.

"posture" for discerning the mind of the whole Church on such important and controversial matters. It is the posture of all orders of the Church in Synod seated, deliberating and voting together – at least until a vote by orders is called. We find this posture in the ACNA Provincial Council and Assembly, where there is no provision for meeting separately, much less voting by orders.[511] The one and only exception to this is in Provincial Council, where a vote by orders is taken to approve the same order on the Court for the Trial of a Bishop, and even then to do so only when the Council is in session as a whole.[512] We also find this posture in the ACNA dioceses, where deliberation and voting is unicameral, even when there is a vote by orders.[513] The same is true for the dioceses of TEC.[514]

This is not the case for the TEC General Convention. In fact, the House of Bishops and the House of Deputies (clergy and laity) are required by Constitution to "sit and deliberate separately."[515] There are only two exceptions to

---

[511] ACNA, [n335], Can. I.1.3: Meetings of Provincial Council shall be conducted under rules approved by the Council. No provision for voting by orders or deliberating separately, and Can. I.2.2: The Assembly shall function as a unicameral body.

[512] Ibid., Can. IV.5.2: "The members of this Court shall be elected by the Provincial Council, each Order electing its representatives by majority vote of that Order."

[513] See *Anglican Diocese of the South,* [n335], Constit. IV.6: "The Synod shall deliberate and vote as one body," except as otherwise provided; *Diocese of Western Anglicans,* [n335], Can. I.2.05: Always unicameral, clergy and laity voting together on all matters.

[514] See *Diocese of Atlanta,* [n335], Constit. II.5: Diocesan Council shall deliberate and act as one body unless otherwise required by constitution or canon, or unless a vote by orders is requested; *Diocese of Los Angeles* [n335], Constit. XVII.38: In all matters before Convention, the clergy and the laity shall deliberate together, and vote together unless a separate vote is requested by any five members of Convention.

[515] TEC, [n335], Constit. I.1.1

this rule – joint sessions of both Houses to consider budget and nominees for Presiding Bishop at a Convention scheduled for such an election.[516] This separation is reinforced by rules that govern the communications between the House of Deputies and the House of Bishops and their priority in the daily order of business.[517] This separation seems at odds with the principle at work in other Churches of seeking the mind of the whole Church together in one sitting.

Unlike the Churches of Australia, Nigeria and Ireland, neither TEC, ACNA nor their dioceses require bishops to wait for the vote of the laity and the clergy in order to discern the mind of the Church.

TECs' General Convention and ACNA's Provincial Council have different thresholds for discerning the mind of the Church when matters are neither extraordinary nor controversial – because they do not involve faith, doctrine, worship or the order of the Church (such as amendments to its constitution and canons). In TEC, such ordinary matters may be resolved in the affirmative by a simple majority of all the Deputies present in the House of Deputies and the Bishops in the House of Bishops. However, if there is a vote by orders in the House of Deputies, both the majority of the clergy and the laity must vote in the affirmative within their order, the votes counted separately in each order, the diocese having one collective vote for each order, and with concurrence in the

[516]Ibid, Cans. I.4.6 (f) (for budget) and I.2.1 (e-f) (Presentation by Nominating Committee of Nominees for Presiding Bishop). See *The Task Force for Re-Imagining the Episcopal Church, Resolution A002* in <http://www.generalconvention.org/gc/2015-resolutions/A002/original_english_text> Accessed 26 October 2015, which calls for the Amendment of I.1.1 and the creation of a unicameral General Convention in which "all members shall meet together as one body."
[517] TEC, [n335], Rules of Order for the House of Bishops, Daily Orders I (8).

affirmative by a majority of the diocese present in that order.[518] In the House of Bishops, there is a consent calendar which "fast tracks" such majority votes.[519]

By contrast, *all legislation* coming from the ACNA Provincial Council, whether ordinary or special, initiated by bishops or not, must be ratified by Provincial Assembly.[520] This Assembly has the authority only to affirm or reject such legislation, and if rejected the legislation simply goes back to Provincial Council for

---

[518] TEC, [n335], Constit. I.5, "Unless a greater vote" is required by TEC constitution or canons. It could be argued that since any two deputies in each order can prevent such an affirmative vote as required in each order, that this represents an inherent "brake" on legislation that does not reflect the mind of the Church; see also Rules of Order for the House of Deputies, XI: Voting, Rule 44: The 2/3 requirement is a collective 2/3 when not voting in orders, and satisfied by a majority vote of ¾ within each order when voting by orders. But see Podmore, *A Tale of Two Churches* [n81] at 130 who argues that quite the opposite is true: "a motion only passes if a majority of the dioceses vote in favor. This means that if opinions are evenly distributed across the church as a whole, a 75 per cent majority is effectively required, but if there were a majority of 3-1 in each of 56 of the 110 dioceses (that is, 168 people in favour), the motion would be passed even if all of the other deputies in that order (which could be as many as 272 people) voted against. *This voting arrangement suggests a lack of weight or 'ecclesial density' at the national level: ultimately. The House of deputies is an assembly of deputations of diocesan churches, and, in that sense, the General Convention is not the synod of a single Church."* (Emphasis added).

[519] Ibid., Rules of Order for the House of Bishops, Daily Orders VI: placed on calendar by Legislative Committee of Bishops upon ¾ vote to adopt (with or without amendments) discharge or reject, heard and voted on after 12noon the day following placement on calendar and no debate is in order. A matter may be removed from consent calendar by objection of any 3 bishops, sponsor or Committee on dispatch of business and placed back on daily regular calendar.

[520] ACNA, [n335], Constit. VI.2; Can.I.2.2.

further consideration.[521] In this sense, Assembly functions as a second level of discerning the mind of the Church on *all legislation* just as the Church of England Houses of Laity and Clergy do so with regards to special matters of faith and order proposed by the House of Bishops – ratifying or rejecting proposals exactly as presented by the Bishops "and not otherwise."[522]

In the dioceses of both Churches, a simple majority vote of the whole synod, or by orders, is required for any matter unless otherwise provided by constitution or canon.[523]

When it comes to important and controversial matters including faith, worship and order, the only overlap TEC and ACNA have is in the area of amending constitution and canons. In both Churches there is a rigorous procedure for such amendments with some differences between them in the notice required, the majorities required at General Convention vs. Provincial Council, and subsequent review. In both Churches the requirements for amending the constitution are higher than for amending canons.[524] In the TEC dioceses constitutional

[521] Ibid, Can I.2.2: "The role of the Assembly in the governance of the Church is to ratify the Constitution and canons and any amendments adopted by the Council. Matters not ratified shall be returned to the Council for further consideration." See also *Diocese of Western Anglicans,* [n335], Can. I.2.06: where actions of the Executive Committee are subject to a simple vote of ratification, and if there is no ratification, the matter is referred back to the Executive Committee for further consideration.
[522] See discussion in Chapter 2, Principle 3.
[523] *Diocese of Atlanta,* [n335], Constit. II.5 and *Diocese of Los Angeles,* [n335], Constit. XVII.38; *Anglican Diocese of the South,* [n335], Constit. IV.6 and *Diocese of Western Anglicans,* [n335], Can. I.2.07(c).
[524] TEC, [n335], Constit. XII: First notice of proposal to amend Constitution at General Convention, then notice to dioceses, then affirmative majority vote of Bishops and by orders in Deputies per Art. I.5 at next General Convention, and Can. V.1: when amending canons, concurrent resolution of the two Houses of GC, introduced first in either House, then referred to

amendments require two successive votes of the synod by a simple majority. Amendments to canons require a referral to the diocesan Committee on Constitution and Canons for ireview, further amendments, and recommendations.[525]

In the ACNA dioceses, *The Anglican Diocese of the South* requires two successive votes of the synod by simple majority to approve constitutional amendments, while the *Diocese of Western Anglicans* requires only one – but both by a 2/3 majority of all delegates entitle to vote.[526] In

---

Committee on Canons in each House for report and recommendation, unless ¾ of each House votes to proceed, and adoption by a simple majority of both Houses; ACNA, [n335], Constit. XV: Amendment of the Constitution requires a 2/3 majority of all members present and voting at any regular or special meeting of Provincial Assembly, and Can. V.1.1: Amendment of the Canons requires majority vote of the Provincial Council and ratification by a majority vote of Provincial Assembly.

[525] Compare TEC *Diocese of Atlanta,* [n335], Constit. 8: Amendment to Constitution, if adopted by simple majority of Council, lies over to next Council where it becomes effective if adopted again by a simple majority, and Can. 45.2: Amendment and additions to Canons must be received by Committee on Constitution and Canons no less than 30 days prior to Council, recommendations made and adoption by simple majority; and *Diocese of Los Angeles,* [n335], Constit. XX.47: Proposed alteration, amendment or addition filed with Secretary of Convention at least 100 days before Convention, or if submitted at Convention with 2/3 approval, then referred to next annual Meeting of Convention where it may be amended at that convention before vote by orders, with a majority in each order, and concurred in by Bishop, and Can. XXXIV: Proposed amendment of Canons filed with Secretary of Convention at least 100 days before Convention or if submitted at Convention by unanimous consent, then referred to Committee on Constitution and Canons, then may be amended to the Report of the Committee at a next or succeeding annual Convention before vote, then Committee may modify the proposed Canon and others for consistency and, finally, affirmative vote by a majority of the delegates.

[526] Compare ACNA *Anglican Diocese of the South,* [n335], Constit. XVI: Two successive votes at Synod by 2/3 majority, and *Diocese of Western Anglicans,* [n335], Constit. VI: 2/3 vote of all delegates present at any

amendments to the canons, *Anglican Diocese of the South* also requires submission first to the diocesan Committee on Constitution and Canons, while *Western Anglicans* does not – but, again, both require a 2/3 majority vote to ratify such changes.[527]

While the synods of both Churches do provide rigorous procedures for the formation and dissolution of dioceses, there are differences in subject matter between the two. In TEC, General Convention has final approval by 2/3 majority of the cession of territory to new dioceses and retrocession of territory when a diocese is dissolved.[528] In ACNA, Provincial Council has final authority to modify the minimum requirements for forming a diocese, as well as to remove from membership an existing diocese.[529]

But there are other differences in subject matter and the pathway by which changes in the faith, worship and order are affirmed by the mind of the Church. In TEC, the election of a Presiding Bishop is subject to the concurrence

---

regular or special meeting of the House of Delegates called for that purpose.

[527] Compare ACNA *Anglican Diocese of the South,* [n335], Can. VI.1 with *Diocese of Western Anglicans,* [n335], Can. VII.I.02

[528] TEC, [n335], Constit. VI.2: First, by ¾ vote of parishes in the ceded or retroceded area, then by ¾ vote of parishes in the originating diocese, then by 2/3 majority of both Houses at General Convention, including 2/3 majority in each order of each diocese present in House of Deputies. See also *Anglican Diocese of the South,* [n335], Can. VI.2, which requires prior approval by 2/3 present and voting at Synod to merge, dissolve, transfer or encumber the Diocese; and *Diocese of Western Anglicans,* [n335], Can. I.1.01: Addition or removal of congregations, with our without cause, upon recommendation/approval of Bishop and 2/3 majority vote of Executive Council.

[529] ACNA, [n335], Can. I.5.1: Modification of minimums only upon recommendation by Executive Committee and 2/3 ratification by Provincial Council; Constit. XIV: removal only after "due warning" to diocese by Executive Committee and 2/3 majority vote of the members of any two of the three orders.

of both Houses of General Convention, whereas there is no such requirement in ACNA, where the election of the Archbishop is within the powers of the College of Bishops alone.[530] Likewise, in TEC, alterations and additions to the Book of Common Prayer are subject to notice to all dioceses and final approval by General Convention, whereas in ACNA such alterations or additions are not, but are again within the powers of the College of Bishops alone.[531]

While both Churches require the mind of the whole Church when electing a diocesan bishop, in ACNA the "*consensus fidelium*" is limited to prior permission from the College of Bishops before an election may be held, and consent by the College to a choice or "choice and consent"

---

[530] Compare TEC, [n335], Constit. I.3: Election first by majority of Bishops, subject to "confirmation of House of Deputies". But in case of resignation, infirmity or death, by special meeting of House of Bishops by majority vote concurred in by majority of the Standing Committees of the dioceses; and ACNA, [n335], Constit. X.2: The College of Bishops shall elect the Archbishop from among its members, and Can. I.3.2: They shall do so during the week immediately prior to the Provincial Council and Assembly marking the end of his term. No ratification or confirmation required by Council or Assembly.

[531] Compare TEC, [n335], Constit. X and Can. I.1.1 (e): First proposed in a session of GC, then notice given to all dioceses of the change at next meeting of their diocesan councils, then at next regular session of General Convention by majority of Bishops entitled to vote and by a vote by orders of Deputies per Art. **I.5** with an affirmative in each order in a majority of the dioceses entitled to vote. But Trial use only requires majority of bishops and clerical and lay deputies voting by orders; and ACNA, [n335], Constit. X.1 and Can. III.8.2: Bishops are guardians and teachers of the faith, doctrine and order of the Church. No provision in the constitution and canons for Council or Assembly to review alterations or additions to the services of the Church.

to nominees sent from the diocese.[532] By contrast, TEC establishes the "consensus fidelium" after election only, by consents from the majority of Standing Committees of the dioceses and bishops having jurisdiction.[533] However, the dioceses of both Churches provide generally for a Standing or Executive Committee of the synod to establish the process and timeline for nominating and electing, by a majority vote of all members present and entitled to vote at synod.[534]

In short, the same rigorous procedures to establish the mind of the Church that we find in other Churches are evident in both TEC and ACNA – including a certain legislative pathway that includes a requirement of the forum in which important matters are raised, and an order in which those matters must be reviewed. Where TEC and

[532] Compare ACNA, [n335], Cans. III.8.4.1: prior consent of College before a diocese may commence election, and III.8.4.4-5: Diocese certifies election of bishop, or 2-3 nominees, to College of Bishops for 2/3 majority vote to consent, or for choice and consent, within 60 days.

[533] TEC [n335], Constit. II.1-2: Bishop chosen "agreeably to rules of prescribed by the convention of that diocese," must receive the consents of 2/3 of the Standing Committees of the diocese and 2/3 of the Bishops having jurisdiction within the Church before ordination and consecration.

[534] See TEC *Diocese of Atlanta,* [n335], Can. 43: Standing Committee of Council initiates, majority in each order elects by concurrent ballot, and *Diocese of Los Angeles,* [n335], Constit. XX.44: Standing Committee of Convention initiates, majority of each order if 2/3 entitled to vote are present, otherwise 2/3 vote in each order by concurrent ballot; See ACNA *Anglican Diocese of the South,* [n335], Constit. V.3: Standing Committee of Synod decides by majority vote whether it will be an election and request for consent by ACNA College of Bishops, or choice and consent to a number of nominees, with election by majority in each order of Synod voting concurrently, and *Diocese of Western Anglicans,* [n335], Can. II.4: Executive Committee appoints a Nominating Committee from its membership and House of Delegates to nominate, vet and recommend a slate of nominees to the House of Delegates for approval and recommendation to ACNA College of Bishops for consent and choice.

ACNA differ most is in the alteration of the services of the Church and in the election of its bishops. In TEC, these matters are within the subject matter jurisdiction of General Convention, and include notice to dioceses of alterations to the services of the Church, and consent from the dioceses for the election of bishops. In ACNA both worship and episcopal elections are in the subject matter jurisdiction of the College of Bishops alone. This suggests that ACNA places more trust in its bishops alone to discern the *consensus fidelium* than TEC, and raises the question why the ACNA does not include among all matters subject to ratification by Provincial Assembly alterations to the doctrine and worship of the Church by its bishops, as well as consent to episcopal elections? For in all other matters, the ACNA has a second level of review of all matters coming out of Provincial Council – both ordinary and special –by the Assembly, a body which is even more representative of all orders of the Church than Provincial Council.

4. That Bishops Have a Particular Role as Guardians of the Faith, Order and Liturgy

Bishops have a particular role as the guardians of the faith and order of the Church and of its liturgy. This conciliar principle is negligible within TEC. The Presiding Bishop *may* from time to time issue "Pastoral Letters," and a diocesan Bishop *may* deliver a charge to the clergy or a "Pastoral Letter" to the people on points of doctrine, discipline and worship. The diocesan bishop may even require the "Pastoral Letter" to be read by the clergy to their congregations. But there is no hint of guarding such doctrine, discipline and order.[535] Instead, both the

[535] TEC, [n335], Cans. I.2.4(b): reports and Pastoral Letters of the Presiding Bishop, and III.12.4(b): Of the life and work of a Bishop

Presiding Bishop and bishops diocesan are defined almost entirely by their administrative duties in relation to clergy and congregations in Title III, and their duty to apply ecclesiastical discipline in Title IV. The Presiding Bishop is Chief Pastor and Primate, leads in policy and strategy, speaks Gods word to Church and to world, represents the Church and episcopate "in its corporate capacity", provides interim Episcopal services for dioceses, convenes bishops and visits every diocese, and more. But there is nothing in the job description about guarding the faith and order of the Church.[536]

Likewise the duties of a Bishop Diocesan, Coadjutor, Suffragan or Assisting prescribed by canon are administrative. They include visiting congregations, recording episcopal acts, making annual reports and licensing visiting bishops to officiate.[537] In the TEC *Diocese of Los Angeles* the Bishop is the Ecclesiastical Authority of the Diocese, Chief Pastor, Ordinary of all organizations, issuer of Pastoral letters, and resolver of all disputes. The bishop has power to appoint various commissions and task forces "as seem necessary for the Mission of the Church," including a Commission on Church Architecture on which he or she sits to approve or reject any new building plans of churches, chapels or parish halls.[538] None of these descriptions includes guarding the faith and order of the Church.

By contrast, the role of bishops in the ACNA is rich in constitution and canons with the reaffirmation of the bishop's role as guardian of the faith and order of the

---

[536] Ibid., Can. I.2.4 (1-6).
[537] Ibid., Can. III.12.3 (a).
[538] See *Diocese of Los Angeles,* [n335], Constit. IV and Can. XVIII.01-05. *The Diocese of Atlanta* has no provision within its constitution or canons defining the duties of a Bishop.

Church. Specifically, the Constitution provides that the chief work of the College of Bishops shall be "the propagation and defense of the Faith and Order of the Church, and in service as the visible sign and expression of the Unity of the Church."[539] In the Canons of the Church the bishop is described according to the requirements for "overseers" in I Peter 5:2-3, called to "propagate, to teach, and to uphold the faith of the Church willingly and as God wants him to – not greedy for money, but eager to serve; not lording it over those entrusted to his care, but being a wholesome example to the entire flock of Christ."[540] While bishops also administer "godly discipline and governance" for the Church, their teaching-guardianship role is paramount.[541] This is equally true of the dioceses that reaffirm this paramount role of the bishop and add to it care of the clergy, evangelism and church planting.[542]

---

[539] See ACNA, [n335], Constit. X.1. Within this charge the Archbishop serves as the convener and President of all meetings of Provincial Council and Assembly and the College of Bishops, "represents the Province in the Councils of the Church and carries out such other duties and responsibilities as may be provided by canon." Ibid., IX.3

[540] Ibid., Can. III.8.1. See also Can. III.8.2, *Concerning the Ministry of Bishops:* "They are chief missionaries and chief pastors, guardians and teachers of doctrine, and administrators of godly discipline and governance."

[541] Ibid., Can. III.8.2, *Concerning the Ministry of Bishops:* "They are chief missionaries and chief pastors, guardians and teachers of doctrine, and administrators of godly discipline and governance."

[542] See ACNA *Anglican Diocese of the South,* [n335], Constit. I: "The Bishop Evangelist" will concentrate on four main things: upholding the Holy Scriptures, ministering to the clergy of the diocese, doing the work of an evangelist and overseeing/supervising the planting of churches," and Constit. V: "the Office of Bishop," citing ACNA Cans. III.8.1 and 2. See also *Diocese of Western Anglicans,* [n335], Constit. I: "The Bishop Evangelist" and see also Can. IV.2.03: In the dissolution of a pastoral relationship between clergy and congregation, the Bishop shall "devote generously of his time and attention so that the matter may be resolved as expeditiously as possible, consistent with Godly process and scriptural principles."

There is probably no greater contrast between TEC and ACNA than in this principle role of the bishop as guardian of the faith and order of the Church. For ACNA, this contrast is rooted in the Biblical requirements for the orders of deacons and presbyters, and the additional requirements for the Bishop as an overseer, spelled out in the canons on ministry.[543]

5. THAT DIOCESAN SYNODS ARE LIMITED IN THEIR SCOPE

There is evidence of the principle of subsidiarity: specifically, that diocesan synods are limited in their scope and may not take unilateral action touching upon the faith and order of the Church. A clearer definition of Anglican subsidiarity can be found in the *Windsor Report* (2004) that:

> "(A) central authority should have a subsidiary function, performing only those tasks which cannot be performed effectively at a more immediate or local level." [544]

This principle of the limitation of powers runs both ways, insofar as dioceses are limited in their power as a lower body of the Church to make doctrinal statements and actions that touch upon the whole church. Of course, the dioceses have authority to legislate *for* the diocese.[545] But in TEC the limitation is not so much on the greater authority of General Convention. In fact, the emphasis is on "unqualified accession" by new dioceses to the constitution and canons of the Church.[546] Such unqualified

[543] ACNA, [n335], Can. III.8.1.

[544]The Lambeth Commission on Communion, *The Windsor Report 2004* [n349], at para. 83; see also *The Report of the Inter-Anglican Theological and Doctrinal Commission*: *The Virginia Report* (1997) [297] at sec. 4.8

[545] See *PCLCCAC,* [n17], Principle 20.5.

[546] TEC, [n335], Constit. V.1 and Can. I.10.4 This may be the result of litigation by recently departing dioceses on the grounds that they never made unqualified accession to the constitution and canons of TEC and therefore had the right to withdraw from General Convention.

accession is a condition precedent to General Convention approving a new diocese's governance by its own constitution and canons not inconsistent with those of the Church.[547]

By contrast, In ACNA the powers not specifically delegated to the Province are reserved to the dioceses,[548] and the Constitution of the Church recognizing the inherent right of each diocese to determine its own governance by constitution and canons with powers "not yielded to the Province" by their own consent.[549] One striking example of the limitation of Provincial authority in ACNA is the right of each diocese to make its own decision with regards to the ordination and ministry of women as deacons and presbyters.[550]

Another example of the "top down" authority of the Church in TEC lies in its Canon governing the reunification or merger of dioceses. As a matter of subsidiarity, such reunification or merger of two dioceses into one requires a mutual agreement between the Conventions of the two Dioceses *and* consent by the Ecclesiastical Authority of each Diocese. But the reunification shall not be considered complete until

---

[547] Ibid., Can. I.10.4.

[548] ACNA, [n335], Constit. VIII.1; see also *Anglican Diocese of the South,* [n335], Constit. I: "Submission to the Church": All powers not granted to the Church are reserved to the diocese and its congregations. This decentralization of power may also be the result of litigation by departing congregations and dioceses who sought to make themselves free in the future from any unqualified claims to their property and governance by the Church.

[549] Ibid, VIII.1: "The member dioceses or networks…and those dioceses banded together as jurisdictions shall each retain all authority they do not yield to the Province by their own consent."

[550] Ibid, VIII.2: The Province "shall make no canon abridging the authority of any member dioceses" with regards to women's ordination.

consents have been received from the majority of Bishops with jurisdiction and Standing Committees of *all* the Dioceses of the Church (if the reunification is more than three months before General Convention), and the consents recorded with the Secretary of General Convention – *and* if the reunification is within three months of General Convention by majority vote of the House of Bishops and the House of Deputies voting by orders.[551] Either way, the ultimate approval and control of the process lies in the governing documents of the Church. There is no such provision in ACNA.

By contrast, the governing documents of ACNA have more to say about congregations – and different emphases – than those in TEC. In ACNA, congregations are defined not only by their formal relationship to the Diocese and the Church, but spiritually as a gathering "where the pure Word of God is preached and the sacraments are duly administered," citing Article XIX of the Thirty-Nine Articles.[552] Whereas TEC focuses on the geographical boundaries of a parish or congregation,[553] ACNA focuses on the local congregation as "the fundamental agency of the mission of the Church to extend the Kingdom of God," and the imperative of Church planting "whenever possible" under the spiritual covering, direction and assistance of the Diocese.[554] Whereas TEC imposes a trust

---

[551] TEC, [n335], Can. I.10.6.

[552] ACNA, [n335], Can. I.6.2

[553] TEC, [n335], Can. I.13.2-3: Parish boundaries, Formation of new Parish within limits of existing Parishes vested in Bishop and Standing Committee only, Boundaries of Parishes when not defined by law.

[554] ACNA, [n335], Can. I.6.1: "the chief agents of this mission are the people of God," and Can. 1.6.7: "With the leadership and consent of the Bishop, a diocese and its congregations, clergy and people should, whenever possible, plant new congregations." As a matter of subsidiarity, the section goes on to state that a new church plant will be considered a congregation

on all real and personal property of the local congregation or mission in favor of the Church and the Diocese,[555] ACNA vests all such property ownership in the local congregation, and expressly removes all claims express or implied by the Church or the Diocese.[556] This has led to the corollary declaration in TEC that while people may leave the local congregation, the congregation itself may not leave – while in ACNA congregations as a whole have an express right to transfer to another diocese or leave the

---

"when it meets the criteria for sustainability *as determined by its diocese and Bishop."* (Emphasis added).

[555] TEC, [n335], Can. I.7.4, II.6.4: "The Dennis canon": "All real or personal property held by or for the benefit of any parish, Mission or Congregation is held in trust for this Church and the Diocese thereof in which such parish, Mission or Congregation is located, The existence of this trust, however, shall in no way limit the power and authority of the Parish, Mission or Congregation otherwise existing over such property *so long as the particular Parish, Mission or Congregation remains a part of, and subject to, this Church and its Constitution and Canons."* (Emphasis added). See also *PCLCCAC* [n17], Principle 80.7, which authorizes the central assembly of the church to "frame laws for the management and use of property held in trust for that church." However, Principle 80.2 provides that such property is to be held by authorities who are recognized as trustees or other entities of a fiduciary nature under civil *as well as* church law. The question of who may function under civil law as a trustee, and whether a church can impose such a trust relationship through legislation at its central assembly *without* express permission of the local congregation, has been the subject of much litigation in civil courts in North America.

[556] ACNA, [n335], Can. I.6.6 "Concerning property Ownership": All congregational property, real and personal, owned by a member congregation, is and shall be solely and exclusively owned by the congregation and shall not be subject to any trust in favor of the Province or other claim of ownership arising out of the canon law of the Church; neither may any Diocese assert any such claim over the property of any of its congregations without the express written consent of the congregation. Where property is held in a different manner by any Diocese or grouping, such ownership shall be preserved.

Church altogether.[557] In other respects, such as the existence of vestries, subject to the laws of the State and the Diocese, as legal agents for the local church as a corporation, and the need for an annual/parochial report, the governing laws of the two Churches are very similar.[558]

In short, in TEC subsidiarity runs from the centralization of power and ownership of all property real and personal in the governing bodies of the Church to specific enumerated powers in dioceses, parishes, missions and congregations. But in ACNA, subsidiarity runs in a different direction: from property ownership vested in the local congregations, to all other powers reserved in the diocese that are not enumerated and given to the Province. It reflects a decentralizing authority that reflects a belief that Church governance may be best which is closer to the people who are the chief agents of the mission of the Church.[559] The only "trust" is that which the Church must

---

[557] Ibid., Can. I.6.9: "Concerning Transfer or Withdrawal": "Congregations reserve the right to seek transfer between Dioceses of the Church with the permission of the Bishops involved. Congregations also reserve the right to disaffiliate from the Church after consultation with their Bishop."

[558] Compare TEC, [n335], Can I.14 "Of Parish Vestries" with ACNA, [n335], Cans. I.6.3 "Concerning Organization" and I.65, "Concerning Governing Boards." Both affirm the same set of laws under which vestries or governing boards operate, and that the Rector shall preside at meetings. But TEC canons also specify how long the Wardens and other members shall hold office, while ACNA leaves such matters to diocesan canons and congregational by-laws. Compare also TEC, [n335], Can. I.6 "Of the Mode of Securing an Accurate View of the State of the Church" with ACNA, [n335], Can. I.6.8: "Concerning Annual Reports," where the subject matter and reporting requirement are virtually the same.

[559] See the "Governing Principles" of both *Anglican Diocese of the South,* [n335], Constit. I and *Diocese of Western Anglicans,* [n335], Constit. I, which define "subsidiarity" as follows: "Wisely has the Church chosen the governance principle of subsidiarity, namely, that whatever can wisely be left to the dioceses should be left to the dioceses, and whatever the dioceses can wisely leave to the local congregations should be left to the

earn from its dioceses, and dioceses from its congregations, as they both function as servants to the people in their "Godly mission and work."[560]

6. THAT SYNODAL GOVERNMENNT MUST EXIST AT THE DEANERY, DIOCESAN AND NATIONAL CHURCH LEVELS, AND MAY EXIST AT THE LEVEL OF THE LOCAL CHURCH

In both Churches, synodal government exists at almost all levels of the Church, including the local church. The governing documents of both Churches cited thus far are evidence of synodal government at the "national" and diocesan level. Both Churches also make provision for dioceses to band together into a Province or "sub-jurisdiction."[561] TEC both enumerates the powers and the limits of its Provinces, whereas ACNA simply reserves to its sub-jurisdictions – like its dioceses – all those powers not specifically delegated to the Province.[562] Otherwise there

---

local congregations. This Diocese exists to serve and to coordinate the work of its Member Congregations; *it must never be a usurper of their Godly mission and work."* (Emphasis added).

[560] Ibid.

[561] TEC, [n335], Constit. VII and Can. I.9: Dioceses may be united into Provinces within the Church provided they do so willingly and by their own consent, and subject to the Constitution and Canons of the Church; ACNA, [n335], Constit. IV.4: "Dioceses or networks (whether regional or affinity based may band together for common mission, or as distinct jurisdictions at the sub-Provincial level." Ibid., Can. I.5.2.

[562] Compare TEC, [n335], Can. I.9.3-12, which specifies the synodal rights and powers of a Province, its composition and representation, regularity of meetings, power to consider the work of General Convention as it applies to the life and ministry of the Province, power to take over work begun by the Execute Council within the Province, and even power to legislate on matters touching the life and ministry of the Province not inconsistent with the Constitution and canons of the Church, while prohibiting a Province from controlling the internal affairs of a diocese; with ACNA, [n335], Constit. VIII.1: "The powers not delegated to the Province by this Constitution nor

are no provisions in the governing documents of ACNA specifying the powers and limits of sub-jurisdictions, or the terms on which they should function synodally. While both Churches seem to empower their dioceses to divide themselves for organizational and missional purposes into deaneries, districts or areas, only TEC's dioceses provided for synodal government at this level.[563]

At the diocesan level, both Churches provide for synodal government within the local church[564] – but some more than others. Almost all of the dioceses provide for an Annual Meeting where Vestry members are elected to serve staggered terms, where the qualifications of both the nominees and the electors are defined, and where the frequency of other Parish Meetings, ordinary and special Vestry meetings are also defined.[565] Only the TEC *Diocese*

---

prohibited by this Constitution to these diocese or jurisdictions, are reserved to these dioceses or jurisdictions respectively."

[563] See TEC *Diocese of Atlanta,* [n335], Can. 6, "Of Convocations": Organized for administrative purposes, mission and extension work, meeting in council once a year as deemed necessary by its Dean, and reporting its work to the Ecclesiastical Authority, and *Diocese of Los Angeles,* [n335], Can. IX, "Deaneries": Organized to facilitate the mission of the Church in the region, including evangelism discipleship and church growth, specifying composition, meetings and by-laws of Deanery Council, reports of its meetings and works to Diocesan Council, and larger "Pastoral care Areas" to which a Deanery may be assigned. By contrast, see ACNA *Anglican Diocese of the South,* [n335], Can. I.7: Districts or regions may be organized to "advance the administration of the diocese," period, and *Diocese of Western Anglicans,* [n335], Constit. Definitions and II: Deanery is to address the concerns of congregations within the region and to intensify their ministry development to expand both the work of the Diocese and the Kingdom of God within the region.

[564] See *PCLCCAC* [n17], Principal 15.6: "A parish also has an assembly."

[565] See TEC *Diocese of Atlanta,* [n335], Can. 31 and *Diocese of Los Angeles,* [n220], Can. 4: Provides for annual meeting only; and ACNA *Anglican Diocese of the South,* [n335], Can. II.4; but see *Diocese of Western Anglicans,* [n335], Can. IV.1: No provision for Annual Meeting; vestry to meet monthly.

of Atlanta requires reports from Rector, Vestry, Warden and all parish Organizations to the Annual Meeting, specifies the majority needed to elect new Vestry,[566] and that the Rector is the presiding officer of the Vestry and has a casting vote in the event of a tie.[567] But the *Anglican Diocese of the South* describes with Biblical precedent how Rector and Vestry are to work together in "mutual submission" with the Rector modeling at all times "servant leadership,"[568] and the Vestry in turn ordinarily expected to support him "in all aspects of his ministry."[569] This comes very close to describing the ideal of the relationships within a council.[570]

---

566 *Diocese of Atlanta,* [n335], Can. 31: Written reports.

567 Ibid., Can. 33.

568 *Anglican Diocese of the South*, [n335], Can. II.2.1: "The Rector should have the cooperation and full support of the Vestry, The Vestry in turn should expect the Rector to model the servant leadership required of all in the fundamental declarations and governing principles of the Constitution and the Diocese and the Church (Mark 10:45). In all matters the Rector and the Vestry shall observe the principles of mutual submission called for by the Apostle Paul in Philippians 2:3 and Ephesians 5:22."

569 Ibid., Can. II.4.7(i)

570 Ibid., see also Can. II.2.3 for extensive process of consultation between Rector, vestry and Bishop when either Vestry or Rector believe the pastoral relationship between the Rector and the Congregation is "imperiled or hindered by reason of dissension." The process involves the Bishop seeking to effect reconciliation through conferences with Rector and Vestry "who shall participate cooperatively in the process." The Bishop may issue interim recommendations before a final judgement, and shall consult with the Standing Committee and the Chancellor before issuing a final judgment. The Standing Committee may also hold conferences with the Rector and Vestry before issuing its recommendation to the Bishop. The final judgement may include steps short of dissolution, and the terms may be appealed by either party to the Standing Committee for modification. Failure to comply results in sanctions for the non-compliant party, whether Rector or Vestry. Again, this comes very close to modelling the relationships that are needed within a council to reach a godly decision.

7. THAT SYNODS MANIFEST ECCLESIAL DENSITY

Ecclesial Density seeks a common good or corporate identity which each member of synod represents above and beyond any personal or group interests. The voting by the House of Deputies, by deputations of dioceses, within a bicameral General Convention that meets only once every three years suggests to Podmore that TEC lacks weight or 'ecclesial density' at the national level ultimately. The House of deputies is an assembly of deputations of diocesan churches, and, in that sense, the General Convention is not the synod of a single Church."[571] In Article I of the Constitution of the ACNA, the existence of seven "Fundamental Declarations" as both characteristic of the "Anglican way and "essential to membership" in Article I is evidence of a corporate identity above and beyond any personal or group interests.

8. THAT THE WHOLE CHURCH GATHERS IN SYNOD AROUND ITS BISHOP(S), BUT NEVER OVER AND AGAINST THEM

Episcopal leadership is fundamental to the polity of a church.[572] In both Churches, episcopal leadership is evident in the right of the Presiding Bishop or Archbishop to summon and preside over the synodal gathering. But there are some differences between TEC and ACNA. In TEC, the Presiding Bishop has the right to summon the Bishops to all meetings of the House or as a Council, to summon Joint Sessions of Bishops and Deputies at General Convention, to preside over both meetings of the House of Bishops and Joint Sessions of general Convention, to

[571] See discussion on Principle 7 in Chapters Two and Three. This is in contrast to ACNA, where all orders sit and deliberate together, annually, in a unicameral Synod.
[572] *PCLCCAC,* [n17], Principle 15.10.

address the House of Deputies at General Convention "upon due notice," and to address the whole General Convention on the state of the Church, with recommendations upon which "its shall be incumbent" for both Houses to consider and act.[573] But in ordinary meetings of General Convention, it is the President of the House of Deputies that both summons that House to order and presides.[574]

In light of the unicameral nature of its synodal gatherings, and by simple contrast, the Archbishop of the ACNA has the right to summon and preside over all meetings of Provincial Council and Assembly, as well as the College of Bishops.[575]

In both Churches, the Presiding Bishop and the Archbishop, respectively, preside over the Executive bodies that carry on the work of the synodal gatherings between meetings.[576]

---

[573] TEC, [n335], Can. I.2.4 (a) (4-5). But note rare exceptions allowing Joint Sessions. See also Rules of Order for House of Bishops, *General Rules for Meetings of this House, Rule V:* Members of the House address the Presiding Bishop during debate, and on motion from any member of the House, or on the motion of the Presiding Bishop alone, may call for a vote to recess for 10 minutes in small groups "to define and clarify the issues of debate" before resuming.

[574] Ibid., Can. I.1(a)(b): President of House of Deputies performs those duties in the House appropriate to such office and canon, and once the House is called to order, appoints a Committee to "wait upon the House of Bishops" and inform them of the Deputies readiness to conduct business. See also Can.I.1.3: The right to call special meetings of General Convention is vested in the Bishops, and such meetings summoned by the Presiding Bishop.

[575] ACNA, [n335], Constit. IX.3, Can. I.1.5.

[576] But compare TEC, [n335], Can. I.4.3(a): Presiding Bishop is the *Ex Officio* President and Chair, with the CEO of the Executive Council as the acting

With the exception of the ACNA *Diocese of Western Anglicans* (where leadership in temporal matters is shared with a Lay President)[577] diocesan bishops summon and preside over their synodal gatherings.[578] Episcopal leadership at the diocesan level is also practiced among some Anglican Churches in the requirement for the Bishop to assent to all acts of the Synod, with provision for an override of the Bishop's non-consent or veto.[579] There is little evidence for this in the dioceses of TEC, and none in ACNA.[580]

Chair, with ACNA, [n335], Can. I.1.4: The Archbishop shall be the chairman of Executive Committee.

[577] *Diocese of Western Anglicans,* [n335], Can. I.4.08: Lay President Co-chairs and facilitates with the Bishop all meetings of the Executive Committee and the House of Delegates, and chairs those meetings in the Bishop's absence.

[578] See TEC *Diocese of Atlanta.* [n335], Constit. II.4, Can. I.1 and *Diocese of Los Angeles,* [n335], Constit. VIII, Can. XVI; and ACNA *Anglican Diocese of the South*, [n335], Constit. IV.5, Can. I.5.2-3: and with Chancellor proposes Rules of Order for Synod.

[579] See *PCLCCAC,* [n17], Principle 20.6: "A diocesan bishop may give or withhold consent to proposed diocesan legislation to such extent as is provided by law, but may not legislate unilaterally."

[580] See TEC, [n335], Can. I.10.6, which requires the consent of the Bishops or Ecclesiastical Authorities of both dioceses seeking a merger or reunification, notwithstanding the affirmative vote of each diocese's Convention for such a merger; see also *Diocese of Atlanta,* [n335], Constit. II.3: No council shall organize or transact any business unless there shall be present the Bishop; but see ACNA *Anglican Diocese of the South,* [n335], Can. I.5.3: Ruling of the Bishop "on any matter" may be overridden by a simple majority of those present and voting at Synod, and *Diocese of Western Anglicans,* [n335], Can. I.4.08, where Bishop need not be present for business of House of Delegates.

9. THAT SYNOD IS CONCERNED WITH THE CHURCH'S MISSION TO THE WORLD, NOT JUST WITH THE INTERNAL LIFE OF THE CHURCH

This is evident among Anglican Churches who have a written statement or articulation of such mission in their governing documents.[581] In TEC, the mission of the Church is defined in a canon on the Standing Committee for Mission and Evangelism, "(A)dvancing, within this Church's jurisdictions, God's mission to restore all people to unity with God and each other in Christ."[582] By contrast, ACNA places the mission of the Church in its Constitution at Article III: "to extend the Kingdom of God by so presenting Jesus Christ in the power of the Spirit that people everywhere will come to pit their trust in God through Him, know Him as savior and serve him as Lord in the fellowship of the Church."[583] This is a modern and close paraphrase of the working definition for evangelism found in the Archbishops' 1945 Report on Evangelism, *Toward the Conversion of England*.[584] Moreover, ACNA

---

[581] See discussion on Principle 9 in Chapetrs Two and Three.

[582] TEC, [n335], Can. I.1.2(n)(4): Advancing the mission includes "patterns and directions for evangelism, Church planting, leadership development, and ministries that engage the diversity of the Church's membership and the communities it serves, and to make recommendations to General Convention."

[583] ACNA, [n335], Constit. III, which goes on to provide that the people are the chief agents of the mission of the Church, and that the work of the Province is to equip each member so that they can "reconcile the world to Christ, plant new congregations and make disciples."

[584] *Towards the Conversion of England: Being a report of a Commission on Evangelism appointed by the Archbishops of Canterbury and York,* (Westminster: Press and Publications Board of the Church Assembly, 1945), para. 1: "To evangelize is so to present Christ Jesus in the power of the Holy Spirit, that men shall come to put their trust in God through him, to accept him as their Saviour, and serve him as their King, in the fellowship of his church."

also sets aside as the chief purpose for its Provincial Assembly the strengthening of this mission and making recommendations accordingly to Provincial Council.[585] In its canons, ACNA goes on to define the local congregation as the fundament agency of mission, and that dioceses are to set standards for the discipleship of all members—including equipping the laity to become "effective ministers of the Gospel of Jesus Christ."[586]

The constitution and canons of TEC *Atlanta* and *Los Angeles* do not define the mission of the Church in the Dioceses. By contrast, both the ACNA *Anglican Diocese of the South* and *Diocese of Western Anglicans* incorporate the ACNA statement of mission into their constitution and canons verbatim, as well as the requirement for laity to be effective ministers of the Gospel,[587] while adding their own emphases on discipleship and church planting.[588]

In short, ACNA has more evidence of a mission focus in its governing documents at all levels than TEC, and a singular focus on mission as conversion to Jesus Christ.

---

585 ACNA, [n335], Constit. VI and Can. I.2.1.

586 Ibid, Cans. I.6.1 and I.10.1.

587 *Anglican Diocese of the South,* [n335], Constit. I: "The Mission and Work of the Diocese," and Can. II.5.1: "Laity: Membership Requirements," and *Diocese of Western Anglicans,* [n220], Constit. I: "The Mission and Work of the Diocese," and Can. III.1.01: "The Ministry of the Laity."

588 Ibid, *Anglican Diocese of the South* [n335], Constit. I: "A principal work of the diocese is to plant new congregations, to encourage and assist Congregations in planting new congregations, and to strengthen newly planted congregations to become self-sustaining member congregations," and II: in addition to the mission of the Church to fulfill the Great Commandment and the Great Commission [cites] by leading people into a growing relationship with Jesus Christ through personal discipleship, evangelism and the nurturing and planting of congregations." See also *Diocese of Western Anglicans* [n335], Constit. I: same emphasis on church planting.

10. A SYNOD ALSO EXPRESSES THE SPIRITUAL LIFE AND EVENT OF THE CHURCH THROUGH DAILY WORSHIP AND PRAYER, AND THE HOLY EUCHARIST

In TEC, as an expression of humble dependence upon the Word and Spirit of God, and the Primitive Councils, a copy of Bible is reverently placed in public view at both Houses of General Convention.[589] General Convention begins with an opening Holy Eucharist for both Houses together, with a sermon by the Presiding Bishop.[590] After that, each session of the House of Bishops begins with devotions (a Bible reading and prayer), and includes noonday prayer and a daily celebration of Holy Eucharist.[591] Each session of the House of Deputies opens with devotions and also includes noonday prayers.[592] In the TEC *Diocese of Atlanta* every Council shall be opened with prayer, and in the *Diocese of Los Angeles* every Convention shall include a celebration of Holy Eucharist.[593]

But there is no provision for daily devotions, prayer or Holy Eucharist at synodal gatherings in the governing documents of ACNA, the *Anglican Diocese of the South* or the *Diocese of Western Anglicans*. This omission raises a fair question whether ACNA understands its synods to be an expression of the spiritual life of the Church.[594]

---

[589] TEC, [n335], Rules of Order for the House of Bishops, Services and Devotions Rules I-VII: Rules of Order for the House of Deputies, I: The Holy Scriptures, Rule I, and II: The Opening of the Daily Session Rule II.

[590] Ibid, Rules of Order for the House of Bishops, Rule VII.

[591] Ibid, Rules II-V.

[592] Ibid, Rules of Order for the House of Deputies, II: The Opening of the Daily Session Rule II.

[593] *Diocese of Atlanta,* [n335], Constit. II.4, *Diocese of Los Angeles,* [n335], Constit. VII.18.

[594] Having attended ACNA Provincial Councils and Assemblies, as well as the Synods of the *Anglican Diocese of the South, Diocese of the Mid-Atlantic,*

11. THE WORK OF SYNODS MUST CONFORM TO THE ULTIMATE AUTHORITY OF THE HOLY SCRIPTURES

This ultimate Biblical authority is typically stated in one or more ways in the governing documents a Church: (1) within a set of Fundamental Declarations or Ruling Principles, (2) in a statement of doctrine which includes the Thirty-Nine Articles, thereby incorporating by reference the Articles on the supreme authority of Scripture over Councils, and/or (3) in a separate statement or appeal to the Scriptures as the source and authority for the law of the Church.[595]

The nearest TEC comes to a Fundamental Declaration is in the Preamble to the Constitution, where it promises to uphold and propagate "the historic Faith and Order as set forth in the Book of Common Prayer."[596] It defines "doctrine" for the purposes of ecclesiastical discipline, and includes the canon of Holy Scripture "as it is understood" in dispersed authorities *not* including the Thirty-Nine Articles.[597] And the only separate statement or appeal to

---

and the Anglican Diocese of Pittsburgh, I can testify that they begin with a celebration of the Holy Eucharist, daily sessions with devotions and prayers, as well as noonday prayer. A Bible is also placed openly and reverently on a table for all to see during Synod. But the omission in the governing documents is one that needs addressing.

[595] The *PCLCCAC* state that "Scripture, tradition and reason are fundamental authoritative sources of law," [n17] at Principle 4.1, they do not establish Scripture as the ultimate standard or authority.

[596] TEC, [n335], Constit. Preamble.

[597] TEC, [n335], Can. IV.2: Doctrine defined as "the basic and essential teachings of the Church and is to be found in the Canon of Holy Scripture as understood in the Apostles and Nicene Creed and in the sacramental rites, the Ordinal and catechism in the Book of Common Prayer. See also "An Outline of the Faith, or Catechism in *The Book of Common Prayer and Administration of the Sacraments and Other Rites and Ceremonies of the Church* (New York: The Church Hymnal Corporation, 1979) at pp. 853-54: "Q: How do we understand the meaning of the Bible? A: We understand the

the authority to scripture is in the subscription at ordination, which limits the authority of the scriptures to all things necessary for salvation.[598]

By contrast, the Preamble to the Constitution of ACNA declares the "trustworthiness of the Holy Scriptures," in the context of repentance for things "done and left undone that have contributed to the rise of false teaching."[599] In its Fundamental Declarations, ACNA confesses the canonical books of the Old and New Testaments to be the inspired Word of God, containing all things necessary for salvation, but adding "*and to be the final authority and unchangeable standard for Christian Faith and Life*" (Emphasis added).[600] In the same Declarations it also receives the Thirty-Nine Articles as 'expressing fundamental principles of authentic Anglican belief," including the authority of Scriptures in Art. XX over and against the works of Church Councils.[601]

---

meaning of the Bible by the help of the Holy Spirit, who guides the Church in the true interpretation of the Scriptures." The exception of the Thirty-Nine Articles (especially Art. XX) and the addition of the Holy Spirit as the ultimate hermeneutic in guiding the church in the "true interpretation of Scripture" has led other Anglican Churches to view TEC as abandoning the authority of Holy Scripture with regards to such essentials as salvation through Christ alone (John 14:6) as well as matters of human sexuality and holy orders (See Chapter 6).

[598] Ibid, Constit. VIII: the subscription for the ordination of deacons and presbyters, and the ordination and consecration of a bishop reads: "I do believe the Holy Scriptures of the Old and New Testaments to be the Word of God, and to contain all things necessary to salvation; and I do solemnly engage to conform to the Doctrine, Discipline and Worship of The Episcopal Church."

[599] ACNA, [n335], Constit. Preamble.

[600] Ibid, Constit. I.

[601] Ibid, Constit. I.7. See also Cans. I.6.2, citing Art. XIX as authority for the definition of a congregation, and II.4.3 (5), citing Art. XXVIII as authority for the qualifications for "rightly receiving "Holy Communion.

ACNA dioceses also subscribe "unreservedly" to these Fundamental Declarations.[602]

Apart from its Fundamental Declarations and reliance upon the Thirty-Nine Articles for the supreme authority of the Scriptures, the canons of ACNA are replete with appeals to Scripture as authority for a variety of matters in the law of the Church.[603] Both *The Anglican Diocese of the South* and the *Diocese of Western Anglicans* repeat these citations in their own canons on the same matters.[604] But it

---

[602] See *Anglican Diocese of the South,* [n335], Constit. Preamble: citing the trustworthiness of the Holy Scriptures and I: "Fundamental Declarations and Governing Principles: Submission to the Church," and *Diocese of Western Anglicans,* [n335], Constit. Preamble: "We subscribe without reservation to the Fundamental Declarations in the Constitution of the Church," ibid., Can. II.1.02.

[603] ACNA, [n335], Cans. II.7.4, II.8.2: Marriage as a lifelong covenant between a man and a woman, divorce as failure and tragedy, and only limited exceptions for remarriage after divorce (Mt 19 and I Cor. 7); III.2.1: Requirements for Deacon according to Holy Scripture (I Tim 3); III.2.3: Requirements for Presbyter according to Holy Scripture (I Tim. 3, 5 and Titus); III.2.4: Requirements for married candidates for Holy orders with or without children (I Tim 3, Titus); III.2.5: Upholding the sanctity of marriage for those to be ordained (no person shall be ordained who has been divorced and remarried; III.2.6: Pastoral exception to pervious section in Matt. 19 and I Cor. 7; III.8.1: Requirements for Bishop according to Holy Scripture (I Peter 5) See also Cans.III.2.7: No person admitted to Holy Orders without properly trained in Holy Scriptures; and III.4.2: Examination upon the Bible, its contents, historical background and interpretive methods a requirement to ordination to the presbyterate.

[604]See *Anglican Diocese of the South,* [n335], Cans. II.7.4 (Marriage as a lifelong covenant and exceptions for remarriage), II.8 (standards of sexual morality and ethics), IV.2 (Biblical qualities for those ordained deacons and presbyters, married, remarriage, and with children) and IV.2.7 (no one ordained unless properly trained in Holy Scripture), IV.4.2(a) (such training in Holy Scripture shall include the Bible, its contents and historical background and interpretive methods; and *Diocese of Western Anglicans,*[n335], Cans.II.1.04 "upholding the sanctity of Christian Marriage and single life for the clergy, II.1.07 "Basic fitness for ministry" (I Tim. 3),

is in the Constitution of *The Anglican Diocese of the South* that the principle of the supremacy of Scripture in synodal gatherings is stated most elegantly:

> "Neither the Bishops nor any governing body of the Diocese shall make any edict or take any action that is contrary to the Scriptures as they have been received by the Church." [605]

In contrast to TEC, this principle is stated and practiced at all levels of the ACNA, in Fundamental Declarations and Governing Principles of the Church and its dioceses, in reliance upon the Thirty-Nine Articles to reaffirm the supremacy of the Scriptures, and in appeals to specific Scriptures on specific matters as authority for Church law.

II.1.08: Standards for sexual morality and ethics "In view of the teaching of Holy Scripture"; and II.4.07 "Concerning the election of a Bishop," the scriptural foundation of overseer according to I Tim 3 and Titus 1, and scriptures for fasting and prayerful discerning in the election.

[605] *Anglican Diocese of the South,* [n335], Constit. III.

A Glossary of Latin Terms

Ambulate: Jean Gerson's sermon at the Council of Constance (1415) which calmed the delegates and allowed proceedings to continue when the Pope left abruptly.

Consensus Fidelium: Also called ***sensus fidelium*** (sense of the faithful) when exercised by the body of the faithful as a whole, is the supernatural appreciation of faith on the part of the whole people, when, from the bishops to the last of the faithful, they manifest a universal consent in matters of faith and morals. Also expressed in the *Commonitorium of St.Vincent of Lerins* as that which has been believed by all Christians at all times and in all places.

Defensor Pacis: Marsilius of Padua wrote *Defensor pacis* in 1324 in the context of a power struggle between Pope John XXII and Ludwig of Bavaria, Emperor of the Holy Roman Empire. Relying heavily on Scripture, Marsilius seeks to show that Jesus did not claim to possess any temporal power and that he did not intend his church to exercise any. On the contrary, Scripture teaches that the church should be thoroughly subordinate to the state in both secular and spiritual matters. All authority in the church lies with the whole body of the faithful, the secular ruler who acts as the people's representative, and general councils called by the secular ruler. Some of Marsilius's arguments on these themes had a marked influence during the Reformation.

Frequens: Edict of the Council of Constance (1417) which held that General Councils of the Church should be held at regular intervals to continually reform the Church: "A *frequent* celebration of general councils is an especial means for cultivating the field of the Lord and effecting the destruction of briars, thorns, and thistles, to wit, heresies, errors, and schism, and of bringing forth a most abundant harvest. The neglect to summon councils fosters and develops all these evils, as may be plainly seen from a recollection of the past and a consideration of existing conditions. Therefore, by a perpetual edict, we sanction, decree, establish and ordain that general councils shall be celebrated in the following manner, so that the next one shall follow the close of this present council at the end of five years. The second shall follow the close of that, at the end of seven years, and councils shall thereafter be celebrated every ten years in such places as the Pope shall be required to designate and assign, with the consent and approbation of the council, one month before the close of the council in question, or which, in his absence, the council itself shall designate."

Haec Sancta: Also called *Sacrosancta*, a decree of the Council of Constance asserting the authority of ecumenical councils over popes. It was issued April 6, 1415, as a part of the council's effort to end the western schism. Finding their authority to deal with the schism at issue, the council fathers included language in the decree that has made it the historical high-water mark of medieval Catholic conciliarism.

Ius Commune: The "common law"– in the context of the Churches of the Anglican Communion, Principles of Canon Law Common to the Churches of the Anglican Communion. The *ius commune*, in its historical meaning, is commonly thought of as a combination of canon law and Roman law which formed the basis of a common system of legal thought in Western Europe from the rediscovery and reception of Justinian's Digest in the 12th and 13th centuries. Some scholars believe that the term, when used in the context of the ecclesiastical courts of England in the fourteenth and fifteenth century, also meant the law that is common to the universal church, as opposed to the constitutions or special customs or privileges of any provincial church.

Lumen Gentium: The *Dogmatic Constitution on the Church*, is one of the principal documents of the Second Vatican Council. This dogmatic constitution was promulgated by Pope Paul VI on 21 November 1964, following approval by the assembled bishops by a vote of 2,151 to 5.– As is customary with significant Roman Catholic Church documents, it is known by its first words, "Lumen gentium", Latin for "Light of the Nations".

Post Factum: After the fact.

Semper reformanda: Short for ***Ecclesia semper reformanda est*** ("the church must always be reformed"). It is a phrase which refers to the conviction of certain Reformed Protestant theologians that the church must continually re-examine itself in order to maintain its purity of doctrine and practice.

Universitas: Meaning "the whole."

Bibliography

Just a note: I'm using the Oxford University rules for legal citation, which state that of you have an author of more than one book, you use the usual citation and then cite all subsequent books under his name beginning with a double hyphen (--) then the title, place of publication, publisher, date, etc.

Primary Sources

Jewell J, *The Apology of the Church of England: An Apology, or answer, in Defense of the Church of England, With a Brief and Plain Declaration of the True Religion Professed and Used in the same* (London: Cassell and Company, Limited, 1888) republished at <http://www.anglicanlibrary.org/jewel/apology/2.htm > Accessed 20 August 2015

The Canons of the Church of England, Seventh Edition (London: Church House Publishing, 2012)

National Institutions Measure 1998 <http://www.legislation.gov.uk/ukcm/1998/1/introduction> Accessed 1 September 2015

Parochial Church Councils (Powers) Measure 1956 <http://www.legislation.gov.uk/ukcm/Eliz2/4-5/3/contents> Accessed 23 October 2015

Synodical Government Measure 1969 (SGM) Introductory Text 25th July 1969 <http://www.legislation.gov.uk/ukcm/1969/2/contents> Accessed 29 August 2015

The Standing Orders and Constitutions of the Exeter Diocesan Synod, <http://www.exeter.anglican.org/wp-content/uploads/2014/10/Diocesan-synod-standing-orders.pdf> Accessed 31 August 2015

The Standing Orders of the Synod of the Diocese of Liverpool, <http://www.bing.com/search?q=Standing+Orders+of+the+Synod+of+the+Diocese+of+Liverpool&form=PRDLCS&pc=MDDCJS&mkt=en-us&refig=c33286b68c3344df985e767bc358c075&pq=standing+orders+of+the+synod+of+the+diocese+of+liverpool&sc=0-26&sp=-1&qs=n&sk=&cvid=c33286b68c3344df985e767bc358c075> Accessed 31 August 2015

"The House of Bishops Working Group on human sexuality: The Pilling Report" (28 November 2013), para, 490.16, page 151. *The Church of England* <http://www.churchofengland.org/media/1890818/pilling%20report.docx.pdf> Accessed 12 January 2014

The Constitution Canons and Rules of the Anglican Church of Australia 2014, Tenth Edition (Sydney: The Anglican Church of Australia Trust Corporation, 2014)

Provincial Synod Constitution Amendment Ordinance 2011 Assenting Ordinance 2011 (New South Wales) <http://www.sds.asn.au/assets/Documents/ords/2011/41ProvSynConstitutionAmendOrd11.AssentOrd2011.pdf> Accessed 12 October 2015

The Constitution, Canons and Regulations of the Diocese of Adelaide, <http://www.adelaide.anglican.com.au/leadership/governance/constitution/> Accessed 6 October 2015

The Constitution of the Anglican Church of Australia in the Diocese of North Queensland, <http://www.anglicannq.org/governance/diocesan-constitution-and-canons> Accessed 6 October 2015

Constitution and Canons of The Province of The Anglican Church in South East Asia (Received by email dated 12 August 2015 from Stephanie Ng, Bishop's Office, Diocese of Singapore)

Constitution of the Diocese of Singapore (Received by email dated 12 August 2015 from Stephanie Ng, Bishop's Office, Diocese of Singapore)

The Constitution of the Synod of the Church in the Diocese of Kuching (Received by email dated 18 August 2015 from Stephanie Ng, Bishop's Office, Diocese of Singapore)

Constitution and Canons of The Church of Nigeria (Anglican Communion) (Received by email dated 22 July 2015 from Gbenga Fatoye on behalf of Abraham Yisa, Registrar of the Church of Nigeria),

The Principles, Constitution and Regulations of the Anglican Diocese of Etsako (Received by email dated 22 July 2015 from Gbenga Fatoye on behalf of Abraham Yisa, Registrar of the Church of Nigeria)

The Constitution and Regulations of the Diocese of Ogbia (Received by email dated 22 July 2015 from Gbenga Fatoye on behalf of Abraham Yisa, Registrar of the Church of Nigeria)

Sheil B, ed., The Constitution of The Church of Ireland as set out in the First Schedule to the Statute of the General Synod, Chapter XV of 2003 and An Appendix comprising the standing orders of General Synod, the provisions relating to the constitution, duties and powers of the Standing Committee and the Board of Education of the General Synod, etc. (Dublin: The General Synod of the Church of Ireland, 2003) (Received by email 21 July 2015 from Dr. Catherine Smith, Synod Officer, Church of Ireland House, Dublin)

Diocese of Connor Diocesan Regulations 2010 with Proceedings and Standing Orders of The Diocesan Synod (Passed by the Diocesan Synod 9 September 2010, Amended 3 October 2013) (Received by email 30 July 2015 from Tracey Taggert, Assistant to the Secretary of the Dioceses of Connor, Down and Dromore, Church of Ireland)

Diocese of Down and Dromore Diocesan Regulations 2010 with Proceedings and Standing Orders of The Diocesan Synod (Passed by the Diocesan Synod 17 June 2010, Amended 20 June 2013), (Received by email 30 July 2015 from Tracey Taggert, Assistant to the Secretary of the Dioceses of Connor, Down and Dromore, Church of Ireland)

Constitution and Canons for The Episcopal Church, Adopted in General Conventions 1789-2012. Together with the Rules of Order, Revised by the 77th General Convention (New York: General Convention Office, 2012)

"Resolutions of the 77th General Convention of The Episcopal Church: Resolution A049 Authorize Liturgical Resources for Blessing Same-Gender Relationships" (2012) in The Archives of The Episcopal Church <http://www.episcopalarchives.org/SCLM/2012-A049/dioceses/2012-A049.pdf> Accessed 10 January 2014

The Task Force for Re-Imagining the Episcopal Church (2015), Resolution A002 <http://www.generalconvention.org/gc/2015-resolutions/A002/original_english_text> Accessed 26 October 2015

"Resolutions of the 78th General Convention of the Episcopal Church: Resolution A054: Adopt Resources and Rites from Liturgical Resource I: 'I will bless you, and you will be a blessing,' expanded and revised" <http://www.generalconvention.org/gc/2015-resolutions/A054/current_english_text> Accessed 21 November 2015

The Constitution of the Diocese of Atlanta, as Adopted by the Council of the Diocese 1987 and amended 2011, < ***https://www.episcopalatlanta.org/Diocese/Governance/Diocesan-Canons-and-Constitution/The-Constitution-of-the-Diocese/***> Accessed 24 October 2015

The Canons of the Diocese of Atlanta <https://www.episcopalatlanta.org/Diocese/Governance/Diocesan-Canons-and-Constitution/The-Canons-of-the-Diocese/> Accessed 24October 2015

The Constitution and Canons of the Church in the Diocese of Los Angeles, adopted 1896 and revised 2012, <http://s3.amazonaws.com/dfc_attachments/public/documents/3168510/The_Constitution_and_Canons_through_2012.pdf > Accessed 24 October 2015

The Anglican Church in North America Constitution and Canons, as ratified by the inaugural Provincial Assembly 2009 and revised 2014, <https://c119b78671d19b8aee34-1ab073aa91389396dfc8b6aabc9b141e.ssl.cf2.rackcdn.com

/Constitution-and-Canons-CURRENT-9-5-14.pdf> Accessed 24 October 2015

Constitution and Canons of the Anglican Diocese of the South, <http://adots.org/?s=Constitution+and+Canons&submit = > Accessed 24 October 2015

The Constitution and Canons of the Diocese of Western Anglicans, <http://www.westernanglicans.org/sites/default/files/attachments/c_cs_dwa_feb_2015_0.pdf > Accessed 24 October 2015

Resolutions of the Lambeth Conference of Bishops 1920: Resolution 9: "Reunion of Christendom," Lambeth Conference Archives 1920, <http://www.anglicancommunion.org/resources/document-library/lambeth-conference/1920/resolution-9-reunion-of-christendom?author=Lambeth+Conference&year=1920> Accessed 19 November 2015

Resolutions of the Lambeth Conference of Bishops 1930: Resolution 48: "The Anglican Communion," Anglican Communion Archives, Lambeth 1930,<http://www.anglicancommunion.org/resources/document-library/lambeth-conference/1930/resolution-48-the-anglican-communion?author=Lambeth+Conference&year=1930 > Accessed 19 November 2015

Resolutions of the Lambeth Conference of Bishops 1930, Resolution 49: "The Anglican Communion," <http://www.anglicancommunion.org/resources/document-library/lambeth-conference/1930/resolution-49-the-anglican-

communion?author=Lambeth+Conference&year=1930> Accessed 10 November 2015

"The Bonn Agreement of 1931," <http://www.willibrord.org/bonn_en.html> Accessed 19 November 2015

Subscription and Assent to the Thirty-nine Articles: A Report of the Archbishops' Commission on Christian Doctrine (London: SPCK, 1968)

Lambeth Conference 1968: Resolution 43: The Ministry-The Thirty-Nine Articles," Anglican Communion Archives, Lambeth 1968 <http://www.anglicancommunion.org/resources/document-library/lambeth-conference/1968/resolution-43-the-ministry-the-thirty-nine-articles?author=Lambeth+Conference&year=1968> Accessed 20 November 2015

Proceedings of the Sixth Meeting of the Anglican Consultative Council, (London: ACC, 1984)

The Report of the Inter-Anglican Theological and Doctrinal Commission: The Virginia Report (London: The Anglican Consultative Council, 1997)

The Kuala Lumpur Statement on Human Sexuality: Second Global South Encounter (1997) <http://www.globalsouthanglican.org/index.php/comments/the_kuala_lumpur_statement_on_human_sexuality_2nd_encounter_in_the_south_10/> Accessed 4 November 2015

The Lambeth Conference Official Website: Resolutions 1998 <http://www.lambethconference.org/resolutions/1998/1998 *of*-1-10.cfm> Accessed 3 November 2015

"A Statement by the Primates of the Anglican Communion, Meeting at Lambeth Palace" (16 October 2003) <http://www.globalsouthanglican.org/index.php/blog/comments/a_statement_by_the_primates_of_the_anglican_communion_meeting_in_lambeth_pa > Accessed 4 November 2015

"Statement of the Primates of the Global South in the Anglican Communion," (2 November 2003) <http://www.globalsouthanglican.org/index.php/blog/comments/statement_of_the_primates_of_the_global_south_2_Nov_2003> Accessed 4 November 2015

The Lambeth Commission on Communion, The Windsor Report 2004 (London: Morehouse, 2004)

"The Primates Meeting Communique, (Dromantine)," (February 2005) <http://www.globalsouthanglican.org/index.php/blog/comments/the_anglican_communion_primates_meeting_communique_february_2005_dromantine> Accessed 4 November 2015

"Anglican Consultative Council (ACC-13) 2005: Resolution 10 Response to the Primates' Statement at Dromantine," and "Resolution 11: Supplementary Resolution of Thanks,"
The Anglican Communion official website-Instruments of Communion-ACC-13 Resolutions <***http://www.anglicancommunion.org/communion/acc/meetings/acc13/resolutions.cfm#s10*** > Accessed 10 January 2014

"The Road to Lambeth: A Statement from the Primates of the Council of Anglican Provinces in Africa (CAPA), Kigali Rwanda" (23 September 2006)

<http://www.globalsouthanglican.org/index.php/blog/printing/the_road_to_lambeth_presented_at_capa> Accessed 10 January 2014

"The Communiqué of the Primates Meeting in Dar es Salaam" (19th February 2007) Anglican Communion-Instruments of Communion-Primates Meetings-Resources <http://www.anglicancommunion.org/communion/primates/resources/downloads/communique2007_english.pdf> Accessed 7 January 2014

"The Jerusalem Declaration (2008)," GAFCON: Global Anglican Future Conference <http://gafcon.org/images/uploads/jerusalemdeclaration.pdf> Accessed 13 November 2015

Communion, Conflict and Hope (London: Anglican Communion Office, 2008)

The Principles of Canon Law Common to the Churches of the Anglican Communion (PCLCCAC) (London: Anglican Communion Office, 2008)

The Anglican Communion Covenant (Ridley-Cambridge Draft, 2009) <http://www.cs.utsa.edu/~wagner/church/gc2009/covenant.pdf> Accessed 21 November 2015

The Anglican Communion Covenant *(Final Text, 2009)* <http://www.anglicancommunion.org/media/99905/The_Anglican_Covenant.pdf> Accessed 13 November 2015

"A Key Letter from Primate of the Middle East Mouneer Anis explaining his resignation from the JSC," TitusOneNine, January 31, 2010,
<

http://www.kendallharmon.net/t19/index.php/t19/article/28019/#comments> Accessed 21 November 2015

"Towards an Understanding of the Purpose and Scope of The Primates' Meeting: A Working Document Approved by The Primates Meeting" (January 29, 2011) The Anglican Communion website-Instruments of Communion-Primates Meetings <http://www.aco.org/communion/primates/resources/downloads/prim_scpurpose.pdf> Accessed 12 January 2014

"Preamble to the Letter of Accession to the Anglican Communion Covenant- Province of South East Asia" (07 May 2011), <http://www.anglicanwestmalaysia.org.my/images/articles/Preamble%20to%20the%20Letter%20of%20Accession.pdf> Accessed 4 November 2015

"What Really Happened in Auckland NZ at ACC-15?" Anglican Ink, 8 November 2012, <http://anglicanink.com/article/what-really-happened-auckland-nz-acc-15> Accessed 21 November 2015

"GAFCON 2013: The Nairobi Communiqué" (26 October 2013) The Global Fellowship of Confessing Anglicans <http://gafcon.org/images/uploads/Nairobi_Communique_Final.pdf> Accessed 13 November 2015

"Responses from Churches of the Anglican Communion to the proposed Anglican Communion Covenant as of 19th January 2015," Anglican Communion Covenant <http://www.anglicancommunion.org/identity/doctrine/covenant/responses.aspx> Accessed 21 November 2015

Books, Journals and Reports

Avis P, *Beyond the Reformation? Authority, Primacy and Unity in the Conciliar Tradition* (London: T&T Clark, 2006)
– *The Identity of Anglicanism: Essentials of Anglican Ecclesiology* (London: Bloomsbury T&T Clark, 2008)
– "Anglican Conciliarity: History, Theology and Practice," (2004) Documents of The Lambeth Commission on Communion <http://www.anglicancommunion.org/commission/process/lc_commission/docs/200402conciliarity.pdf> Accessed 11 November 2015

Black A, *Council and Commune* (London: Burns and Oats, 1979)

Bray G, "Editorial: A Canterbury Tale," *The Churchman: Journal of the Church Society*, <http://archive.churchsociety.org/churchman/documents/Cman_127_4_Editorial.pdf> Accessed 15 November 2015
– *Tudor Church Reform: The Henrician Canons of 1535 and the Reformatio Legum Ecclesiasticarum* (Woodbridge: Suffolk: Boydell Press and the Church of England Record Society, 2008)

Brown R, *The Churches the Apostles Left Behind* (New York and Ramsey NJ: Paulist Press, 1984)

Burns, J. H. and Izbicki T, eds., *Conciliarism and Papalism* (Cambridge: Cambridge University Press, 1997)

Cameron G, "A Tortoise in a Hurry: The Ordering of the Anglican Communion," *International Journal for the Study of the Christian Church*, Vol. 8, No. 2, May 2008

Doe N, *The Legal Framework of the Church of England* (Oxford: Clarendon Press, 1996)

– *Canon Law in the Anglican Communion: A Worldwide Perspective* (Oxford: Oxford University Press, 1998)
– *Christian Law: Contemporary Principles* (Cambridge: Cambridge University Press, 2013)

– "The Instruments of Unity and Communion in Global Anglicanism "in Ian Markham, J Hawkins, Justyn Terry and Leslie Steffensen, eds. *The Wiley-Blackwell Companion to the Anglican Communion* (Chichester, West Sussex: John Wiley & Sons, Ltd., 2013)

Dunn J.D.G, *Unity and Diversity in the New Testament: An Inquiry into the Character of Earliest Christianity*, 2nd ed. (London: SCM Press, 1990)

Goddard A, "The Anglican Communion Covenant" in Ian Markham, J Hawkins, Justyn Terry and Leslie Steffensen, Eds. *The Wiley-Blackwell Companion to the Anglican Communion* (Chichester, West Sussex: John Wiley & Sons, Ltd., 2013) – "Communion and Covenant: A Theological Exploration." *International Journal for the Study of the Christian Church*, Vol. 8, No. 2, May 2008

Gomez D and Sinclair M, eds., *To Mend the Net: Anglican Faith and Order for Renewed Mission* (Carrollton TX: Ekklesia, 2001)

Hill M, *Ecclesiastical Law, Third Edition* (Oxford: OUP, 2007)

Hind J, "The Idea of an Anglican Covenant: A faith and Order perspective," *International Journal for the Study of the Christian Church*, Vol. 8, No. 2, May 2008

Huillier P, *The Church of the Ancient Councils: The Disciplinary Work of the First Four Ecumenical Councils* (Crestwood NY: St. Vladimir Seminary Press, 1996)

Humphrey E, "The Nature of the Church: Apostolic, Conciliar and Concrete," lecture delivered at the International Anglican Catholic Conference, Ft. Worth TX (USA), July 15 2015, <http://www.kendallharmon.net/t19/index.php/t19/article/61253/> Accessed 16 August 2015

James G, "Resolving to Confer and Conferring to Resolve: the Anglican way," in Kenneth Stevenson, ed., *A Fallible Church: Lambeth Essays* (London: Dartman, Longman & Todd, 2008)

Keble J, ed., *The Works of That Learned and Judicious Divine, Mr. Richard Hooker: Of the Laws of Ecclesiastical Polity, Vol. 1* (Books One through Four) (Oxford: Oxford University Press, 1836)

Kung H, *Structures of the Church* (New York: Thomas Nelson & Sons, 1964)

MacMullen R, *Voting about God in Early Church Councils* (New Haven and London: Yale University Press, 2006)

Martin R, *Carmen Christi: Philippians 2:5-11 in Recent Interpretation and in the setting of early Christian worship* (Grand Rapids, MI: Eerdmans Publishing, 1983) (First published 1967 as Volume 4 in the Society for New Testament Studies Monograph Series by the Syndics of the Cambridge University Press, London)

McGrath A, *Christian Theology: An Introduction, Third Edition* (London: Blackwell, 2001)

Noll, S, "Sea Change in the Anglican Communion," (November 11, 2013) Anglican Mainstream <http://www.anglican-mainstream.net/2013/11/11/sea-change-in-the-anglican-communion-2/ > Accessed 11 January 2014 – "Communion Governance: The Role and

Future of the Historic Episcopate and the Anglican Communion Covenant," *Stephen's Witness*, February 2, 2010 <http://www.stephenswitness.org/2012/02/communion-governance-role-and-future-of.html> Accessed 21 November 2015
– "Communion Governance: A Revised Anglican Covenant," *Stephen's Witness*, August 1, 2010 <http://www.stephenswitness.org/2010/08/communion-governance-revised-anglican_01.html> Accessed 21 November 2015

Oakley F, *The Conciliarist Tradition: Constitutionalism in the Catholic Church 1300-1870* (Oxford: OUP, 2003)

Orsy L, "Episcopal Collegiality Revisited" in Alberto Melloni, Silvia Scatena *Synod and Synodality: Theology, History, Canon Law and Ecumenism in new contact, International Colloquium Bruges 2003* (Piscataway NJ: Transaction Publishers, 2005)

Packer J.I, *The Thirty-nine Articles: Their Place and Use Today* (Oxford: Latimer House, 1984)

Podmore C, *Aspects of Anglican Identity* (London: Church House Publishing, 2005)

– "A Tale of Two Churches: The Ecclesiologies of The Episcopal Church and the Church of England Compared," *International Journal for the Study of the Christian Church*, Vol. 8, No. 2, May 2008, 124-154 at 131. First published in *Ecclesiastical Law Journal* (2008), 10 Ecc. LJ 34-70.
– "The Governance of the Church of England and the Anglican Communion," General Synod Miscellaneous Paper 910 (January 2009) <https://www.churchofengland.org/media/38963/gsmisc910.pdf> Accessed 21 November 2015

Rees J, "Covenant and Communion," *Ecclesiastical Law Journal* (2012) 14 Ecc LJ 235-255.

Report of the Lambeth Conference of 1930 (London: SPCK, 1930), at 154

Runyon A and McCall M, "Title IV Revisions:Unmasked," *The Anglican Communion Institute,* September 12, 2010 at <*http://www.anglicancommunioninstitute.com/wp-content/uploads/2010/09/title_iv.pdf*> Accessed 6 November 2015

Schmemann A, *Church, World, Mission: Reflections on Orthodoxy in the West* (New York: St. Vladimir's Seminary Press, 1979)

Sigmund P, ed. *Nicholas of Cusa: The Catholic Concordance* (Cambridge: Cambridge University Press, 1996)

Slack S, "Synodical Government and the Legislative Process," *Ecclesiastical Law Journal* (2012), 14 Ecc LJ 43-81

The Book of Common Prayer and Administration of the Sacraments and Other Rites and Ceremonies of the Church (New York: The Church Hymnal Corporation, 1979)

The Commonitorium of St. Vincent of Lerins, <https://www.crossroadsinitiative.com/library_article/1049/Commonitorium_Vincent_of_Lerins.html> Accessed 16 August 2015

"The Episcopal Church: Overbearing and Unjust Episcopal Acts." *The American Anglican Council*, February 2, 2010 < https://americananglican.org/wp-content/uploads/2014/02/TEC-Overbearing-and-Unjust-Episcopal-Acts-Feb-2010.pdf > Accessed 10 November 2015

The Lambeth Conference 1948, (London: SPCK, 1948)

The Lambeth Conference 1958, (London and New York: SPCK/Seabury Press, 1958)

The Lambeth Conference 1968 (London and New York: SPCK/Seabury Press, 1968)

The Lambeth Conference 1978 (London: CIO, 1978)

"The New Episcopal Church: What Hath General Convention 2015 Wrought?" *The Anglican Communion Institute*, July 27, 2015, <http://www.anglicancommunioninstitute.com/2015/07/the-new-episcopal-church-what-hath-general-convention-2015-wrought/> Accessed 6 November 2015

The Six Lambeth Conferences 1867-1920 (London: SPCK, 1920)

Thollander M, "The conciliar intent of Richard Hooker's theological hermeneutic," *Reformation and Renaissance Review*, Vol. 16, No. 1 April 2014

Tierney B, *Foundations of the Conciliar Theory* (Cambridge: CUP, 1955)

– *Towards the Conversion of England: Being a Report of a Commission on Evangelism appointed by the Archbishops of Canterbury and York*, (Westminster: Press and Publications Board of the Church Assembly, 1945)

Valliere P, *Conciliarism: A History of Decision Making in the Church* (Cambridge: Cambridge University Press, 2012)

Van Cullin S. and Terry A, "Anglican Consultative Councils" in Ian Markham, J Hawkins, Justyn Terry and Leslie Steffensen, Eds. *The Wiley-Blackwell Companion to the Anglican Communion* (Chichester, West Sussex: John Wiley & Sons, Ltd., 2013)

Whalon P, "The Tale Needs Retelling: A Reply to Colin Podmore's 'A Tale of Two Churches," *Theology (SPCK Sage Journals online)* January/February 2011, no. 1 at 3-12. Available for download at <http://www.collegeforbishops.org/assets/1145/the_tale_needs_finalrevision.pdf> Accessed 6 November 2015

Whitby M, "An unholy crew? Bishops behaving badly at Church Councils," in R Price and M Whitby, eds., *Chalcedon in Context: Church Councils 400-700* (Liverpool: Liverpool University Press, 2009)

Williams R, "Communion, Covenant and our Anglican Future: Reflections on The Episcopal Church's 2009 General Convention," *Anglican Communion News Service* <http://www.anglicannews.org/news/2009/07/communion,-covenant-and-our-anglican-future.aspx> Accessed 20 November 2015

Zizioulas J, *The One and the Many: Studies on God, Man, the Church and the World today* New York: St. Vladimir's Seminary Press, 1993)
– *Lectures in Christian Dogmatics*, edited by Douglas Knight (London: T&T Clark, 2008)

Articles

"Nigerian Church New Constitution Redefines Relationship with Canterbury," *Christianity Today* (19 September 2005) <http://www.christiantoday.com/article/nigerian.church.new.constitution.redefines.relationship.with.canterbury/3994.htm> Accessed 13 November 2015

"Half of the Church of England's dioceses reject unity covenant," *BBC News UK Website* (12 March 2012)

<http://www.bbc.co.uk/news/uk-17500144> Accessed 21 November 2015

"Covenant voting continues," *The Living Church*, (26 March 2012) < http://www.livingchurch.org/covenant-voting-continues> Accessed 21 November 2015

"Primates Meet as Conference Opens," *GAFCON Media Release, Leaders Conference, London, 23 April 2012*, <http://gafcon.org/news/primates-meet-as-conference-opens> Accessed 13 November 2015

"Anglican Structures need updating, says Archbishop," *Christianity Today*, 13 October 2013, <http://www.christiantoday.com/article/anglican.structures.need.updating.says.archbishop/34431.htm> Accessed 13 November 2015

"GAFCON Chairman's Advent Letter" (7 December 2013) <http://gafcon.org/news/chairmans-advent-letter> Accessed 12 January 2014

"Archbishop of Canterbury calls for Primates gathering," *Justin Welby, The Archbishop of Canterbury* (16 September 2015) <http://www.archbishopofcanterbury.org/articles.php/5613/archbishop-of-canterbury-calls-for-primates-gathering> Accessed 17 October 2015

Brown A, "Archbishop of Canterbury plans to loosen ties of divided Anglican Communion," in *The Guardian* (16 September 2015) <http://www.theguardian.com/world/2015/sep/16/archbishop-of-canterbury-urges-breakup-of-divided-anglican-communion> Accessed 17 October 2015

Gledhill R, "How to understand Justin Welby's vision for Christian unity," *Christian Today* (17 September 2015) <*http://www.christiantoday.com/article/how.to.understand.justin.welbys.vision.for.christian.unity/65040.htm*> Accessed 17 October 2015

Communique of the Standing Committee of the Church of Nigeria, October 1, 2015 <http://anglicanmainstream.org/nigerian-anglican-communique/> Accessed 7 October 2015

"Chairman's October Pastoral Letter 2015: Archbishop Eliud Wabukala, Primate of Kenya and Chairman of the GAFCON Primate's Council," *GAFCON NEWS*, October 24, 2015, <http://gafcon.org/news/chairmans-october-pastoral-letter-2015> Accessed 11 November 2015

"Subsidiarity" in *Wikipedia*, <https://en.wikipedia.org/wiki/Subsidiarity> Accessed 29 August 2015

"Blessing of same-sex unions in Christian churches," *Wikipedia: The Online Encyclopedia* < http://en.wikipedia.org/wiki/Blessing_of_same-sex_unions_in_Christian_churches > 11 January 2014

www.ingramcontent.com/pod-product-compliance
Ingram Content Group UK Ltd.
Pitfield, Milton Keynes, MK11 3LW, UK
UKHW021838270726
14058UKWH00002B/214

9 780997 9211